INFORMATION

INFORMATION

Keywords

EDITED BY
MICHELE KENNERLY,
SAMUEL FREDERICK, AND
JONATHAN E. ABEL

Columbia University Press
New York

Columbia University Press
Publishers Since 1893
New York   Chichester, West Sussex
cup.columbia.edu

Copyright © 2021 Columbia University Press
All rights reserved

Library of Congress Cataloging-in-Publication Data
Names: Kennerly, Michele, editor. | Frederick, Samuel, editor. | Abel, Jonathan E., 1971– editor.
Title: Information : keywords / edited by Michele Kennerly, Samuel Frederick, and Jonathan E. Abel.
Other titles: Information (Kennerly, Frederick, Abel)
Description: New York : Columbia University Press, [2021] | Includes bibliographical references and index.
Identifiers: LCCN 2020024849 (print) | LCCN 2020024850 (ebook) | ISBN 9780231198769 (hardback) | ISBN 9780231198776 (trade paperback) | ISBN 9780231552806 (ebook)
Subjects: LCSH: Information science—Miscellanea.
Classification: LCC Z665 .I582525 2021 (print) | LCC Z665 (ebook) | DDC 020—dc23
LC record available at https://lccn.loc.gov/2020024849
LC ebook record available at https://lccn.loc.gov/2020024850

Cover design: Milenda Nan Ok Lee
Cover art: Sylverarts Vectors © Shutterstock

CONTENTS

Acknowledgments vii

Introduction: Information + Humanities   1
MICHELE KENNERLY, SAMUEL FREDERICK, AND JONATHAN E. ABEL

Abundance   17
DAMIEN SMITH PFISTER

Algorithm   31
JEREMY DAVID JOHNSON

Archive   44
LAURA HELTON

Bioinformatics   57
HAUN SAUSSY

Cognition   72
N. KATHERINE HAYLES

Gossip   89
ELIZABETH HORODOWICH

Index   100
DENNIS DUNCAN

Intel 110
GEOFFREY WINTHROP-YOUNG

Keyword 121
DANIEL ROSENBERG

Knowledge 133
CHAD WELLMON

Noise 148
MATTHEW F. JORDAN

Screen 162
FRANCESCO CASETTI AND BERNARD DIONYSIUS GEOGHEGAN

Search 174
DAVID L. MARSHALL

Self-Tracking 187
DEBORAH LUPTON

Tele (Τῆλε) 199
WOLF KITTLER

Contributors 213
Index 217

ACKNOWLEDGMENTS

Were this a medieval manuscript, we would order these acknowledgments to allow us to open the page with a large incipit χ.

The idea for this volume originated in 2016, coinciding with the launch of the Center for Humanities and Information (CHI) at Penn State. We thank its founder and director, Eric Hayot, along with codirectors Pamela VanHaitsma and John Russell, for entrusting us with assembling, editing, and introducing it. Eric dreamed up the idea for companion volumes—one, this one, a Keywords volume, and the other a Reader, also published with Columbia University Press in 2021—and he designed the intellectual and social architectures of CHI. We are grateful, too, to the inaugural group of CHI fellows—particularly Anatoly Detwyler, Lea Pao, Bonnie Mak, and Laura Helton—for their savviness and support. For administrative assistance of various types at Penn State, we thank Olivia Brown, Alysa Hickey, Dina Mahmoud, and Yiming Ma. At Columbia University Press, we have benefited from the good humor of Monique Briones, editorial assistant extraordinaire, and appreciate the stewardship of senior editor Philip Leventhal and production editor Susan Pensak. The press sent our manuscript to two astute readers, who helped us articulate better the relationships between this volume and volumes from information scientists. Thanks to Partha P. Chakrabartty for their thoughtful and thorough copyediting, and to Sarah Osment for compiling the index.

The ingenuity and insightfulness of the contributors to this volume helped us sustain our energy over the past four years. We would also like to thank Ann

Blair, whom CHI brought to Penn State in September of 2016 for a stunning lecture on early modern amanuenses, and one of the editors—along with Paul Duguid, Anja-Silvia Goeing, and Anthony Grafton—of *Information: A Historical Companion* (Princeton University Press, 2020). We are delighted that volume and ours have a few contributors in common and can only laugh at the fact that the Princeton University Press posse secured a few scholars who had turned us down.

The keyword entries were written no later than fall 2018, and the three of us finalized the intro in the summer of 2019, which may go some way toward explaining missing bibliography.

INFORMATION

INTRODUCTION

Information + Humanities

MICHELE KENNERLY, SAMUEL FREDERICK,
AND JONATHAN E. ABEL

Generally, humanists prefer to use the absolute article modestly. For that reason, the common designation of our time as "the information age" and of our social structure as "the information society," as well as the recent claim that information is "the keyword of our time," might irk in form alone.[1] Maybe, as historian Robert Darnton has insisted, "every age is an age of information, each in its own way and according to the media available at the time."[2] Maybe, as a coeditor of the companion volume to this one, Eric Hayot, submits, "all societies are information societies; the social is, in some strong sense, both the outcome of a series of processes for managing, organizing, and passing information on, as well as itself a process for managing future outcomes."[3] Maybe the idea of *information* as a standout, standalone keyword is antithetical to the concept of keywords, which take relative meaning within a vocabulary.[4] But some humanists might find those particular absolutes unsettling for different reasons: *information* seems to index practices, terminologies, and technologies far removed from those of the humanities. Furthermore, information, whatever its history, seems more inescapable now than ever before. In "the information age," do the humanities have a place? What do the humanities have to do with information?

From this latter perspective, it makes sense to ask: what, as a matter of genuine and perhaps even urgent inquiry, might it mean to imagine information as a humanistic concept? What might a humanities-informed conceptualization of information look like?

We offer two responses to such questions. The first is that we do not have to use our imaginations only: scholars of the theoretical-critical and traditional humanities have been treating information as a humanistic concept—or as a concept for the humanities—for some time, and with increasing regularity. Some early work takes terms from the engineering-oriented study of information and applies them to a humanistic area of inquiry. Consider, for example, the work of rhetoricians H. Hardy Perritt on "Cybernetics and Rhetoric," from 1954, and Daniel Marder on "Entropy in Rhetoric," from 1974.[5] By the 1980s, information was everywhere—and posing as without a past. In 1986, sociologist and communication theorist James R. Beniger gave it one, feeling pressed to answer why, given that "information plays an important role in all human societies, . . . it has only recently emerged as a distinct and critical commodity." His answer is what he names "the Control Revolution, a complex of rapid changes in the technological and economic arrangements by which information is collected, stored, processed, and communicated, and through which formal or programmed decisions might effect societal control," a revolution Beniger situates in the final quarter of the nineteenth century.[6] Two years later, communication theorist John Durham Peters pursued the intellectual origins of the information concept, offering a critical history that begins with the medieval uptake of Aristotle's theories on *hulē* and *morphē*.[7] The second half of the 1990s saw "the information age" trilogy of sociologist Manuel Castells, which attempts to name emergent social formations, most notably what he terms the "network society."[8] Early-modern historian Ann Blair's 2010 *Too Much to Know: Managing Scholarly Information before the Modern Age* marked the first book-length application of information concepts—foremost among them, information overload—to a historical period far removed from the centuries usually claimed for "the information age."[9] In 2015, medievalist Kathleen E. Kennedy considered in *Medieval Hackers* "how the medieval norms of commonness, openness, and freedom of information" were used in late medieval England by translators of the Bible into English, and "how these norms challenge modern copyright law."[10] 2018 books by political scientist Virginia Eubanks and information scientist Safiya Umoja Noble demonstrated the disproportionate effects of algorithmic data discrimination on, respectively, poor people and people of color, especially Black women.[11] Classicist Andrew M. Riggsby's 2019 book *Mosaics of Knowledge: Representing Information in the Roman World* attends to what he calls "conceptual developments" in information technology in the ancient Latin-speaking world, such as lists, tables, weights and measurements, and maps.[12]

This sampling shows the range of information work undertaken across the humanities (and in domains whose practitioners sometimes lean humanist), from confronting the information technologies of a given time (including our own), to enlarging the historical scope of information's lifespan.[13] The trouble is that one might never have thought to read all of those items together. Certainly the humanistic work being done on information would look more unified and less informous if those who write it and read it were to establish some common concepts or corpus of readings.[14] What is therefore needed is work that alters, augments, and enriches the set of referents and histories conjured when one hears "information."

And that brings us to our second response: this volume. *Information: Keywords* articulates information as a humanistic concept to present forms of "information thinking" that include but do not begin with information's twentieth-century, engineering-oriented heritage. *Keywords* recognizes information as a long-standing feature of social, cultural, and conceptual management; as a matter of social practice; and as a fundamental challenge for the humanities today. In this way, it aims to lay out a humanistic vision of the information concept, and in that way to define a field that is just now coming into existence. Our fifteen keywords proceed from the conviction that thinking about information and the humanities requires more than a knowledge of the history of information in all its guises: it requires the opening of new angles of inquiry into the idea of information itself.

Information: Keywords is, we hope, an accessible book for students, teachers, and ambitious readers interested in learning how information shapes our daily lives, but also in how thinking about information can produce new understandings of the present—and the past. The collected entries showcase inventive and invitational thinking about the methods of description, classification, and organization that shape the idea of information from a global and transhistorical perspective. The volume features fifteen keywords that highlight the humanistic nature of information practices and concepts ordinarily linked to the 1940s, when the so-called information age was born.[15] "Information" continues to be a cultural keyword, and thinking through the historical and social dimensions of information concepts often associated exclusively with science and engineering (e.g., *noise*) or that are dismissed by those areas as not technical enough to warrant consideration (e.g., *gossip*) gives those concepts new textures and patterns.[16]

Acknowledging the interdependence of information and the human, *Information: Keywords* forges connections with the following fields without comfortably residing in any one of them: information studies, cybernetics, engineering, media studies, library sciences, computer science, communication/s, ethics of information, digital humanities, and big data. Therefore, this volume is something of a synecdoche for that which it enumerates, elaborates, and emancipates. That is, if we treat the volume the way information has been treated—titling it, categorizing it, periodizing it, organizing it, characterizing it, tagging it—we create another layer of information about it, thus not only introducing but also instantiating it. How do we categorize the methods of inquiry in the present volume with contributors from the disciplines of rhetoric, history, literature, sociology, and philosophy? Is there a coherent method for these studies or is listing and labelling the various and sundry techniques for considering information itself enough to be informative? The simple answer is "no," yet these are not questions to be answered with a monosyllable—if at all.

Anticipatory Rejoinders

But perhaps we are moving too quickly. Let's dwell for a bit on information resistance, which, after all, also has a history. Resistance to engaging information through humanistic inquiry or as a humanistic concept could come in several dispositions, from avoiding the (ostensibly) faddish to, more seriously, abjuring the abandonment of humanistic haunts for the land and language of science and technology, which commonly enjoy more public recognition and epistemic weight than that of the humanities. After all, phrases like "the information society" or "the information age" were not developed by humanists but rather by social scientists and engineers looking to brand their pursuits with a potentially popular term that seemed unlikely to go away any time soon. Thinking about the growth of "information industries," anthropologist Tadao Umesao seems the first to have proposed the arrival of an "information society" (*jōhō shakai*), in a roundtable discussion published in January 1964.[17] Futurologist Yoneji Masuda followed Umesao's lead in 1968 with the first book publication to use the term, *Jōhō shakai nyumon: Conpyūta wa ningen shakai wo kaeru* (*Introduction to an Information Society: Computers Are Transforming Human Society*), which would be reworked and published in English several years later as *The Information Society as Post-Industrial Society*.[18] Masuda attempts to predict the growth of information industries and societies, proposing policy that anticipates the coming "computopia."[19] His approach is ostensibly neutral, technical, and practical: this is coming, here's how we ought to prepare and prioritize. For that reason, fifty years later, "computopia" seems quaintly utilitarian, and even utopian. Also in the early 1970s, Tibor Charles (T. C.) Helvey, at one time an associate professor of cybernetics, appears to be the first to christen the age in his 1971 book *The Age of Information: An Interdisciplinary Survey of Cybernetics*.[20] None of the disciplines Helvey connects or goes between are humanistic. Perhaps, then, humanists are right to be wary of totalities so large as to be epochic but so narrow as to exclude the humanities.

In fact, distrusting information has long been a heavily weighted criterion for being a good humanist. As a catch-all concept for concrete data, information represents dead knowledge, fixed facts that must correspond to some pre-established and unquestioned notion of objective reality. As such, information is what Heidegger would call "correctness," which is important for determining one's taxes or the proper dosage of medication, but not for making sense of the world. That sense—which Heidegger would call "truth," though we would prefer not to—cannot be reduced to an equation or a list of data or even a definition. It can only be approached (in Heidegger-speak, encountered in its "unconcealment") through methods of inquiry predicated on the understanding that there can be no final or singular answer.[21]

We need not, though, dwell in the philosophy of Heidegger or climb to some high plateau upon which Deleuze reads Lacan to find a critique of cybernetic-style correctness. Instead, we can look to a brief discourse about the game of odds and evens delivered by the master detective in Edgar Allan Poe's "The Purloined Letter," upon which Lacan and, following suit, Deleuze built their schema for psychoanalytical/schizo-interventions into information studies.[22] In that short story, the Prefect of the Parisian police, who had maligned poetic sensibilities and instead opted for a scientific approach to problem solving, comes to C. Auguste Dupin for help in solving a mystery. Dupin, the world's first superhero private detective, tells the narrator that he had to adopt the mindset not only of the poet but also of the mathematician to grasp the solution hiding in plain sight—but not before railing specifically against a mathematical mode of thinking that reaches too far:

> I dispute the availability, and thus the value, of that reason which is cultivated in any especial form other than the abstractly logical. I dispute, in particular, the reason educed by mathematical study. The mathematics are the science of form and quantity; mathematical reasoning is merely logic applied to observation upon form and quantity. The great error lies in supposing that even the truths of what is called pure algebra, are abstract or general truths. And this error is so egregious that I am confounded at the universality with which it has been received. Mathematical axioms are not axioms of general truth. What is true of relation—of form and quantity—is often grossly false in regard to morals, for example. In this latter science it is very usually untrue that the aggregated parts are equal to the whole. . . . There are numerous other mathematical truths which are only truths within the limits of relation. But the mathematician argues, from his finite truths, through habit, as if they were of an absolutely general applicability—as the world indeed imagines them to be.[23]

Rather than adopting the singular approach of the Prefect who searches for the titular stolen letter by examining every inch of its known vicinity, Dupin chooses a mixed methodology examining the micro facial reactions of thieving Minister D as different parts of the room in which the letter is are mentioned. In this way, Poe shows us that opting for either the poetic or mathematic alone will fail. The origins of this dualistic conception of inquiry coincides with the modern institutional origins of the humanities themselves, articulated and defined against the mechanistic and positivistic.[24]

Defending tradition, embodiment, and orality, Walter Benjamin rejected the increased prevalence of information in his essay "The Storyteller," in which he goes so far as to blame the decline of true storytelling and authentic experience on the ramped up spread and speed of reports made possible by new media (radio, newspapers, etc.).[25] What Benjamin finds insidious about information is its immediate verifiability, its intrinsic comprehensibility, and its unambiguous plausibility. These qualities spell the death of life and art in all its slowness, uncertainty, strangeness, and wonder. Shot through with information, existence becomes permeated by explanation, the impulse to make everything we encounter digestible and intelligible, which is to shut down any independent critical thought and to entice the recipient with the next morsels, already dispatched and on their way. Benjamin's picture of information dependency resonates even more forebodingly in today's social-media-saturated world. Who wouldn't want to shun such a corrupting flow of information and reclaim the humanistic pursuit of lived experience through art?

The problem with Benjamin's view is twofold: first, it lacks the recognition that the altered experience of time and space itself is a perception rationalized by a deterministic view of what the then-new media of radio and newspaper afforded, and, therefore, is no different than what previous media afforded. In other words, the fetish for new technologies has a much longer history; this fetish attests to our long-standing infatuation with too much information (see the "abundance" keyword). Second, it promotes the notion that wonder is somehow antipodal to information. Is not the experience of speed and transparency of meaning itself capable of inspiring a sense of awe? Isn't big data the source of a new religion which places faith in numbers to predict the future? In Benjamin's day, furthermore, the shift in our fundamental experience of the world and our place in it was the fertile ground for an aesthetic revolution in which the inseparability of man from machine was seen as a positive and productive development of modern existence. The name for this movement was *Neue Sachlichkeit* (New Objectivity or New Sobriety), a return to *die Sache*, the matter at hand, the objective facts in front of our eyes, that which is indisputable and clearly intelligible. The art, literature, and film produced by *Neue Sachlichkeit* celebrated these new perspectives both through mechanistic spectacles of sights and sounds as well as through dispassionate, critical reportage, emphasizing in each case the functionality and utility of life and art while also suggesting that the new man could be re-built like a machine for the collective, utopian age.[26] As Bertolt Brecht's 1926 play *Man Equals Man* has it, "a man is reassembled like a car."[27] What Benjamin's view of the technical interruption of awe and wonder in "The Storyteller" refuses—though, to be fair, his other writings, including the contemporaneous essay on the technological reproducibility of artwork, do acknowledge and affirm it—is the potential for the dazzlement and entrancement of the masses, whether by the flickering glow of the cinema projector or by the intense blue light of today's OLED screens.[28] If Guy Debord's view of the "society of spectacle" draws on and expands Benjamin's understanding of our screened life, it does so precisely to expound on the humanist fears of our immersion in propaganda and information.[29]

This humanist fear of information ultimately grows from a sense that data alone cannot provide answers, that, dig as we might to uncover new facts, the old human problems will remain: Who am I? Why am I here? What is my relationship to others? If there is an impetus in sociology to reject the nonscience of the humanities by answering questions about, say, the individual in relation to the community with data, there is an implicit (sometimes overt) humanist rejection of social science as pseudo-science, an alchemy that renders the gold of causation from the base metal of correlation. If knowledge acquisition reproduces a vanishing point of Zeno's paradox, then the notion that more data will give us answers is illusory, because our most pressing questions will always exceed the answers provided by our information. This is why humanists are wont to use "positivist" as a critique, if not an insult. The conclusions humanist scholars arrive at are not meant to be definitive, admitting no question, but rather, while considering the data, to demand further questioning, a process which comprises the project of inquiry itself.

The methodologies employed by the contributors to this volume remain firmly humanistic: they criticize, contextualize, and historicize. The objects of their inquiry, however, are the ways information structures and determines those aspects of life we typically consider distinct from or in opposition to data/information. We reject the notion that human experience can be separated from our experience of an information-saturated world, and thus insist that questions of the human must also include questions about information, even as such questions fail to account for the infinity of human experience. There is no need to fear information, since there is no place for the human outside or beyond information. There is no human without information; there is no information without the human.

Of course, the discipline of library and information science (LIS)—which includes, now, information studies—has been addressing the entanglement of humans and information since the mid-1930s, when it was known as documentation science. Belgian pacifists Henri la Fontaine (1854–1943) and Paul Otlet (1868–1944) are commonly credited with founding the field of documentation, and we have Otlet to thank for the catalog card, that medium of classification and organization ubiquitous in various institutions well into the computer age.[30] The study of the recording and retrieval of information underwent a shift in nomenclature and technology in the 1960s, coinciding with the dawn of "the information age." For instance, in 1968, the American Society for Information Science emerged from the American Documentation Institute. Traditional LIS focal points—such as bibliometrics, information architectures, and knowledge organization—are mirrored in entries in this volume, but LIS concerns tend toward theories, technics, and pragmatics of information storage, access, and retrieval in archives, libraries, and museums.[31] When scholars in LIS give that tendency a critical edge, however, their work moves into the information + humanities intersection.[32] From the other direction, humanists have been writing about archives, libraries, and museums for a few decades.[33] Increasingly more common are collaborations between scholars with humanities appointments and those with LIS appointments, as well as humanists with appointments in schools and departments of information.[34] Clearly, information pulls diverse disciplines into alignment, and even creates new intellectual formations.

Threading the Needle; or, A Clew for Reading *Keywords*

Readers expecting to learn more about this volume's titular concept of "keywords" should turn promptly to the "keyword" entry authored by Daniel Rosenberg, for we understand our objective quite literally: an introduction ought to "lead into" what follows. Here, we lead by demonstration rather than by definition, selecting a word that has long been of importance to culture. Having multifarious meanings, and all of them unassuming, the file recommends itself as an ideal structuring thematic to prepare the way. Like the other keywords featured in this volume, it too has a history that threads the humanistic and the informatic. "File" gestures to textiles and to technologies of ordering, points to the continuity of a narrative throughline and to a discrete unit, belongs in ancient *officinae dicendi* (speech workshops) as well as modern offices, and indexes both material and digital storage. "File" originates from the Latin noun *filum*, originally meaning a thread of something woven, usually wool or linen.[35] As such, the word has a textile, tactile origin—and emerges from the fingertips of women.

Histories of information, technology, computation, and digital networks are recovering the consequential though largely uncredited roles played by women and their work. Whether they cast a view toward the *longue durée* or focus tightly on the twentieth century, many of these studies recognize weaving as a throughline. In "Losing the Thread," Virginia Postrel ties together a sequence of stories about technology that tend to forget or exclude women. For instance, in considering the binary system that is so central to twentieth-century information work, Postrel recalls that "[w]eaving is the original binary system, at least 9,000 years old. Warp threads are held in tension, and weft threads go over or under them. Over-under, up-down, on-off, one-zero. Punch cards could control looms because weaving is intrinsically binary."[36] Reflecting upon the gendered patterns she finds while constructing a history of "net(-)work," Mari Lee Mifsud adds that the prolonged forgetfulness "about ancient rhetorics of network is cultural amnesia of women's lives, work, authority, art, and the very basis of technology."[37] According to Postrel and Mifsud, the weaving of women continually underlays cultural ages and organizations celebrated for achievements overwhelmingly treated as disembodied, or else attributed to men.

NASA, that darling of the information age, is a case in point. The promotional materials and public memory of NASA have long skewed male. Lately, however, scholars, science writers, and now even pop culture have been remembering the women who made U.S. space work possible.[38] For example, in the 1950s and 1960s, NASA spacecraft guidance systems "stored information in core memory ropes: threaded wires, passed through or around magnetized rings. NASA engineers nicknamed this hardware 'LOL memory' for the 'Little Old Ladies' who carefully wove wires around small electro-magnetic ferrite cores by hand."[39] Wishing to memorialize and materialize magnetic-core memory weaving, Daniela Rosner, Samantha Shorey, Brock Craft, and Helen Remick launched the Making Core Memory project, which "examin[ed] the forms of technical labor performed in early processes of core memory production" through a patch-kit-based quilting project.[40] Among NASA's plentiful information-related remits has been to gather climate data. In our post-2016 moment, when all public archives in the U.S. are under threat and the current U.S. administration refuses to attempt to mitigate climate change, Marissa and Justin Connelly and Emily McNeil founded The Tempestry Project, which "blends fiber art with temperature data to create a bridge between global climate and our own personal experiences through knitted or crocheted temperature tapestries."[41] Like the Making Core Memory project, it is kit-based and participatory. Whereas most climate infographics represent temperature change over years, The Tempestry Project kits visualize data from only one year and one location, manifesting local impacts that become more dramatic looking when kits come together in installations. These projects criss-cross citizen science with citizen crafting, restoring the connection between textiles and technologies of the information age.[42]

NASA was not the only information-age entity to benefit from the weaving skills of women. In her study of the Fairchild Semiconductor plant built in 1965 on the Navajo reservation in Shiprock, New Mexico, Lisa Nakamura attends to how "Indian-identified traits and practices such as painstaking attention to craft and an affinity for metalwork and textiles were deployed to position the Navajo on the cutting edge of a technological moment precisely because of their possession of a racialized set of creative cultural skills in traditional, premodern artisanal handwork."[43] Navajo women, in particular, excelled at assembling integrated circuits. In 1970, *Businessweek* assessed that "after years of rug weaving, Indians were able to visualize complicated patterns and could, therefore, memorize complex integrated circuit designs and make subjective decisions in sorting and quality control."[44] Nakamura details how Fairchild exploited Navajo practices to position the assembling of circuits as "culture work for the nascent information age."[45] This ostensible negotiation of tradition and innovation, and past and future, was meant to hold appeal for stakeholders and consumers.

The histories and projects we have threaded here add the social to the technical, demonstrating how humanistic inquiry orients attention: toward culture, power, memory, touch. Though our volume is, in places, light on gender, race, and class, readers will find within all entries attention to constructions that organize (and therefore hierarchize) social relations.

File also helps us speak to the style and arrangement of *Information: Keywords*. While the women of ancient Rome wove, its orators and poets began to apply *filum* to style; namely, to a way of speaking or writing that was thin, delicate, filamentous. There is, of course, a gendered dimension to that turn of the word. Further, those who speak or write in that way must stick with small themes or risk an embarrassing incongruity between form and content. More generally, *textum*, a woven thing, becomes the English "text," composed of many *fila*. Such threads of meaning, tugged through a foot of verse or prose, are early units of information.[46] The keywords in this volume evince a variety of styles. In terms of scholarly genres, they fall between encyclopedia entries and argumentative essays. Each enjoys its own texture. For that reason, each entry *could* be read standalone, in the manner in which they were composed. But the keywords are best enjoyed in combination, a point to which we return momentarily.

We have arranged the volume alphabetically, a trusted (and Hellenistic in origin) filing system. According to Ann Blair and Peter Stallybrass, scholars of the early modern period, by the mid-15th century a "file" was an actual thread strung up across a room to keep papers organized for easy finding and viewing.[47] As they detail, a 1699 itemized bill delivered to the House of Commons included "'6 large Needles, ½ lb. of Thread' for filing documents."[48] Media theorist Craig Robertson has embarked on a history of the filing cabinet, which was until the rise of the personal computer the most familiar filing system of the twentieth century, and may still continue to be as it has been remediated into the very structure of everyday information gadgets for future generations.[49] Because the design of the "desktop" of the personal computer proceeded on the principle of the skeuomorph, computer "documents" and "files" can be named and placed in folders. With the establishment of the digitally networked mediascape came comment "threads" and "threaded" tweets on Twitter, attempts to keep bursts of communication integrated into something like a conversation—or a soliloquy.

With this short history of *file*, we prepare readers for what they can expect to find as they move deeper into the volume: familiar words made strange, new words made historical, old words made new, humanistic words made informatic, informatic words made humanistic. In this volume, we have opted for an organizational form long found in the steely cases of twentieth-century offices organizing paper bureaucracies: the alphabetical. Of course, other organizational schema are possible. For the sake of readers primed to push against the randomness of the alphabetical, we provide here some thematic file drawers and folders.

Readers interested in questions of *history and periodization* will find that numerous entries evoke concepts of media archeology and the deep time of information.[50] In this historical grouping, we might place into one folder the essays on "archive," "rumor," "index," "intel," "screen," and "tele," all of which take the long view on how their subjects engage with information, often since antiquity. In another folder, we might place those pieces with a shorter timespan, beginning at the dawn of "the information age," and thus enfolding "cognition," "noise," "bioinformatics," "keyword," and "knowledge." These essays foreground the questions of knowledge formation that arose with computerization. Finally, using this method of periodization, we could file those chapters that deal with our present computer-saturated moment of ubiquitous digitization such as "abundance," "algorithm," "cognition," "search," and "self-tracking." But such cutting up of the book in terms of the age of the material covered itself risks overemphasizing the historicity of information rather than similarities over time—in other words, privileging the diachronic over the synchronic. Prioritizing history in this way would also risk losing precisely what the entries that engage ancient sources suggest; namely, that ancient people too had their information overloads, telecommunications nightmares, and gadget failures.

Readers interested in the *theory of information as communication*, following the Shannon model, will find the essays dealing directly and indirectly with source, signal, and receiver of particular value.[51] The entries on "self-tracking," "intel," "gossip," and "abundance" speak to issues of *source*, attending as they do to questions of the production and proliferation of information, and the different ways messages originate and terminate. Under the label of *signal*, we might group "index," "keyword," "tele," "algorithm," and "noise," because these entries are concerned with how information is organized, manipulated, transmitted, and interrupted. In the *receiver* folder, the files for "cognition," "bioinformatics," "archive," "screen," and "knowledge" might provide the start of an alternative history of witnessing, digesting, and consuming the signal.

There could be yet another folder based on the *ontological or material formation of information*. These might be divided into three sub-categories: organism, machine, and institution. Filed together under *organism*, we would find the files on "cognition," "bioinformatics," "abundance," and "self-tracking," each of which consider information in terms of the body and attendant questions of growth, health, and survival. A second folder with the label *machine* would contain those files concerned with matters external to or extended from the body: "screen," "index," "algorithm," "noise," "search," and "tele." That would still leave four files that either resist fitting into one of these folders, calling into question the body-machine dualism, or cut across both machine and body. This folder, labeled *institution*, would feature the files concerned with information as constituted by and for the social and those organizations that establish and structure our interactions with each other and our world. In this folder, we might find filed the entries on "knowledge," "archive," "keyword," "intel," and "gossip." The fun of this grouping is that, depending on one's interpretation, entries could be sorted differently, or challenge the categories; for instance, "self-tracking" might just as well belong with the files in the *machine* folder or call into question the separation between organism and machine.

Yet another grouping might organize entries according to their engagement with information *functions*, such as collecting, sorting, storing, and transmitting. In a folder on *collecting*, "self-tracking," "intel," "gossip," "abundance," and "search" would illustrate the various modes by which information might be identified and gathered. What is gathered must be sorted and organized before it is stored. In the second folder, therefore, which would be labeled *sorting*, one would find the documents that work through questions of distinction, classification, analysis, and exclusion. This folder would include the entries on "index," "keyword," "algorithm," and "noise." A focus on *storing* would bring "archive," "bioinformatics," and "cognition" to the fore. That abc of storage would reveal the materiality of information, at once a gesture toward the infinity of the world as well as a material attempt to record it, reducing it to the markable. Finally, a third folder would contain files concerned with the movement of information implied by the activities of collecting, sorting, and storing. We might label this folder *transmitting*. Etymologically, both "trans-" (Latin "across") and "mission" (from Latin *mitto*, send) are animated by movement, and even the successful delivery and receipt of a transmission does not guarantee one has "gotten through" to someone. Sending something can be a straightforward, orderly process, but messiness sets in across time and distance, or is a feature of the message from the outset, whether the message is symbolic, electrical, or biological. For that reason, we place "tele," "screen," "gossip," and "bioinformatics" in the transmitting folder.

We intend the foregoing files and folders to serve as a tagging or flagging of possible read-throughs, even as we admit most will come to *Information: Keywords*—as we tend more and more to come to our "too much information" spaces and archives—with already piqued interest in particular searches.

Notes

1. T. C. Helvey, *The Age of Information: An Interdisciplinary Survey of Cybernetics* (Englewood Cliffs, NJ: Educational Technology, 1971); Tadao Umesao, "Jōhō sangyō," *Chūō kōron* 78, no. 3 (March 1963); "keyword" quote from Ronald R. Kline, *The Cybernetics*

Moment, or Why We Call Our Age the Information Age (Baltimore: Johns Hopkins University Press, 2017), 204.
2. Robert Darnton, "5 Myths About the Information Age," *Chronicle of Higher Education*, April 17, 2011, https://www.chronicle.com/article/5-Myths-About-the-Information/127105.
3. Eric Hayot, "Introduction," in *Information: A Reader*, ed. Eric Hayot, Lea Pao, Anatoly Detwyler (New York: Columbia University Press, forthcoming).
4. Raymond Williams, *Keywords: A Vocabulary of Culture and Society* (New York: Oxford University Press, 1976).
5. H. Hardy Perritt, "Cybernetics and Rhetoric," *Southern Speech Journal* 20 (1954): 7–15; Daniel Marder, "Entropy in Rhetoric," paper presented at the Annual Meeting of the Conference on College Composition and Communication, Anaheim, CA, April 1974.
6. James R. Beniger, *The Control Revolution: Technological and Economic Origins of the Information Society* (Cambridge, MA: Harvard University Press, 1986), vi.
7. John Durham Peters, "Information: Notes Toward a Critical History," *Journal of Communication Inquiry* 12, no. 2 (1988): 9–23. Peters reviewed Beniger's book in John Durham Peters, "The Control of Information," *Critical Review: A Journal of Books and Ideas* 1, no. 4 (1987): 5–23.
8. Manuel Castells, *The Rise of the Network Society* (Oxford: Blackwell, 1996); Manuel Castells, *The Power of Identity* (Oxford: Blackwell, 1997); Manuel Castells, *End of Millennium* (Oxford: Blackwell, 1998).
9. Ann Blair, *Too Much to Know: Managing Scholarly Information Before the Modern Age* (New Haven, CT: Yale University Press, 2010).
10. Kathleen E. Kennedy, *Medieval Hackers* (New York: Punctum, 2015), 2.
11. Virginia Eubanks, *Automating Inequality: How High-Tech Tools Profile, Police, and Punish the Poor* (New York: St. Martin's, 2018); Safiya Umoja Noble, *Algorithms of Oppression: How Search Engines Reinforce Racism* (New York: New York University Press, 2018). Both Eubanks and Noble are sensitive to intersectionality.
12. Andrew M. Riggsby, *Mosaics of Knowledge: Representing Information in the Roman World* (New York: Oxford University Press, 2019).
13. 2020–2021 has already seen one, and will see another volume explicitly about the history of information: Ida Nijenhuis, Marijke van Faassen, Ronald Sluitjer, Joris Gijsenbergh, and Wim de Jong, eds., *Information and Power in History: Toward a Global Approach* (New York: Routledge, 2020); Ann Blair, Paul Duguid, Anja-Silvia Goeing, and Anthony Grafton, eds., *A Companion to the History of Information* (Princeton: Princeton University Press, forthcoming).
14. *Information: A Reader*, the companion volume to this one, does this latter work.
15. For an overview of disputes since the 1940s over the history and meaning of "information," see Bernard Dionysius Geoghegan, "The Historiographic Conceptualization of Information: A Critical Survey," *IEEE Annals of the History of Computing* (January–March 2008): 66–81.
16. See the entries for those keywords. See also, e.g., Victoria Rimmell, "Let the Page Run On: Poetics, Rhetoric, and Noise in the *Satyrica*," in *Petronius: A Handbook*, ed. Jonathan R. W. Prag and Ian D. Repath (Malden, MA: Wiley-Blackwell, 2009), 65–81; Pamela VanHaitsma, "Gossip as Rhetorical Methodology for Queer and Feminist Historiography," *Rhetoric Review* 35, no. 2 (2016): 135–47.
17. Youichi Ito, "Birth of *Joho shakai* and *Johoka* Concepts in Japan and Their Diffusion Outside Japan," *Keio Communication Review* 13 (1991): 3–12; Yoshimi Shunya, "Information," *Theory, Culture, and Society* 23, nos. 2–3 (May 2006): 271–78. For attention to the development of "the information society" in China in the 1980s, see Xiao Liu,

Information Fantasies: Precarious Mediation in Postsocialist China (Minneapolis: University of Minnesota Press, 2019).
18. Yoneji Masuda, *Jōhō shakai nyumon: Konpyuta wa ningen shakai o kaeru* (Tokyo: Perikansha, 1968); Yoneji Masuda, Seiichirō Yahagi, and Shirō Shimaya, *Jōhōka shakai no yukue: sore wa nani o motarasu ka?* (Tokyo: Nihon keizai shinbun, 1972).
19. Yoneji Masuda, *The Information Society as Post-Industrial Society* (Washington, DC: Word Future Society, 1983), 146–56; Tessa Morris-Suzuki, *Beyond Computopia: Information, Automation, and Democracy in Japan* (New York: Routledge, 2011).
20. Helvey, *The Age of Information*. Its title shows that, at that point, *information* had overtaken *cybernetics* as the leading moniker of the era, earning top billing. Most chapters, though, have "cybernetic" in their titles. Kline, a historian of science and engineering, traces the contest between cybernetics and information in *The Cybernetics Moment*.
21. Martin Heidegger, "On the Essence of Truth," trans. John Sallis, in *Pathmarks*, ed. William McNeill (Cambridge: Cambridge University Press, 1998), 138. With "correctness" Heidegger appeals to the formula of a correspondence theory of truth: *veritas est adaequatio intellectus ad rem*.
22. See Lydia H. Liu, "The Cybernetic Unconscious: Rethinking Lacan, Poe, and French Theory," *Critical Inquiry* 36, no. 2 (2010): 288–320.
23. Edgar Allan Poe, "The Purloined Letter," in *The Selected Writings of Edgar Allan Poe*, ed. G. R. Thompson, Norton Critical Texts (New York: Norton, 2004), 941–52.
24. Chad Wellmon, *Organizing Enlightenment: Information Overload and the Invention of the Modern Research University* (Baltimore: Johns Hopkins University, 2015).
25. Walter Benjamin, "The Storyteller: Observations on the Works of Nikolai Leskov," in *Selected Writings*, vol. 3: *1935–1938*, ed. Howard Eiland and Michael W. Jennings (Cambridge, MA: Harvard University Press, 2002), 143–66. Info-panic often results from new communication technologies. Scholars in early modern Germany (to use an anachronism) wrote warily of "die Bücherflut" (the book-flood) raging forth from printing presses. See Dirk Werle, "Die Bücherflut in der Frühen Neuzeit—realweltliches Problem oder stereotypes Vorstellungsmuster?" in *Frühneuzeitliche Stereotype: Zur Produktivität und Restriktivität Sozialer Vorstellungsmuster*, ed. Miroslawa Czarnecka, Thomas Borgstedt, and Tomasz Jablecki (Bern: Peter Lang, 2010), 469–86. See also Pericles Lewis, "Walter Benjamin in the Information Age? On the Limited Possibilities for a Defetishizing Critique of Culture," in *Mapping Benjamin: The Work of Art in the Digital Age*, ed. Hans Ulrich Gumbrecht and Michael Marrinan (Stanford: Stanford University Press, 2003), 221–29.
26. See, e.g., John Willett, *Art and Politics in the Weimar Period: New Sobriety, 1914–33* (New York: Pantheon, 1978).
27. Bertolt Brecht, *Man Equals Man*, trans. Gerhard Nellhaus, in *The Collected Plays: Two*, ed. John Willett and Ralph Manheim (London: Bloomsbury, 2007), 38.
28. Walter Benjamin, "The Work of Art in the Age of Its Technological Reproducibility: Second Version," in *Selected Writings*, vol. 3: *1935–1938*, 101–33.
29. Guy Debord, *The Society of the Spectacle* (New York: Zone, 1994).
30. For an example of their work together, see Henri La Fontaine and Paul Otlet, *Sur la création d'un Répertoire Bibliographique Universel*, Conference bibliographique internationale (Brussels: Larcier, 1895). See also Alex Wright, *Cataloguing the World: Paul Otlet and the Birth of the Information Age* (New York: Oxford University Press, 2014).
31. For an overview, see David Bawden and Lyn Robinson, eds., *Introduction to Information Science* (London: Facet, 2012).

32. The literature here is vast, and includes Ronald E. Day, *The Modern Invention of Information: Discourse, History and Power* (Carbondale: Southern Illinois University Press, 2001); Ronald E. Day, *Indexing It All: The Subject in the Age of Documentation, Information, and Data* (Cambridge, MA: MIT Press, 2014); Noble, *Algorithms of Oppression*; Melissa Adler, *Cruising in the Library: Perversities in the Organization of Knowledge* (New York: Fordham University Press, 2017); Tonia Sutherland, "Archival Amnesty: In Search of Black American Transitional and Restorative Justice," *Journal of Critical Library and Information Studies* 1, no. 2 (2017).

33. The literature here, too, is vast, so we give but a few examples: Michel Foucault, *The Order of Things: An Archaeology of the Human Sciences* (New York: Pantheon, 1970); Jacques Derrida, *Archive Fever*, trans. Eric Prenowitz (Chicago: University of Chicago Press, 1996); Jason König, Katerina Oikonomopoulou, and Greg Woolf, eds., *Ancient Libraries* (New York: Cambridge University Press, 2013); Kate Eichhorn, *The Archival Turn in Feminism: Outrage in Order* (Philadelphia: Temple University Press, 2013); Boris Jardine and Matthew Drage, "The Total Archive: Data, Subjectivity, Universality," *History of the Human Sciences* 31, no. 5 (May 2019): 3–22; Laura Helton, author of the entry on "archive" in this volume, is working on a book titled *Collecting and Collectivity: Black Archival Publics, 1900–1950*. As Helton stresses, humanists often do not engage with LIS work on the archive and archives. For evidence of humanists overlooking archival studies, see Michelle Caswell, "'The Archive' Is Not an Archives: Acknowledging the Intellectual Contributions of Archival Studies," *Reconstruction: Studies in Contemporary Culture* 16, no. 1 (2016). For a less polemical overview of interest in archives across disciplines, see Marlene Manoff, "Theories of the Archive from Across the Disciplines," *Portal: Libraries and the Academy* 4, no. 1 (2004): 9–25. Thanks to Helton for several of those references.

34. Many such collaborations happen under the aegis of the digital humanities. For an example of a large team, see The Colored Conventions Project, cofounded and codirected by P. Gabrielle Foreman and Jim Casey and currently housed at the University of Delaware but soon to move to Penn State (http://coloredconventions.org/). For examples of humanists in information schools, consider medievalist Bonnie Mak (University of Illinois; associate professor in the School of Information Sciences, with cross appointments in history and medieval studies); Americanist Jonathan Senchyne (University of Wisconsin-Madison; assistant professor in the Information School and director of the Center for the History of Print and Digital Culture); and Helton (Delaware; a Ph.D. in history, a background in anthropology and information and library science, and an assistant professor position in English).

35. S.v. *filum*, Lewis and Short, *A Latin Dictionary*, http://www.perseus.tufts.edu/hopper/text.jsp?doc=Perseus%3Atext%3A1999.04.0059%3Aalphabetic+letter%3DF%3Aentry+group%3D15%3Aentry%3Dfilum.

36. Virginia Postrel, "Losing the Thread," *Aeon*, June 5, 2015, https://aeon.co/essays/how-textiles-repeatedly-revolutionised-human-technology.

37. Mari Lee Mifsud, "On Network," in *Ancient Rhetorics and Digital Networks*, ed. Michele Kennerly and Damien Smith Pfister (Tuscaloosa: University of Alabama Press, 2018), 28–47, 37.

38. See, e.g., Margot Lee Shetterly, *Hidden Figures: The American Dream and the Untold Story of the Black Women Mathematicians Who Helped Win the Space Race* (New York: William Morrow, 2016); Theodore Melfi, dir., *Hidden Figures* (Fox 2000 Pictures, 2016); for the British (nonastronomical) technological scene, see Mar Hicks, *Programmed*

Inequality: How Britain Discarded Women Technologists and Lost Its Edge in Computing (Cambridge, MA: MIT Press, 2017).

39. Daniela K. Rosner, Samantha Shorey, Brock Craft, Helen Remick, "Making Core Memory: Design Inquiry Into Gendered Legacies of Engineering and Craftwork," *Proceedings of the 2018 CHI Conference on Human Factors in Computing Systems*, Paper No. 531, 1. Thanks to Damien Smith Pfister for this reference.
40. Rosner, Shorey, Craft, Remick, "Making Core Memory," 4.
41. "About," The Tempestry Project, November 15, 2018, https://www.tempestryproject.com/about/. Sara J. Grossman stresses the exigence of work on historical weather and climate data in "Archiving Weather Data," *Process: A Blog for American History*, May 4, 2017, http://www.processhistory.org/archiving-weather-data/. Grossman is working on a monograph titled *A Natural History of Data*.
42. For more on the past and present of "knitting as protest," check out Jennifer LeMesurier, "Knitting as Protest," *Academic Minute Blog, Inside Higher Ed.*, January 4, 2019, https://www.insidehighered.com/audio/2019/01/04/knitting-protest#.XFp_pBgN-R9.link. Media archaeology, too, has taken to textiles; see, e.g., artist Sarah Rooney's crochet patterns of early Apple computers at https://mediaarchaeologylab.com/blog/soft-computers-crochet-patterns-by-sarah-rooney/.
43. Lisa Nakamura, "Indigenous Circuits: Navajo Women and the Racialization of Early Electronic Manufacture," *American Quarterly* 66, no. 4 (2014): 919–41, 925. For an earlier history of how Navajo craft was capitalized upon, see Erika Marie Bsumek's *Indian-Made: Navajo Culture in the Marketplace, 1868–1940* (Lawrenceville: University Press of Kansas, 2008).
44. Quoted in Nakamura, "Indigenous Circuits," 926.
45. Nakamura, "Indigenous Circuits," 930.
46. See, e.g., Lea Pao, "Informational Practices in German Poetry: Ernst Meister, Oswald Egger, Friedrich Gottlieb Klopstock," Ph.D. diss., Pennsylvania State University, 2017. Pao's approach to information and poetry is markedly different from that of Paul Stephens, *The Poetics of Information Overload: From Gertrude Stein to Conceptual Writing* (Minneapolis: University of Minnesota Press, 2015).
47. Ann Blair and Peter Stallybrass, "Mediating Information, 1450–1800," in *This Is Enlightenment*, ed. Clifford Siskin and William Warner (Chicago: University of Chicago Press, 2010), 139–63, 139, 152–53.
48. Blair and Stallybrass, "Mediating Information," 153.
49. Craig Robertson, "Learning to File: Reconfiguring Information and Information Work in the Early Twentieth Century," *Technology and Culture* 58, no. 4 (October 2017): 955–81. For a history of hierarchical filing on digital machines from Xerox through Apple, see Jesse Hunter, "Authoring Literacy: From Index to Hypermedia," *Canadian Journal of Communication* 19, no. 1 (1994); Aaron Marcus, "Managing Metaphors for Advanced User Interfaces," *ACM '94 Proceedings of the Workshop on Advanced Visual Interfaces* (1994): 12–18.
50. Erkki Huhtamo and Jussi Parikka, *Media Archaeology: Approaches, Applications, and Implications* (Berkeley: University of California Press, 2011); Jussi Parikka, *A Geology of Media* (Minneapolis: University of Minnesota Press, 2015); Siegfried Zielinski, *Deep Time of the Media: Toward an Archaeology of Hearing and Seeing by Technical Means* (Cambridge, MA: MIT Press, 2006).
51. C. E. Shannon, "A Mathematical Theory of Communication," reprinted with corrections from *The Bell System Technical Journal* 27 (July, October 1948): 379–423, 623–56. In his entry on "noise," Matt Jordan analyzes this model in detail.

ABUNDANCE

DAMIEN SMITH PFISTER

Public discourse about information often mirrors Homer Simpson's famous line about beer: it is the cause of and solution to all the world's problems. Critics of digital culture frequently highlight the ongoing crisis of "information overload" as the cause of multiplying epistemic problems. According to these critics, the abundance of available data makes it much more difficult to decide what to believe about political dramas, scientific controversies, consumer purchases, and other human obsessions. The characterization of information overload in a digital context is increasingly creative: it has been variously referred to as information glut, infobesity, infoxication, and data smog. The fear of digital information abundance has been as creatively explored, with its drawbacks including information anxiety, information pollution, paralysis by analysis, continuous partial attention, attention deficit disorder, and multimultimultitasking, in addition to the proliferation of con artists and computational propaganda. At the same time, information is positioned as a marvelous antidote for that which ails us: with more data, we might finally be able to meaningfully assess political dramas, scientific controversies, and consumer purchases, in other words the very human obsessions that the abundance of data complicated. What is needed to guide human affairs more wisely and efficiently is "Big Data" about human (and increasingly nonhuman) practices, better algorithms to acquire, sort, and analyze, and artificial intelligence that can crunch, output, and iterate. We are invited to fantasize about the plenitude of digital information, which entails benefits like pervasive computing passively gathering data on everything from health and activity to ambient air quality and traffic; digital devices detecting the previously unseen and unthematized in order to serve the public good; and digital personal assistants who learn your habits and seamlessly make sure your latte is paid for and waiting when you go to pick it up.

Fears and fantasies of information abundance have accompanied every inscription technology since alphabetic writing but seem to have intensified in what many call "The Information Age."[1] If the experience of acquiring information for most of human history was like waiting for water from a slowly dripping faucet, it is now, as Richard Lanham observes, like "drinking from a firehose."[2] In 2008, *Wired* magazine announced the advent of what they dubbed "The Petabyte Age," reflecting the "Big Data" rhetoric then beginning to circulate in public discourse.[3] The Petabyte Age, when we considered the possibilities of mere millions of gigabytes, was short lived, eclipsed by the Zettabyte Age in 2016, in which trillions of gigabytes now constitute the horizon of abundance. To trace "abundance" as a keyword of information theory, then, is to illustrate the fantasies and fears related to interpretation, control, and emotion that are baked into the very concept of information, especially as that term is pulled into the orbit of culture and governance. In relating an abbreviated account of the history of information abundance as a concept, I aim to trouble the naturalized connection between information and epistemics. From *copia*, the prescription to produce abundance as an inventional aide for rhetorical performance, to computers, capable of producing and managing abundance, the concept of information has typically been articulated to epistemology.[4] Information is knowledge is power, or at least close enough that the gaps between them are often elided.[5] To acquire abundant information about web searches for "flu" gives public health organizations knowledge about where flu outbreaks are occurring, authorizing the power to focus their curative resources on areas of need. In an epistemic frame, questions of information are steered toward variants of "How can information gathering, analysis, and circulation be optimized so that power might be deployed differently or more efficiently?" This is why the epistemic frame induces rhetorics of fantasy and fear: because the politics of information often have life or death consequences. How information abundance is managed matters, but a middling approach between fantasy and fear might offer a more pragmatic way to think about information abundance in all its complexity. What kinds of questions might be asked if information, in all its abundance, is thought of not as a question of epistemics but of technics? Put differently, how might questions related to information abundance change when information itself is seen not as a transparent window into the real but as the product of a technical infrastructure that has its own politics?

To answer that question invites a turn to an early clash between epistemics and technics: between Plato and the sophists. Yes, it is well-trodden terrain. Nonetheless, recasting the contest between Plato and his sophistic foils in the context of information abundance offers a new path through this familiar conflict. In short, Platonic reservations about the sophists are primarily expressions of fear about information abundance, and the sophistic celebration of never-ending rhetorical performances is primarily about the fantasy of better living through more communication. This communication was still primarily oral, but newly abundant because the new infrastructures of democracy created frequent opportunities for speech. Moreover, the new media technology of writing produced an abundance of texts. For Nathan Crick, the sophistical attitude is "marked by a respect for the diversity and reality of human experience as reflected in the multiplicity of *logoi*."[6] Abundance is necessary in order to provide an accounting of all the various perspectives that might be voiced on an issue. Gorgias, Protagoras, and Prodicus—to name three prominent sophists—embraced the perspective that any claim was but an interpretation of events that "discloses new possibilities in the world."[7] Of course, not all interpretations were equally compelling. In the proliferation of differently styled interpretations, and the subsequent winnowing down of these plausible interpretations through competing rhetorical performances, rests the experimentalist ethos of democracy. Sophistic pedagogy, then, emphasized playing with language, with rhetorical figuration, with different ways of interpreting shared experience in order to surface "unrecognized qualities of things and then suggesting new possibilities of action based on their analysis and comparison."[8] In abundance lies not just pleasure but the belief that more words will open up more worlds.

Against the endless proliferation of interpretation prized by the sophists stands Plato's Socrates. From Plato's critique of Protagoras' penchant for making the weaker argument appear the stronger, to his unsympathetic portrayal of the wordsmithing of Prodicus, to offhand characterizations of sophists as buzzing about on any subject, the very idea of abundant interpretations rivaled the Platonic assumption that one true meaning could be found if enough dialectical pressure were applied to a particular topic. Plato's *The Sophist* most explicitly takes on this issue, tackling a fundamental question of ontology: is being many or one? Can a person or a thing be described in manifold ways, or is there one way that best—truly, essentially—describes the essence of a thing? If alphabetic writing makes common life *"available to interpretation* (by citizens debating it in the *logos*)," as Bernard Stiegler explains, then Plato's philosophical approach was oriented towards the *"logical reduction of interpretability."*[9] Stiegler elaborates how the invention of writing technology precipitated this clash over the value of interpretability:

> Contrary to what Plato would have us believe (Plato, who understood truth as univocity and exactitude (*orthotēs*), as universality in this sense, and not as the plurivocal singularity of meanings variously conferred on a statement by the

multiplicity of readers), this participation [of citizens arguing over texts] is an interpretation (*hermeneia*), an activity by which the *logos*, far from limiting itself to *a* meaning, opens *unlimited* interpretive possibilities.... The statement, when it has become text, proves to be interminably interpretable.[10]

The circulation of written materials, and the democratic wrangling about their meanings, disturbed Plato's assumption that the natural joints of the world could be carved up through dialectic.[11] The merger of rhetoric with the technology of writing, Plato warns in *The Phaedrus*, only exacerbates this abundance of interpretation about the likely and the possible, rather than the real and actual.[12] The stakes, for Plato, could not be starker: proliferating interpretations—embracing plurivocality—was a poor way to decide court cases or govern a *polis*, when the truth could be at hand with more rigorous dialectical methods.

Plato's warning hardly forestalled rhetoricians working in his wake from prescribing abundance. Indeed, rhetorical theorists since Plato have been abundant in their prescriptions for abundance. In *The Rhetoric*, Aristotle suggests that different situations call for *onkos*, expansiveness, instead of *syntomia*, concision, as when a metaphor might help clarify a point.[13] The abundant use of conjunctions evokes this sense of expansiveness, as with the rhetorical figure of polysyndeton (a linking together of clauses with, for example, "and" instead of commas in order to amplify the feeling of piling on). Indeed, many rhetorical figures are oriented around the abundant: *exergasia*, the repetition of the same idea in different words; *epimone*, the repetition of the same idea in similar words; *ekphrasis*, a vivid, abundantly detailed description that brings a scene before the eyes (and that's just some of the e's!). Ancient pedagogies like the *progymnasmata*, a set of rhetorical exercises that asked students to refigure a fable or elaborate on a maxim, were grounded in *imitatio*: do it more, and do it differently, and then do it again, more and differently. This ancient tradition was modified and codified centuries later by the Renaissance humanist Erasmus. In chapter 8 of *Copia: Foundations of the Abundant Style*, Erasmus extends the fantasy that rhetorical abundance is useful for elevating one's eloquence, maintaining the attention of an audience, and developing a store of knowledge one can tap into for extemporaneous speaking in public life. Famously, in chapter 33, Erasmus demonstrates his command of *copia* by writing almost 200 variants of the sentence "Your letter pleased me greatly."

Erasmus's defense of abundant style did not cause the explosion of book publication in the wake of the printing press's diffusion throughout Europe, though it might be seen as authorizing the rapid increase in printed materials throughout the 16th and 17th centuries. If *copia* was a good practice, then let's exercise it by printing lots of books! Despite his defense of *copia*, Erasmus is famous for opining that the hip new writings proliferating in print culture were crowding out the more venerable ancient texts: "Is there anywhere on earth exempt from these swarms of new books?"[14] The irony should not be lost: defenders of abundance often become skittish when it's not their kind of abundance, just as skeptics of abundance are often fast to praise new flows of information when their own interests are served. Ann Blair's catalog of the abundance of books as a theme in early modernity includes this plaint from Erasmus and similar luminaries over two centuries: John Calvin complains about the "confused forest of books"; Conrad Gessner scoffs at the "harmful and confusing abundance of books"; René Descartes decided that starting philosophy from scratch would be easier than sorting through the stock of published books where knowledge is "mixed in with many useless things and confusingly heaped in such large volumes"; and Gottfried Leibniz warned of the "return to barbarism" if the "horrible mass of books" keeps proliferating.[15] Information abundance in the age of print thus required the invention of new methods of management, hence the development of commonplace books, reference guides like encyclopedias and almanacs, and journals that focused on reviewing the never-ending waves of books. In other words, the early moderns managed information abundance by inventing the idea of metadata. An underappreciated dimension of the print-powered democratic revolutions in the modern era is the rise of these new masters of metadata, editors and professional critics who felt themselves capable of reviewing and synthesizing the conversations unfolding in the world of print as a way to manage the perceived information overload of the time.[16] Information about information doesn't seem much of a cure for abundance, but concise treatments of larger topics did offer a way to cull more efficiently a large body of specialty literature for a public audience and, more importantly, cut through the confusion of competing claims by systematically attesting to the veracity of some kinds of information over others.

Despite the promise that these modern innovations in synthesizing knowledge would forge order out of the confusing buzz of books, the politics of curation that inheres in the editorial taste-making process prevented the consensus about information that so many Enlightenment figures assumed would inevitably emerge through rational and open discussion.[17] Indeed, as Chad Wellmon documents, the new technologies of encyclopedias and periodicals "failed to deliver on the promise of universal knowledge," and so a new technology had to be invented to control the chaos of information abundance: the research university.[18] Wellmon's account underlines that the concern about information abundance was really about control over epistemic authority, or "what counted as *authoritative* knowledge."[19] Authoritative knowledge would be established by organizing information into discrete disciplines and credentialing subjects authorized to speak about particular research areas, producing a respectable run for universities as organizers of information abundance. However, the contemporary research university, with ever-expanding disciplinary, interdisciplinary, subdisciplinary, and transdisciplinary program offerings, alongside a publishing landscape designed primarily to reward abundance, addresses the problem of information abundance little better than the encyclopedia did earlier.

Critical reactions to information abundance in the modern era were certainly not uniformly fearful. In Europe, cracking the Church and State's hegemony over the flow of information was historically crucial to setting in motion the processes of democratization. Habermas's account of the early modern development of the bourgeois public sphere provides the most obvious example of how more abundant and freely flowing information cultivated subjects who, fortified with facts gleaned from the new sources of print media, saw themselves as capable of self-governance.[20] The democratic imagination has figured information abundance as a way to address the scale of the nation-state ever since. This is especially the case in the United States, where pamphleteering in the early republic and affordable newspapers later on were seen as fundamental to the enterprise of being a citizen. Based on his observations from the 1830s, Alexis de Tocqueville remarked, using the aristocrat's typical device of a backhanded compliment, that the United States' constitution vested a frightening amount of faith in the ability of citizens to gather and evaluate information about civic goings on.[21] Bruce Bimber goes so far as to argue that information abundance is historically the motor driving changes in democratic practice in the United States. The creation of the Postal Service and the burgeoning newspaper industry produced political parties as information brokers in the early republic; industrialization increased the complexity of information, spurring the advent of interest groups; and by the mid-twentieth century electronic broadcast media opened up new possibilities for mass politics reconfigured around voices and bodies. Responding to these changes in the communicative infrastructure and to de Tocqueville's shade about the prospects of democracy in the U.S., progressive reformers in the early twentieth century pushed for universal literacy, public education, and, following John Dewey, "the improvement of the methods and conditions of debate, discussion, and persuasion."[22] Muckraking magazines of the time bloomed with the subsidies provided by new advertising revenue, rooting out corruption in democratic institutions by whipping up public discontent. Indeed, the progressive ideal of the "informed citizen" embeds access to and facility with information into broadly shared cultural assumptions of what makes a good citizen.[23]

The effects of information abundance are so hotly contested because they threaten (for better or worse, depending on perspective) control over information routines: treasured sources of epistemic authority, trustworthy intermediaries and gatekeepers, tried-and-true genres and styles of communication. Add to this list a recurring thematization of the relationship between information abundance and emotion. New forms of mediation expand the range of expressivity; these new forms of expressivity are often coded as emotional; and stakeholders associated with established media work to control that emotional expressivity. Whereas critics of writing technologies such as Plato feared the loss of richness that a move away from face-to-face dialogue implied, many critics of electronic mass media feared that the return of that richness of voice, intonation, pace, pitch, gesture—all of the intensities of embodiment—would threaten the more controlled intellectual environment of print. Consider, for example, Habermas's declinist tale of the public sphere: rational-critical debate reigned during the heyday of print culture, but electronic mass media degraded the press's historical focus on public argument in favor of celebrity bodies, the pomp and circumstance of consumerism, and entertainment divorced from reason-giving talk.[24] Or take Walter Lippmann's diagnosis of media, emotion, and stereotyping in the context of new electronic mass media. "In the great blooming, buzzing confusion of the outer world," Lippman claims, alluding to William James's theory of attention and perception, "we pick out what our culture has already defined for us, and we tend to perceive that which we have picked out in the form stereotyped for us by our culture."[25] These stereotypes recur because "memory and emotion are in a snarl. . . . In the uncriticized parts of the mind there is a vast amount of association by mere clang, contact, and succession."[26] Humans have limited attention and time, Lippmann argues, so stereotyping is a predictable defense mechanism in response to the explosion of media sources in the early twentieth century. (Big technology platforms will spin this more positively when defending their use of algorithmically contoured feeds: there is so much information that we need to make sense of it for you, and the way that we'll do that is by stereotyping you based on past preferences). However, for Lippmann, since stereotypes are grounded in unruly emotion, they make poor guides for public action. Lippmann's educational ideal is quite explicitly a Socrates for every citizen, an interlocutor focused on cross-examining an advocate until clarity of thought and expression—a limitation on interpretability—are achieved.[27] Acknowledging the impossibility of such a scenario, Lippman prescribes more realistically a system of "organized intelligence," experts able to make sense of the flow of information in a way that more capably controls those mystic chords of memory and emotion.[28]

Concerns about the relationship between information abundance and excesses of emotion increased after the experience of propaganda in World War I, the development of more sophisticated methods of advertising based on psychological principles, and the later use of the radio to whip up public emotion by polarizing figures like Father Coughlin in the United States and Adolf Hitler in Germany. Mark Wollaeger captures the complexities surrounding information abundance and emotion during this time: "Mass media thus became both cause and cure: the propagation of too much information by the media created a need for the propagandistic simplifications disseminated by the media as well as a receptive audience for modernism's deep structures of significance.... [B]oth modernism and propaganda provided mechanisms for coping with information flows that had begun to outstrip the processing capacity of the mind; both fabricated new forms of coherence in response to new experiences of chaos."[29] Indeed, propaganda was advanced by World War I propagandist Harold Lasswell as a necessary "concession to the rationality of the modern world. A literate world, a reading world, a schooled world prefers to thrive on argument and news.... The new antidote to [individual] wilfulness [sic] is propaganda. If the mass will be free of chains of iron, it must accept its chains of silver. If it will not love, honor, and obey, it must not expect to escape seduction."[30] Lasswell registers the shifting sensibility from print to electronic mass media, advancing the claim that the affective power of radio and film must be yoked to the interest of the state or else chaos, under the guise of individual wills to power, will reign. Managing—or manipulating—the emotions of the masses in this new era of information abundance was as necessary for the good of the state as it was for the good of the next stage of industrial capitalism.[31]

There was a thin line between propagandists and the new rhetorical entrepreneurs of radio, film, and later, television: stir the emotions of an audience, but not so much that the subsequent riling up cannot itself be managed. Thus, in the United States, teachers of public speaking during the early radio years prescribed emotional self-control for citizens speaking on the radio. "Faced with the cacophony of chaotic voices that were believed to characterize the Great Society," Brenton J. Malin explains, "speakers were to restrain their own emotions—to sound 'natural'—even as they sought technologically sophisticated ways to amplify their voices above the crowd."[32] After World War II, this thin line seemed thinner than ever. In Max Horkheimer and Theodor Adorno's famous critique of mass culture, popular radio had prepared German citizens for fascism by standardizing the listening public's attitudes in such a way as to make them more susceptible to the "omnipresence of his [Hitler's] radio addresses."[33] This observation about the radio's production of information abundance is the "gigantic fact" that they argue must be acknowledged as the most consequential effect of electronic mass media.[34] A Disney short film produced during World War II, *Reason and Emotion*, tried to draw attention to this gigantic fact by showing how the new abundance of information was sowing confusion in the United States, too.[35] The turning point of the short film features a man in a plush chair gradually becoming overwhelmed by the flow of information from the radio, newspapers, and personal social networks that spread rumor, innuendo, and fear. "Go ahead, put reason out of the way," says the narrator, "that's great, fine ... for Hitler." *Reason and Emotion* then dissects how Hitler's appeals to emotions like fear, sympathy, pride, and hate through the radio negatively shaped German attitudes. Unironically, the short cartoon closes by noting that Reason, personified in the cartoon as an eggheadish man, should keep on reasoning, and that Emotion, personified as a Neanderthal, should be strong and love their country—all of this as the short film concludes with sweeping, patriotic music playing over scenes of United States' military bombers in flight. Emotion, it turns out, is difficult to tamp down, even for those dedicated to controlling it.

The diffusion of television in the mid-twentieth century and eventually internetworked media in the late twentieth century paired this anxiety about information abundance, control, and emotion with some more hopeful messages about allowing a broader range of experiences to gain access to the power of publicity. Marshall McLuhan's claim that electric technology recovers the acoustic and the visual from oral cultures entails a return to the world of primordial feelings structured by speech events. "Our experience is not exclusive of other people's experience," McLuhan probes, "but inclusive—symphonic and orchestral, rather than linear and melodic. . . . We may be drowning. But if so, the flood of experience in which we are drowning is very much a part of the culture we have created."[36] McLuhan's optimism about this phenomenon was rarely as high as his interpreters and acolytes led a wider public to believe; nonetheless, his aphoristic legacy prompted a recuperative analysis of televisual media in the wake of Newton Minow's scarcity-inflected claim that television sets were gateways to a "vast wasteland."[37] For example, Kevin DeLuca traces McLuhan's impact on Greenpeace as a representation of how the new social movements of the 1960s and 70s relied on emotionally intense "image events" that spurred public action around environmentalism.[38] Of course, television spectacles were not universally embraced; indeed, debates about the "society of the spectacle" initiated by Guy Debord and extended by Jean Baudrillard and Murray Edelman are fundamentally critiques of televisual information abundance in late capitalism.[39]

Arguments about media, information, control, and emotion intensified as digital media technology diffused in the late twentieth century. Charitable interpreters of digital information abundance like Henry Jenkins and David Thorburn praise the growth of digital communication channels for expanding "the range of voices that can be heard in a national debate."[40] Jenny Edbauer Rice suggests that the affective investments of bloggers are foundational to the rise of networked publics capable of shaping broader deliberative currents.[41] The rage over #TheDress, a picture of a dress that could be perceived as either white and gold or black and blue which, as they say, broke the internet in February 2015, could be interpreted as evidence of the emotional poverty and surplus inanity of these new networks of digital communication *or* as evidence of how emotionally intense controversies in digital culture strengthen informal social networks that can then be redirected toward more serious civic issues.[42] What is distinctive about contemporary network societies is that they balance scale and richness of communicative encounter better than any prior media ecology: "what makes today's networks so profoundly different from traditional social networks is that, for the first time, they scale well.... The resulting relationships among the different [network] nodes are rich and specific."[43] The widespread production of "ambient intimacy" simultaneously offers new ways of maintaining diachronic and synchronic relationships with others while producing a culture where the charge of TMI—too much information—is frequently leveled.[44]

And so we cycle back around to the theme of interpretability and its discontents. In many ways, Yochai Benkler's foundational work on the networked public sphere echoes the sophistic attitude toward the benefits of expanding interpretability. For Benkler, the distributed communication architecture and the practical elimination of communication costs, the combination of which precipitates the ongoing information explosion, is accompanied by a transformation in how citizens see themselves as capable interlocutors.[45] Benkler's position conceals class privilege, as elite voices have the rhetorical savvy and social networks to flourish in the attention economy. Nonetheless, there are more vernacular voices participating in the networked public sphere, which animates boundary work around who can and should participate in the processes of interpretability. Case in point: in 2004, during the U.S. presidential election contest between incumbent George W. Bush and Senator John Kerry, a discussion board commenter at the conservative hub *Free Republic*, writing under the pseudonym "Buckhead," debunked the Killian memos—documents that called into question Bush's service in the National Guard during the 1970s. Buckhead used his background in the typewriter business to note that the memos were proportionally spaced instead of monospaced, a technical style that was not widespread until the mid-1990s. The ensuing controversy ultimately cost venerable news anchor Dan Rather, who had broken the Killian memos story on *60 Minutes*, his job. The press couldn't resist the David vs. Goliath framing of the story, with plucky internet commenter Buckhead taking down an icon of journalism. However, the backlash against Buckhead echoed many of the fears of information abundance that have appeared in other media ecologies. Former vice president of *CBS News* Jonathan Klein defended the traditional broadcast media against criticism by everyday citizens through internetworked media: "you couldn't have a starker contrast between the multiple layers of checks and balances [at *60 Minutes*] and a guy sitting in his living room in his pajamas writing."[46] *The Weekly Standard* echoed Klein's perspective: "if you trawl the posting boards at *FreeRepublic.com* long enough, you'll go mad. Hundreds of voices are shouting, spitting, and clamoring for attention at any given moment."[47] Both of these assessments express commitments to a prior mode of information management and anxieties about the prevalence of new modes of iteration and interpretability.

The early blogosphere represented what Manuel Castells calls a "network of hope," an avenue for democratic participation that potentially represented (for a moment, at least) an improvement over prior media ecologies with regards to inclusion. Yet, the expansion of information abundance, and the interpretability it invites, also facilitates what Castells identifies as "networks of outrage."[48] These networks of outrage can fuel anti-authoritarian movements, like Occupy Wall Street, the Arab Spring, and the *indignadas* in Spain. But they can also fuel populist movements that flirt with—or marry—fascism. The post–Great Recession growth of right-wing populism, in Hungary and Poland, in the Philippines and Russia, and in the United States with the election of Donald Trump to the presidency, is deeply entangled with the emotional currents that are made possible by a newly abundant information ecology. Rhetorical provocateurs like Alex Jones of *Infowars* inflame the passions of a small but committed audience; white supremacists and neo-Nazis have leveraged the reduction in communication costs to circulate their own messages of hate; the manosphere spreads misogyny and toxic masculinity; Russian computational propagandists aim to exacerbate the feelings of tension between racialized identities.[49] These phenomena are all enabled by the underlying abundance of information that encourages the creation of echo chambers or filter bubbles, which, in the wake of the events of 2016, have been understood as sites where "alternative facts" have ushered in "post-truth" politics. The anxieties around this outburst of proto-fascist emotion are warranted at the same time that they may be somewhat misplaced: truth has always been slipperier than philosophers and politicians have assumed, and today's neo-fascist revival can be traced to liberalism's latest crisis as a public philosophy and a widening rich/poor gap as much as information abundance.

In many ways, "The Information Age" seems as committed as ever to an epistemic perspective on information, though there are glimmers of a perspective on information as a product of technics that might offer a more capacious way to think about information abundance and scarcity. Daniel Czitrom, following McLuhan, identifies this tension between epistemics and technics as a key theme in media history: "ever since Socrates used dialectics against the rhetoric of his sophist teachers, a continuing quarrel has raged over whether grammar and rhetoric on the one hand or dialectics on the other should prevail in organizing knowledge."[50] The most recent instantiation of this quarrel is over the possibilities of "Big Data," the codeword for contemporary information abundance. The epistemic approach seeks to engage in a computationally driven "Big Dialectic," relying on data-mining techniques in order to establish actionable information. The technical approach recognizes that those data-mining techniques are not neutral or natural: they impose a grammar on data, a grammar that is rhetorically struggled over and that has rhetorical effects. In other words, behind every good epistemic process is a good technics. While the epistemic approach can be characterized as prevailing in the context of big data, the seeds of a technics turn have been planted by scholars like Lisa Gitelman, who boldly claims "raw data is an oxymoron."[51] The technics turn in information theory orients us to the affordances and constraints of information's grammars, to the political economy in which information production is nested, and to the various cultural uses that information is put toward. The turn to technics encourages us to ask: How does a given technical apparatus shape what is perceived as information? How is information, and by extension human claims to knowing, structured by technical infrastructures? Flu outbreaks might become able to be mapped in more granular detail through an aggregation of web searches, but only because the middle class produces search trails when they are afflicted. Poverty kills more people than the flu, but the problems of poverty do not neatly fit into the dominant grammar of digital technology, since there is little economic incentive to adjust the grammar to account for poverty, and information about poverty is a poor substitute for structural redress. Instead of complaining that there is too much or too little information, we might focus our efforts on understanding how information is made to be information, who information works for and who works on information, and how information comes to be naturalized as knowledge. Therein lies the middle path between fear and fantasy.

Notes

Thanks to Robert Hariman, Michele Kennerly, Samuel Frederick, and Jonathan Abel for their feedback on earlier drafts.

1. Consider, as evidence, a Google n-gram for "information overload" and for "information scarcity," both of which skyrocket after 1960.
2. Richard Lanham, *The Electronic Word: Democracy, Technology, and the Arts* (Chicago: University of Chicago Press, 1993), 227.
3. See "The Petabyte Age: Because More Isn't Just More—More Is Different," *Wired*, June 2008, https://www.wired.com/2008/06/pb-intro/.
4. Robert L. Scott, "On Viewing Rhetoric as Epistemic," *Communication Studies* 18, no. 1 (1967): 9–17.
5. See E. Johanna Hartelius, "Big Data and Global Pulse: A Protagorean Analysis of the United Nations' Global Pulse," in Michele Kennerly and Damien Smith Pfister, eds., *Ancient Rhetorics and Digital Networks* (Tuscaloosa: University of Alabama Press, 2018): 67–87.
6. Nathan Crick, "The Sophistical Attitude and the Invention of Rhetoric," *Quarterly Journal of Speech* 96, no. 1 (2010): 41.
7. Crick, "Sophistical Attitude," 41.
8. Crick, "Sophistical Attitude," 33–34.
9. Bernard Stiegler, *Symbolic Misery*, vol. 1: *The Hyper-Industrial Epoch* (Cambridge: Polity, 2014), 56–57. Italics in original.
10. Bernard Stiegler, *Symbolic Misery*, vol. 2: *The Catastrophe of the Sensible* (Cambridge: Polity, 2015), 38.

11. *Phaedrus*, 266e in Plato, *Euthyphro. Apology. Crito. Phaedo. Phaedrus.*, trans. Harold North Fowler, Loeb Classical Library 36 (Cambridge, MA: Harvard University Press, 1914), 536.
12. Plato, *Phaedrus*, 272d.
13. *The Rhetoric*, 1408a; in Aristotle, *On Rhetoric: A Theory of Civic Discourse*, trans. George A. Kennedy (Oxford: Oxford University Press, 2007), 209.
14. Desiderius Erasmus, *The Adages of Erasmus*, selected by William Barker (Toronto: University of Toronto Press, 2001), 145.
15. Ann Blair, *Too Much to Know: Managing Scholarly Information Before the Modern Age* (New Haven, CT: Yale University Press, 2010), 55–61.
16. Jürgen Habermas, *The Structural Transformation of the Bourgeois Public Sphere: An Inquiry Into a Category of Bourgeois Society*, trans. Thomas Burger (Cambridge, MA: MIT Press, 1989), 41.
17. See E. Johanna Hartelius, *The Rhetoric of Expertise* (Lanham, MD: Lexington, 2010) and Krista Kennedy, *Textual Curation: Authorship, Agency, and Technology in Wikipedia and Chambers's Cyclopædia* (Columbia: University of South Carolina Press, 2016).
18. Chad Wellmon, *Organizing Enlightenment: Information Overload and the Invention of the Modern Research University* (Baltimore: Johns Hopkins University Press, 2015), 9.
19. Wellmon, *Organizing Enlightenment*, 12, emphasis in original.
20. Habermas, *Structural Transformation*, 27; see also Charles Taylor, *Modern Social Imaginaries* (Durham, NC: Duke University Press, 2003).
21. Alexis de Tocqueville, *Democracy in America*, trans. and ed. Harvey C. Mansfield and Debra Winthrop (Chicago: University of Chicago Press, 2000), 155.
22. John Dewey, *The Public and Its Problems* (Athens: Ohio University Press, 1927), 208.
23. Michael Schudson, *The Good Citizen: A History of American Civic Life* (New York: Free Press, 1998).
24. Habermas, *Structural Transformation*, chapter 18.
25. Walter Lippmann, *Public Opinion* (New York: Free Press, 1997), 55.
26. Lippmann, *Public Opinion*, 254.
27. Lippmann, *Public Opinion*, 255.
28. Lippmann, *Public Opinion*, part 8.
29. Mark Wollaeger, *Modernism, Media, and Propaganda: British Narrative from 1900 to 1945* (Princeton: Princeton University Press, 2006), xiii.
30. Quoted in Peter Simonson and John Durham Peters, eds., *Mass Communication and American Social Thought, Key Texts 1919–1968* (Lanham, MD: Rowman and Littlefield, 2004), 50.
31. Edward Bernays, "Manipulating Public Opinion: The Why and the How," *American Journal of Sociology* 33, no. 6 (1928): 958–71.
32. Brenton J. Malin, *Feeling Mediated: A History of Media Technology and Emotion in the United States* (New York: New York University Press, 2014), 110.
33. Max Horkheimer and Theodor Adorno, *The Dialectic of Enlightenment: Philosophical Fragments*, ed. Gunzelin Schmid Noerr, trans. Edmund Jephcott (Stanford: Stanford University Press, 2002), 129.
34. Horkheimer and Adorno, *Dialectic of Enlightenment*, 129.
35. *Reason and Emotion*, directed by Bill Roberts, Walt Disney Productions, August 27, 1943. The sexist representation of reason and emotion in this short propaganda film hints at how fears and fantasies of information abundance are also articulated to gender and other social identities.

36. Marshall McLuhan, *Counterblast* (London: Rapp & Whiting, 1970), 13, 115.
37. Newton N. Minow, "Television and the Public Interest," speech delivered to the National Association of Broadcasters, May 9, 1961, http://www.americanrhetoric.com/speeches/newtonminow.htm.
38. Kevin DeLuca, *Image Politics: The New Rhetoric of Environmental Activism* (New York: The Guilford Press, 1999).
39. Guy Debord, *Society of the Spectacle*, trans. Donald Nicholson-Smith (New York: Zone, 1994); Jean Baudrillard, *Simulacra and Simulation*, trans. Sheila Glaser (Ann Arbor: University of Michigan Press, 1994); Murray Edelman, *Constructing the Political Spectacle* (Chicago: University of Chicago Press, 1988).
40. Henry Jenkins and David Thorburn, eds., *Democracy and New Media* (Cambridge, MA: MIT Press, 2003), 2.
41. Jenny Edbauer Rice, "The New 'New': Making a Case for Critical Affect Studies," *Quarterly Journal of Speech* (May 2008): 211.
42. "#TheDress/What Color Is This Dress," Know Your Meme, http://knowyourmeme.com/memes/thedress-what-color-is-this-dress.
43. Felix Stalder, *Manuel Castells: The Theory of the Network Society* (Cambridge: Polity, 2006), 181.
44. I have detailed this development in *Networked Media, Networked Rhetorics: Attention and Deliberation in the Early Blogosphere* (University Park: Pennsylvania State University Press, 2014), chapter 4.
45. Yochai Benkler, *The Wealth of Networks: How Social Production Transforms Markets and Freedom* (New Haven, CT: Yale University Press, 2006), 225, 230.
46. Jonathan Last, "What Blogs Hath Wrought," *Weekly Standard*, September 27, 2004, http://www.weeklystandard.com/Content/Public/Articles/000/000/004/640pgolk.asp?pg=2.
47. Last, "What Blogs Hath Wrought."
48. Manuel Castells, *Networks of Outrage and Hope: Social Movements in the Internet Age* (Cambridge: Polity, 2012).
49. See John B. Judis, *The Populist Explosion: How the Great Recession Transformed American and European Politics* (New York: Columbia Global Reports, 2016); Angela Nagle, *Kill All Normies: Online Culture Wars from 4chan and Tumblr to Trump and the Alt-Right* (Croydon, UK: Zero, 2017); Samantha Bradshaw and Philip Howard, "Challenging Truth and Trust: A Global Inventory of Organized Social Media Manipulation," *Computational Propaganda Research Project*, 2018, http://comprop.oii.ox.ac.uk/wp-content/uploads/sites/93/2018/07/ct2018.pdf.
50. Daniel Czitrom, *Media and the American Mind: From Morse to McLuhan* (Chapel Hill: University of North Carolina Press, 1982), 168.
51. Lisa Gitelman, ed., *"Raw Data" Is an Oxymoron* (Cambridge, MA: MIT Press, 2013). Although I have emphasized the relationship between information abundance and public deliberation as it coevolves with the development of new media technologies, the technics turn in information theory might also encourage consideration of abundance as an anthropological condition. Humans produce abundant information, and greater attention to the aesthetics and symbolic forms of that information might yield deeper insight about the world. Robert Hariman and John Louis Lucaites have made such a point in the context of the technical apparatus of photography in their chapter "The Abundant Image," in *The Public Image: Photography and Civic Spectatorship* (Chicago: University of Chicago Press, 2017): 227–60.

11. *Phaedrus*, 266e in Plato, *Euthyphro. Apology. Crito. Phaedo. Phaedrus.*, trans. Harold North Fowler, Loeb Classical Library 36 (Cambridge, MA: Harvard University Press, 1914), 536.
12. Plato, *Phaedrus*, 272d.
13. *The Rhetoric*, 1408a; in Aristotle, *On Rhetoric: A Theory of Civic Discourse*, trans. George A. Kennedy (Oxford: Oxford University Press, 2007), 209.
14. Desiderius Erasmus, *The Adages of Erasmus*, selected by William Barker (Toronto: University of Toronto Press, 2001), 145.
15. Ann Blair, *Too Much to Know: Managing Scholarly Information Before the Modern Age* (New Haven, CT: Yale University Press, 2010), 55–61.
16. Jürgen Habermas, *The Structural Transformation of the Bourgeois Public Sphere: An Inquiry Into a Category of Bourgeois Society*, trans. Thomas Burger (Cambridge, MA: MIT Press, 1989), 41.
17. See E. Johanna Hartelius, *The Rhetoric of Expertise* (Lanham, MD: Lexington, 2010) and Krista Kennedy, *Textual Curation: Authorship, Agency, and Technology in Wikipedia and Chambers's Cyclopædia* (Columbia: University of South Carolina Press, 2016).
18. Chad Wellmon, *Organizing Enlightenment: Information Overload and the Invention of the Modern Research University* (Baltimore: Johns Hopkins University Press, 2015), 9.
19. Wellmon, *Organizing Enlightenment*, 12, emphasis in original.
20. Habermas, *Structural Transformation*, 27; see also Charles Taylor, *Modern Social Imaginaries* (Durham, NC: Duke University Press, 2003).
21. Alexis de Tocqueville, *Democracy in America*, trans. and ed. Harvey C. Mansfield and Debra Winthrop (Chicago: University of Chicago Press, 2000), 155.
22. John Dewey, *The Public and Its Problems* (Athens: Ohio University Press, 1927), 208.
23. Michael Schudson, *The Good Citizen: A History of American Civic Life* (New York: Free Press, 1998).
24. Habermas, *Structural Transformation*, chapter 18.
25. Walter Lippmann, *Public Opinion* (New York: Free Press, 1997), 55.
26. Lippmann, *Public Opinion*, 254.
27. Lippmann, *Public Opinion*, 255.
28. Lippmann, *Public Opinion*, part 8.
29. Mark Wollaeger, *Modernism, Media, and Propaganda: British Narrative from 1900 to 1945* (Princeton: Princeton University Press, 2006), xiii.
30. Quoted in Peter Simonson and John Durham Peters, eds., *Mass Communication and American Social Thought, Key Texts 1919–1968* (Lanham, MD: Rowman and Littlefield, 2004), 50.
31. Edward Bernays, "Manipulating Public Opinion: The Why and the How," *American Journal of Sociology* 33, no. 6 (1928): 958–71.
32. Brenton J. Malin, *Feeling Mediated: A History of Media Technology and Emotion in the United States* (New York: New York University Press, 2014), 110.
33. Max Horkheimer and Theodor Adorno, *The Dialectic of Enlightenment: Philosophical Fragments*, ed. Gunzelin Schmid Noerr, trans. Edmund Jephcott (Stanford: Stanford University Press, 2002), 129.
34. Horkheimer and Adorno, *Dialectic of Enlightenment*, 129.
35. *Reason and Emotion*, directed by Bill Roberts, Walt Disney Productions, August 27, 1943. The sexist representation of reason and emotion in this short propaganda film hints at how fears and fantasies of information abundance are also articulated to gender and other social identities.

36. Marshall McLuhan, *Counterblast* (London: Rapp & Whiting, 1970), 13, 115.
37. Newton N. Minow, "Television and the Public Interest," speech delivered to the National Association of Broadcasters, May 9, 1961, http://www.americanrhetoric.com/speeches/newtonminow.htm.
38. Kevin DeLuca, *Image Politics: The New Rhetoric of Environmental Activism* (New York: The Guilford Press, 1999).
39. Guy Debord, *Society of the Spectacle*, trans. Donald Nicholson-Smith (New York: Zone, 1994); Jean Baudrillard, *Simulacra and Simulation*, trans. Sheila Glaser (Ann Arbor: University of Michigan Press, 1994); Murray Edelman, *Constructing the Political Spectacle* (Chicago: University of Chicago Press, 1988).
40. Henry Jenkins and David Thorburn, eds., *Democracy and New Media* (Cambridge, MA: MIT Press, 2003), 2.
41. Jenny Edbauer Rice, "The New 'New': Making a Case for Critical Affect Studies," *Quarterly Journal of Speech* (May 2008): 211.
42. "#TheDress/What Color Is This Dress," Know Your Meme, http://knowyourmeme.com/memes/thedress-what-color-is-this-dress.
43. Felix Stalder, *Manuel Castells: The Theory of the Network Society* (Cambridge: Polity, 2006), 181.
44. I have detailed this development in *Networked Media, Networked Rhetorics: Attention and Deliberation in the Early Blogosphere* (University Park: Pennsylvania State University Press, 2014), chapter 4.
45. Yochai Benkler, *The Wealth of Networks: How Social Production Transforms Markets and Freedom* (New Haven, CT: Yale University Press, 2006), 225, 230.
46. Jonathan Last, "What Blogs Hath Wrought," *Weekly Standard*, September 27, 2004, http://www.weeklystandard.com/Content/Public/Articles/000/000/004/640pgolk.asp?pg=2.
47. Last, "What Blogs Hath Wrought."
48. Manuel Castells, *Networks of Outrage and Hope: Social Movements in the Internet Age* (Cambridge: Polity, 2012).
49. See John B. Judis, *The Populist Explosion: How the Great Recession Transformed American and European Politics* (New York: Columbia Global Reports, 2016); Angela Nagle, *Kill All Normies: Online Culture Wars from 4chan and Tumblr to Trump and the Alt-Right* (Croydon, UK: Zero, 2017); Samantha Bradshaw and Philip Howard, "Challenging Truth and Trust: A Global Inventory of Organized Social Media Manipulation," *Computational Propaganda Research Project*, 2018, http://comprop.oii.ox.ac.uk/wp-content/uploads/sites/93/2018/07/ct2018.pdf.
50. Daniel Czitrom, *Media and the American Mind: From Morse to McLuhan* (Chapel Hill: University of North Carolina Press, 1982), 168.
51. Lisa Gitelman, ed., *"Raw Data" Is an Oxymoron* (Cambridge, MA: MIT Press, 2013). Although I have emphasized the relationship between information abundance and public deliberation as it coevolves with the development of new media technologies, the technics turn in information theory might also encourage consideration of abundance as an anthropological condition. Humans produce abundant information, and greater attention to the aesthetics and symbolic forms of that information might yield deeper insight about the world. Robert Hariman and John Louis Lucaites have made such a point in the context of the technical apparatus of photography in their chapter "The Abundant Image," in *The Public Image: Photography and Civic Spectatorship* (Chicago: University of Chicago Press, 2017): 227–60.

ALGORITHM

JEREMY DAVID JOHNSON

The algorithm dwells in both the palaces of server racks and in the public imagination: we turn to algorithms to manage information when it is simply too much for humans to sort through. Algorithms determine much on our behalf, from the mail routes for our Amazon packages to the order of our timelines on Facebook. They have become both everything and nothing, ever central yet obscured by the magical portrayal of technology "in the cloud."[1] As the fanciful title of a computer science book suggests, we have followed our *Algorithmic Adventures*, advancing *From Knowledge to Magic*.[2] And, according to News Corp CEO Robert Thomson, this "algorithmic alchemy is redefining our commercial and social experiences, turning base matter into noble metals. But like the alchemists of old, algorithms are also a charlatan's charter, allowing claims of pure science when human intervention is clearly doctoring results to suit either commercial imperatives or political agendas."[3] While the rest of Thomson's presentation is best described as a tirade, his argument is not unfounded: despite the assertions of some companies to the contrary, algorithms are inextricably entangled with human commerce and politics.[4] Algorithmic alchemy, like all alchemy, withers away upon closer scrutiny; what is mystical at first glance often is simpler than it seems. As this entry will lay out, demystifying algorithms is an exercise in understanding the intersections of our technics, our material realities, and ourselves.[5] The enterprise is messy and treacherous, but then again, studying *information* has always been precisely so.

As pervasive and powerful as algorithms are, precisely *what* they are is not settled. The term *algorithm* is quite old, having been roughly transliterated from the name of ninth-century Persian mathematician Al-Khwārizmī, who is also credited with theorizing algebra.[6] The algorithm, in its simplest form, is a mathematical procedure, such as a set of steps for calculating a long-division problem. Considered in this way, "Algorithms have been a part of human technology ever since the Stone Age."[7] Michael Kearns and Aaron Roth claim that "*all* decision-making—including that carried out by human beings—is ultimately algorithmic."[8] Take filtering, for example: systems for indexing, organizing, and winnowing have long been part of human technology. Eli Pariser similarly notes that filtering has "been around for millions of years—indeed, it was around before humans even existed."[9] In this view, sensation itself is algorithmic, and so too is reasoning about the world. As John Durham Peters points out, Al-Khwārizmī "was a student of sundials" who wrote not "strings of code, but modelings of sky paths."[10] Through mathematical calculations for understanding the observable universe, algorithms offered their users a method of recognizing the fundamental truths of the world. Since then, the algorithm has been and remains central to human reasoning about the universe and our place within it.

Today, in popular imagination, the term "algorithm" is most commonly associated with computers and digital environments. Algorithms take a great variety of forms, so much so that Nick Seaver understands "terminological anxiety to be one of critical algorithm studies' defining features."[11] Research on algorithms is interdisciplinary, as algorithms can "leap from one field to the next, and they often do."[12] Even within disciplines, however, algorithms are ill-defined and contested. In computer science, for example, there is no settled definition, which is why Robin Hill attempts to clear the air, offering: "An algorithm is a finite, abstract, effective, compound control structure, imperatively given, accomplishing a given purpose under given provisions."[13] Hill's precise definition leaves something to be desired, however, especially as the "effective" parameter specifies "no judgment (except objective evaluation of conditions that may appear), learning, insight, or understanding; . . . not subject to interpretation."[14] As a humanist, I have great unease with such a characterization: algorithms are precisely in the business of judgment, even if they are not exactly like human interpreters. Instead, I would characterize an algorithm as a sequence of instructions, often carried out by a computer, that translates input data into new outputs. This could resemble a routine, a recipe, or any bounded, regular set of procedures that governs behavior, be it human or nonhuman.

Algorithms organize many of the world's basic functions. They simplify and streamline, saving precious human time, energy, and attention. For those stressed about the complexity of the world, suggest Brian Christian and Tom Griffiths, "They don't need a therapist; they need an algorithm."[15] Such glibness belies the scale and seriousness of algorithmic decision-making, however. As Damien Smith Pfister explains, "While people are still involved at various levels in designing algorithms, they have a diminished day-to-day role as attention gatekeepers in an era where complex computer systems filter large-scale information flows."[16] As algorithms exhibit power over information flows and shape networked engagement, they exceed the parameters of efficiency and enter the realm of politics. Antoinette Rouvroy offers that we "rely more and more on algorithms even though they function according to a type of rationality that is no longer our own and that decides for us."[17] Escaping the bounds of human intelligibility, algorithms "[create] invisible powers," reaffirming Wendy Chun's observation that "our media matter most when they seem not to matter at all."[18] Algorithmic control quietly normalizes the informational power of Facebook, Google, Amazon, and other networked platforms that rely on algorithms to deliver a distinct user experience.

This informational power forms the foundation of digital spaces. When faced with abundant information, claims James Gleick, "Strategies emerge for coping. There are many, but in essence they all boil down to two: filter and search."[19] Or, as Taleb suggests, "Information *wants* to be reduced."[20] Filtering, searching, sorting, and ranking are perhaps the most common forms of algorithmic reduction, rendering comprehensible massive information structures. As a result, "algorithms have become an outright pervasive force in our social world."[21] Today, "information connectivity is more layered because it comes with algorithms—software and computation that allow these technologies to do things beyond just connecting people."[22] What, then, do these technologies do? Undoubtedly, they direct human attention. Attention, after all, is "the new scarcity that economics seeks to describe," a resource required to "make sense of information."[23] Yet, directing attention does not quite capture the cosmological capabilities of networked algorithms. Despite being designed by humans to direct attention, algorithms give order to a broad universe of information in ways much more complicated than "filter and search." Through analysis, sorting, filtering, arrangement, and creation, algorithms in-form the world, creating order through computational cosmology.[24]

In the second half of the twentieth century, cybernetic theorists connected information and materiality through algorithmic models of communication. When Claude Shannon offered his "Mathematical Theory of Communication," claims Ted Striphas, he actually "produced among the first algorithmic theories of information."[25] Shannon and Norbert Wiener, among others, seemed to view communication as a fundamentally model-able process, simplifying it to the transmission of information or data. Wiener, in particular, heralded a "cybernetic" theory of information, explaining, "Information is a name for the content of what is exchanged with the outer world as we adjust to it, and make our adjustment felt upon it."[26] According to Jeff Pruchnic, "The ancient Greek term *kybernetes* ... was often used in the fourth century BCE to denote objects ... or individuals ... that directed, but did not fully control, some other object or system, often through artificially simulating a natural process or force. *Kybernetes* would later be the basis for the Latin *guberno*, and thus our root for 'governance.'"[27] Cybernetics implicates information as a director or governor of order in the world, suggesting both a heuristic and an ethic rooted in movement and flow. The result, suggests N. Katherine Hayles, is a "cybernetic man-machine: light on its feet, sensitive to change, a being that both is a flow and knows how to go with the flow."[28] All of these descriptions are apt for algorithms: they direct and govern networked information flows; they create cycles of sensation and adjustment; and they craft human-machine hybrids through the development of algorithmic identity.

Algorithms are part of a computational revolution that has transformed the material world. In contrast to the middle ages when, Peters details, "*informatio* and *information* were used ... to account for the way that the universe is ordered," information long seemed incompatible with the abstracted bits and bytes of the digital world.[29] However, the rise of mobile devices, wearables, and the Internet of Things (IoT) has drawn attention to the material effects of digital technologies. Indeed, as Peters offers, "Digital devices invite us to think of media as environmental, as part of the habitat, and not just as semiotic inputs into people's heads."[30] In this sense, media are material drivers of information, directing movement and behaviors in the world. Often, these media are rendered invisible, obfuscating the agents of material change; for example, the telegraph "was a[n] instance of an apparently immaterial force having powerful effects."[31] Following the proliferation of information in World War II, computers took on a similar role, with machines "being seen not merely as useful things but as custodians of orderliness," as Striphas has put it.[32] Since World War II, the computer has turned from a great marvel of engineering to a mundane, everyday artifact, small enough to fit on our wrists. In the "information age," the physical elements of computing have faded to the background, even as their material effects shape the ground.

As the often-invisible cornerstone of digital media, algorithms are mathematical agents of networked life. Pariser explains, "The algorithms of Google and Facebook may not be made of steel and concrete, but they regulate our behavior just as effectively."[33] Through their material and symbolic power, algorithms are "civilizational ordering devices," capable of altering flows of information, behavior, and material movement.[34] To remain cohesive and comprehensible, digitally networked spaces rely on algorithms, which in turn have become the fundamental arbiters of human experience. Rather than claiming an unchanging essence to things, algorithms offer dynamic but predictable procedures in the digital universe. Thus, algorithms continue an ancient proto-scientific tradition carried by Heraclitus, Plato, and other philosophers who theorized a "rationally ordered *kosmos*" governed by mathematical rules.[35] Richard Lanham clarifies this view, noting, "The ultimate reality of [Plato's] world was a mathematics similar to the computer code that creates the world of computer graphics. So, too, in a different way, the Greek philosopher Heraclitus thought that the ultimate reality of things lay in structure not stuff."[36] A new "ultimate reality" has arisen, with networked order constantly in-formation through the world's most powerful algorithms.

The alchemic mysticism of algorithms is due in large part to their opacity, hiding from view how they govern networked reality. Democratic governance in networked spaces seems increasingly out of reach, particularly as algorithmic systems become "black boxes" hidden from public view. In response to exploits and security concerns, and with the promise of more cash, many central tech developers have closed off the code to their systems. As Frank Pasquale explains, "The less known about our algorithms—by spammers, hackers, cheats, manipulators, competitors, or the public at large—the better, went the new reasoning."[37] Algorithmic "secret sauce" recipes are protected by a broken patent system, even as the tech sector is increasingly deregulated and protected from government intervention, leaving the tech industry free to cash in on its algorithmic power, entrenching the information regimes of Google, Facebook, and Amazon in particular. As a result, the "increasingly de- and unregulated commercially driven Internet raises significant issues about how information is accessed and made available."[38] Among those significant issues, Pasquale points to "a paradox of the so-called information age: Data is becoming staggering in its breadth and depth, yet often the information most important to us is out of our reach, available only to insiders."[39] As Tufekci notes, "the function of gatekeeping for access to the public sphere is enacted through internet platforms' policies, algorithms, and affordances."[40] Networked gatekeeping is more subtle than "old media," but it is just as strong. If ever there was promise of a cyberutopia, it faded as our inability to take everything in gave power to those who could brew an algorithmic elixir and sell to us a new, distinctly dystopian Web 2.0.

With opaque systems, constant change, and copious information, studying algorithmic world-making is difficult. A "big data" approach is tempting: gather more and more data so we can get a sense of the bigger algorithmic picture. But such an approach is fraught with complications, such as the inability to gather data without violating website terms of service.[41] My approach is rhetorical and critical, reading textual patterns and phenomena to understand algorithmic culture. As Christopher Ingraham contends, "Algorithms are rhetorical at a structural level. Their rhetoricity is an inherent quality of what they are."[42] The rhetoricity of algorithms underscores their world-making power: by making persuasive choices about how the world should be structured, algorithms shape communication and informational practices. Tracing textual patterns reveals an "ongoing struggle between different groups and structures" that requires the recognition of "complex, shifting negotiations . . . between people, algorithms, and institutions, always acting in relation to each other."[43] Similarly, Seaver articulates an intriguing view of "algorithms as culture," wherein "algorithms are not technical rocks in a cultural stream, but are rather just more water."[44] Studying the stream without understanding its ecological effects seems myopic and relatively useless; rather, in attending to the broad impacts of algorithms, we need to read them as co-constitutive with the artifacts they carry. Taina Bucher rightly declares: "Precisely *because* of their entangled and complex nature, there is an obvious need to disentangle [algorithms'] meanings and ways of acting in the world."[45] Because we are part of those streams, complete disentanglement is impossible. Still, we can begin to demystify the algorithm through self-reflection and critical reading, lest we be caught in an algorithmic whirlpool.

In a networked society, information attains tremendous velocity. Algorithms regulate movement, in many cases slowing down the world just enough for human consumption. Algorithms operate on the level of the micro-second, but they also account for the sluggishness of human life, layering patterns in different scales of time and space.[46] As a result, algorithms often seem like magic, identifying patterns humans could never hope to notice, crafting a sensible world from unfathomable mountains of data. These algorithmic arrangements are dynamic but tend to repeat, creating distinct patterns. In networked culture, insists Chun, "what remains is not what is static, but instead what constantly repeats and is repeated."[47] Similarly, Lanham claims, "An information economy naturally assumes that pattern, design, comes first."[48] Fittingly, the rise of algorithms coincides with a scholarly turn away from the study of *things* to the study of *process*.[49] Algorithms illuminate the processes and procedures that inform the world, "imbuing people and objects with shape, quality or character."[50] Shape, quality, and character have always been dynamic, but the pace of the so-called information age has made their dynamism more apparent. The challenge for critics, then, is to slow down and work backward, tracing algorithmic patterns to understand their computational cosmology.

Perhaps the most common pattern of algorithms is for designers to praise their mathematical objectivity, creating a "natural" digital landscape. Problematically, a data-based world is neither objective nor neutral—nor indeed are its algorithmic stewards. The algorithm makes subjective, ethical choices about what the world should be, training us to live according to its warped ethic. As Cathy O'Neil proclaims, "If we back away from them and treat [algorithms] as a neutral and inevitable force, like the weather or the tides, we abdicate our responsibility."[51] Unfortunately, mathematics, algorithms, and data are commonly treated as objective, neutral, and inevitable, despite being crafted and maintained by humans. When companies like Google claim that "the algorithm

[has] spoken" and that's that, they absolve themselves of the responsibility to create more fair and ethical networked environments.[52] They make this excuse over and over, even suggesting that algorithms transcend human judgment in reducing bias: this is a "problem [that] cannot be solved by humans and ... shouldn't be solved by humans," according to Google's Philipp Schindler.[53] When mere chemistry cannot suffice, tech companies turn to algorithmic alchemy, offering a magical mysticism beyond human capability. More damagingly, this portrayal is powerful, captivating the public imaginary and positioning tech companies as the mouthpieces of computational gods.

This portrayal is also seductive because, in melding into neoliberal logics of popularity and profit, many of the most vital networked algorithms reproduce what seems to be an order natural to the world. As a result, these algorithms more closely resemble what claims to be a universal principle of governance than a human hierarchy. Kate Crawford claims that "algorithms are designed to produce clear 'winners' from information contests."[54] Algorithms, she continues, "may be rule-based mechanisms that fulfill requests, but they are also governing agents that are choosing between competing, and sometimes conflicting, data objects."[55] While natural processes undoubtedly pick winners and losers, it is worth repeating that algorithms are human creations, designed, programmed, and implemented by imperfect people who exist in a profit-first kind of world. But as human creations that pretend to be universal principles, algorithms, like many other technologies, are especially dangerous in silently normalizing unjust and unequal structures. As Virginia Eubanks points out, public assistance algorithms operate in the name of efficiency while creating a "digital poorhouse"; they're "framed as a way to rationalize and streamline benefits, but the real goal is what it has always been: to profile, police, and punish the poor."[56] The call of the age of the algorithm is to reify the structures of the old through the rhetoric of the new. By heralding the magical power of data, algorithmic operators ensure their control over networked information regimes.

Google, Facebook, and other data-based companies use algorithms to create or reinforce human economic and social hierarchies. "Google's algorithm," for example, "billed as a purely artificial intelligence in contrast to Yahoo's partly curated (human-filtered) searches, was supposed to be neutral and universal in its indifference."[57] But as Safiya Umoja Noble interjects, "Ranking is itself information that also reflects the political, social, and cultural values of the society that search engine companies operate within."[58] Algorithms are more a reflection of human bias than a deflection of it. Siva Vaidhyanathan contends that Google's "biases (valuing popularity over accuracy, established sites over new, and rough rankings over more fluid or multidimensional models of presentation) are built into its algorithms."[59] For others, organizational priorities create algorithmic biases: all algorithms are programmed to prefer some information and some relationships over others. Google favors popularity,

Facebook favors positive engagement, YouTube favors shares—all of these priorities create social hierarchies, often predicated on neoliberal logics. In almost every case, the bottom line is a redline, reinforcing "oppressive social and economic relations."[60] Either add to the tally, or get out of the way.

By encouraging habits and behavioral patterns, algorithms create our understanding of self and other, situated in relation to the rest of a datafied world. As John Cheney-Lippold argues, "The knowledge that shapes both the world and ourselves online is increasingly being built by algorithms, data, and the logics therein."[61] In an algorithmic world, identity formation is altered fundamentally: "we can no longer think of our lives as mediated by information and software, but that they are increasingly constituted by or comprised of them."[62] We are not just represented by media; we are also *made* by media. For their part, algorithms infer us from the inside-out. Based on small kernels of data, algorithms determine which advertisements, which posts, which links, and which people we should see and connect with. The result is what Cheney-Lippold calls "a 'new algorithmic identity,' an identity formation that works through mathematical algorithms to [impose] categories of identity on otherwise anonymous beings."[63] The formulation of who we were, who we are, and what we can be is inflected through computational data. Even "categorical definitions," such as race and ethnicity, are "reconfigured through an algorithmic locum."[64]

By inferring identity and providing dynamic content in response to our behaviors, algorithms exert subtle control over individual behaviors. Everything we do is boiled down to a data point, rendered intelligible for algorithms. Algorithms, in turn, limit our available resources by narrowing the incoming stream for us; they "guide our discovery of information and argument," both of which are key to the formulation of identity.[65] Thus, algorithms quietly work toward identity formation: "A documentary or interpolated subject may not necessarily feel the 'Hey, you!' hail of a police officer but will sense the accompanying introjection."[66] Noble highlights these limitations for African American identity, which is affected by results about African Americans offered in search engines and social networks; when Google offers search results for "black girls" related to sex and sexuality, its algorithms reify racist notions of black bodies.[67] For Noble, this interpellation has "real social and economic impact" in objectifying black women and flattening African American communities.[68] Algorithms establish information regimes that, despite the protestations of their creators, are complicit and culpable in spreading injustice, discrimination, and oppression.

By sustaining information regimes, algorithms shape material power relations, harming communities and subverting democratic power. Recounting her experience of watching #Ferguson unfold, Zeynep Tufekci details, "it appeared that Facebook's algorithm—the opaque, proprietary formula that changes every week . . . may have decided that the Ferguson stories were lower priority to show to many users than other, more algorithm-friendly ones."[69] What resulted, according to Tufekci, was an "algorithmic spiral of silence," stunting the spread of stories about #Ferguson and, once again, disproportionately harming a minority community.[70] Algorithmic discrimination is appalling, but it should not be all that surprising: networked information regimes centralize power rather than democratizing it.[71] The power relations of algorithmic culture may reflect a new hierarchy, but it is a hierarchy nonetheless: at the top, young, white, and overwhelmingly male Silicon Valley stars herald the magic of their technologies, asserting their own values while disguising them as objective and fair.

Ultimately, claims to algorithmic alchemy portray a false magic we ought to reject. Critics of information, algorithms, and communication can recognize the fundamental world-making power of algorithms while simultaneously rejecting, in part or in whole, the networked universe being constructed by them. The most important step in dealing with algorithms is demystifying them. Be it through algorithmic audits, through playing and experimenting with algorithms, or through tracing their effects, algorithms are legible and readable.[72] Resisting the temptation to describe algorithms as "black boxes," Bucher contends: "While it is true that proprietary algorithms are hard to know, it does not make them *unknowable*."[73] In truth, algorithms are as knowable as people. We may not always be able to predict their behaviors, but habits and patterns repeat. Algorithms may be "black boxes" insofar as their code is locked away from the view of public citizens (including scholars), but we can capture glimpses of their inner workings. We can adapt to algorithmic ordering, as have political and social movements both liberal and conservative.[74] For all of the often-warranted pessimism about algorithmic life, there is yet room to change the future. Such changes will require critical attention, consideration, and, at times, opposition.

An algorithmic world is the aggregation of billions of inferred selves. In an algorithmic world, the self is simultaneously everywhere and the center of everything. In other words, we live in the age of ultimate solipsism. Our networked experiences are personalized and packaged according to our past preferences. Pariser writes, "algorithmic induction can lead to a kind of information determinism, in which our past clickstreams entirely decide our future."[75] Such determinism sounds bleak and dystopian, reflecting the very worst of networked landscapes and their attendant information regimes. Many algorithms divide and conquer in the name of efficiency and capital, but alternative paths exist. What kind of a world can we imagine if the priorities built into algorithms aren't greedy and selfish? Rather than reflecting us like a mirror, could algorithms turn our attention outward, toward the other?[76] Wendy Chun declares: "The 'we' is a temporary network weapon."[77] Through concerted action, "we" can see beyond algorithmic alchemy. We can know the algorithm, for it is no *deus ex machina*: algorithms, despite being entangled in complex networks of humans, nonhumans, and material things, are grounded in graspable technics. The algorithm is no mystical being but rather the *antistrophos* to the human.[78] The human is more than information stored in server racks, more than the transmutation of being into data, more than the magical product of algorithmic alchemy. What, then, can the algorithm be?

Notes

1. For a thorough account of the phenomenon that is "the cloud," including its rich history, see Tung-Hui Hu, *A Prehistory of the Cloud* (Cambridge, MA: MIT Press, 2015).
2. Juraj Hromkovič, *Algorithmic Adventures: From Knowledge to Magic* (New York: Springer, 2009).
3. Robert Thomson, "The Almighty Algorithm," *Fox News*, June 15, 2017, http://www.foxnews.com/opinion/2017/06/15/news-corp-ceo-almighty-algorithm-fake-news-and-other-consequences-google-amazon-and-facebooks-relentless-focus-on-quantity-over-quality.html.
4. For example, see Google's claim that its Waze software only maps the "ground truth": Cyrus Farivar, "Waze's Crazy Routing Over a 32% Grade Road Is Driving Residents Nuts," *Ars Technica*, April 5, 2018, https://arstechnica.com/tech-policy/2018/04/waze-blamed-for-rise-in-accidents-along-one-of-steepest-streets-in-us/.
5. I am drawing most explicitly from Damien Smith Pfister's characterization of "technics." For more, see Pfister's entry in this volume.
6. Brian Christian and Tom Griffiths, *Algorithms to Live By: The Computer Science of Human Decisions* (New York: Holt, 2016), 3.
7. Christian and Griffiths, *Algorithms to Live By*, 3.
8. Michael Kearns and Aaron Roth, *The Ethical Algorithm: The Science of Socially Aware Algorithm Design* (Oxford: Oxford University Press, 2020), 190, https://search.ebscohost.com/login.aspx?direct=true&scope=site&db=nlebk&db=nlabk&AN=2255401.
9. Eli Pariser, *The Filter Bubble: How the New Personalized Web Is Changing What We Read and How We Think.* (London: Penguin, 2012), 84.
10. John Durham Peters, *The Marvelous Clouds: Toward a Philosophy of Elemental Media* (Chicago: University of Chicago Press, 2015), 204.
11. Nick Seaver, "Algorithms as Culture: Some Tactics for the Ethnography of Algorithmic Systems," *Big Data and Society* 4, no. 2 (2017): 2.
12. Cathy O'Neil offers a view of algorithms and models that largely overlaps, essentially concluding that algorithms have become, in many cases, "Weapons of Math Destruction." For more, see in particular Cathy O'Neil, *Weapons of Math Destruction: How Big Data Increases Inequality and Threatens Democracy* (New York: Crown, 2016), 31.
13. Robin K. Hill, "What an Algorithm Is," *Philosophy and Technology* 29, no. 1 (2016): 47, https://doi.org/10.1007/s13347-014-0184-5.
14. Hill, 45.
15. Christian and Griffiths, *Algorithms to Live By*, 2.
16. Damien Smith Pfister, *Networked Media, Networked Rhetorics: Attention and Deliberation in the Early Blogosphere* (University Park: Pennsylvania State University Press, 2014), 186.

17. Antoinette Rouvroy and Bernard Stiegler, "The Digital Regime of Truth: From the Algorithmic Governmentality to a New Rule of Law," *La Deleuziana*, no. 3 (2016): 26.
18. On the creation of invisible powers, see Frank Pasquale, *The Black Box Society: The Secret Algorithms That Control Money and Information* (Cambridge, MA: Harvard University Press, 2015), 193; Wendy Hui Kyong Chun, *Updating to Remain the Same: Habitual New Media* (Cambridge, MA: MIT Press, 2016), 1.
19. James Gleick, *The Information: A History, a Theory, a Flood* (New York: Vintage, 2011), 409.
20. Nassim Nicholas Taleb, *The Black Swan: The Impact of the Highly Improbable* (New York: Random House, 2010), 64.
21. Chris Ingraham, "Toward an Algorithmic Rhetoric," in *Digital Rhetoric and Global Literacies: Communication Modes and Digital Practices in the Networked World*, ed. Gustav Verhulsdonck and Marohang Limbu (Hershey, PA: IGI Global, 2013), 62.
22. Zeynep Tufekci, *Twitter and Tear Gas: The Power and Fragility of Networked Protest* (New Haven, CT: Yale University Press, 2017), 129–30.
23. Richard A. Lanham, *The Economics of Attention: Style and Substance in the Age of Information* (Chicago: University of Chicago Press, 2007), 7.
24. While "computational cosmology" is, to my chagrin, not a neologism, my meaning here is different from other uses of the phrase. Rather than referring to computational studies of cosmology, I am arguing that computation creates cosmologies. For more on the traditional sense of computational cosmology, see Peter Anninos, "Computational Cosmology: From the Early Universe to the Large Scale Structure," *Living Reviews in Relativity* 1, no. 1 (1998): 9, https://doi.org/10.12942/lrr-1998-9.
25. Ted Striphas, "Algorithmic Culture," *European Journal of Cultural Studies* 18, nos. 4–5 (2015): 405.
26. Norbert Wiener, *The Human Use of Human Beings: Cybernetics and Society* (London: Free Association, 1989), 17.
27. Jeff Pruchnic, *Rhetoric and Ethics in the Cybernetic Age: The Transhuman Condition* (London: Routledge, 2016), 4.
28. N. Katherine Hayles, *How We Became Posthuman: Virtual Bodies in Cybernetics, Literature, and Informatics* (Chicago: University of Chicago Press, 1999), 104.
29. John Durham Peters, "Information: Notes Toward a Critical History," *Journal of Communication Inquiry* 12, no. 2 (1988): 10.
30. Peters, *The Marvelous Clouds*, 4.
31. Peters, "Information," 17.
32. Striphas, "Algorithmic Culture," 400.
33. Pariser, *The Filter Bubble*, 175.
34. Here I am adapting Peters's claim that "media are civilizational ordering devices." See Peters, *The Marvelous Clouds*, 5.
35. Christopher Lyle Johnstone, "Introduction," in Christopher Lyle Johnstone, ed., *Theory, Text, Context: Issues in Greek Rhetoric and Oratory* (Albany: State University of New York Press, 1996), 13.
36. Lanham, *The Economics of Attention*, 6.
37. Pasquale, *The Black Box Society*, 193.
38. Safiya Umoja Noble, *Algorithms of Oppression: How Search Engines Reinforce Racism* (New York: New York University Press, 2018), 154.
39. Pasquale, *The Black Box Society*, 191.
40. Tufekci, *Twitter and Tear Gas*, 134.

41. As an example of this problem, consider the case of Sandvig v. Sessions: Christian Sandvig, an algorithm researcher at the University of Michigan, filed a suit to challenge the Computer Fraud and Abuse Act, which allowed companies to ban automatic web scraping in their terms of service. According to the Electronic Frontier Foundation, "the plaintiffs have refrained from using automated tools out of an understandable fear of prosecution," which stunted their social media research, including on algorithms. See: Jamie Williams, "D.C. Court: Accessing Public Information Is Not a Computer Crime," *Electronic Frontier Foundation*, April 12, 2018, https://www.eff.org/deeplinks/2018/04/dc-court-accessing-public-information-not-computer-crime.
42. Ingraham, "Toward an Algorithmic Rhetoric," 68.
43. Kate Crawford, "Can an Algorithm Be Agonistic? Ten Scenes from Life in Calculated Publics," *Science, Technology, and Human Values* 41, no. 1 (2015): 7.
44. Seaver, "Algorithms as Culture," 5.
45. Taina Bucher, *If . . . Then: Algorithmic Power and Politics* (New York: Oxford University Press, 2018), 38.
46. For example, algorithms engage in high-frequency trading on Wall Street, making hundreds of financial calculations in the time it takes a person to blink. See Nick Baumann, "Too Fast to Fail: How High-Speed Trading Makes Wall Street Disasters Worse," *Mother Jones*, 2013, https://www.motherjones.com/politics/2013/02/high-frequency-trading-danger-risk-wall-street/.
47. Chun, *Updating to Remain the Same*, 90.
48. Lanham, *The Economics of Attention*, 5.
49. I am referencing in particular the ecological turn in English, communication studies, and other fields. Ecological studies are primarily concerned with movement and change over time, rather than static meaning or being. For a terrific account of ecological studies, see Margaret A. Syverson, *The Wealth of Reality: An Ecology of Composition* (Carbondale: Southern Illinois University Press, 1999).
50. Striphas, "Algorithmic Culture," 407.
51. Here I have substituted "algorithms" for "mathematical models." In O'Neil's writing, the distinction between algorithm and mathematical model is unclear. In my reading, they are interchangeable. See O'Neil, *Weapons of Math Destruction*, 218.
52. Steven Levy, *In the Plex: How Google Thinks, Works, and Shapes Our Lives* (New York: Simon and Schuster, 2011), 275.
53. Mark Bergen, "Google Updates Ads Policies Again, Ramps Up AI to Curtail YouTube Crisis," *Bloomberg*, April 3, 2017, https://www.bloomberg.com/news/articles/2017-04-03/google-updates-ads-polices-again-ramps-up-ai-to-curtail-youtube-crisis.
54. Crawford, "Can an Algorithm Be Agonistic," 1.
55. Crawford, 9.
56. Virginia Eubanks, *Automating Inequality: How High-Tech Tools Profile, Police, and Punish the Poor* (New York: St. Martin's, 2017), 38.
57. Peters, *The Marvelous Clouds*, 336.
58. Noble, *Algorithms of Oppression*, 148.
59. Siva Vaidhyanathan, *The Googlization of Everything: (And Why We Should Worry)* (Berkeley: University of California Press, 2011), 6.
60. Noble, *Algorithms of Oppression*, 10.
61. John Cheney-Lippold, *We Are Data: Algorithms and the Making of Our Digital Selves* (New York: New York University Press, 2017), xiii.
62. David Beer, "Power Through the Algorithm? Participatory Web Cultures and the Technological Unconscious," *New Media and Society* 11, no. 6 (2009): 987.

63. John Cheney-Lippold, "A New Algorithmic Identity: Soft Biopolitics and the Modulation of Control," *Theory, Culture, and Society* 28, no. 6 (2011): 165.
64. Cheney-Lippold, *We Are Data*, 30–31.
65. Aaron Hess, "You Are What You Compute (and What Is Computed for You): Considerations of Digital Rhetorical Identification," *Journal of Contemporary Rhetoric* 4, nos. 1/2 (2014): 15.
66. Cheney-Lippold, *We Are Data*, 170.
67. Noble, *Algorithms of Oppression*, chapter 2.
68. Noble, 179.
69. Tufekci, *Twitter and Tear Gas*, 156.
70. On "spiral of silence," see Tufekci, 159; indeed, algorithms often harm minority communities, especially various African American publics. This is a repeated theme of algorithmic discrimination, or, as Noble calls them, "algorithms of oppression." For a full account of algorithmic harm to minorities, see Noble, *Algorithms of Oppression*.
71. Hindman covers the centralization of power and the "long tail" of networked culture in a slightly dated but nonetheless illuminating work: Matthew Scott Hindman, *The Myth of Digital Democracy* (Princeton: Princeton University Press, 2009).
72. Christian Sandvig et al., "Auditing Algorithms: Research Methods for Detecting Discrimination on Internet Platforms" (Conference Presentation, May 22, 2014).
73. Bucher, *If . . . Then*, 26.
74. Alexander Burns, "Rick Santorum Contacted Google, Says Company Spreads 'Filth,'" *POLITICO*, September 20, 2011, http://www.politico.com/news/stories/0911/63952.html; LuckyGoGo, "The Cucks Are Trying to Google Bomb 'Dangerous Donald Trump,' We Can Play That Game Too.," reddit—/r/The_Donald, accessed September 25, 2017, https://www.reddit.com/r/The_Donald/comments/4i4wkz/the_cucks_are_trying_to_google_bomb_dangerous/.
75. Pariser, *The Filter Bubble*, 136.
76. Pariser, 3.
77. Chun, *Updating to Remain the Same*, 28.
78. I borrow here from Aristotle, who describes rhetoric as the *antistrophos*—commonly translated as "counterpart"—to dialectic. See: Aristotle, *Rhetoric*, trans. W. Rhys Roberts (New York: Modern Library, 1984), chapter 1.1.1.

ARCHIVE

LAURA HELTON

Archive, an etymologist might tell us, is a curious noun, one that changes neither in quantity nor essence when made plural. As it ticks through a sequence of meanings, the *OED* reminds us that each definition operates *sing. & in pl.* An archive, it notes, can connote a place (a "repository for documents") or a collection ("records so kept"). But so can *an archives*, plural.[1] Both usages, singular and plural, have been called upon by scholars to think through wide-ranging questions of memory, evidence, authority, canon, and classification. And yet, while grammatically proper, that very elasticity has proven nettlesome as the "archival turn" has reworked (and perhaps overworked) the term archive, asking it to do critical labor for an ever-growing number of disciplines.[2] In fact, debates around archival grammar register a stark conceptual distance between archives (with an *s*) and archive (without)—the latter's singularity underscored by the frequent use of a definitive article that brands *the* archive as a favorite keyword of the humanities.

For humanists, archives have long served as research sites; that is, repositories that hold objects of study. Archive, in its singular form, has more recently become a subject of humanistic inquiry as well, invoked to theorize historical forms and silences. For some, archives are places; for others they are bodies, traces, sounds, or data. An ever-growing corpus of digital records and environments has prompted a rethinking of divides between material, imaginary, and dispersed archives, as well as the power relationships underlying questions of what we can and should save, and how to represent it. Digital life has also embedded archival functions into personal information habits, from Gmail's "Archive" command to the "Archive" tab ubiquitous in web design. In short, the term archive has proliferated across humanistic practice. Whereas archival theory once delimited a professional discourse on the appraisal, preservation, and description of records, it has, with the archival turn, taken on metaphorical and "extraterritorial" connotations.[3] Building on a Foucauldian notion of archive as a discursive system that governs the enunciability of statements, scholars across a range of disciplines have invoked the term to denote a particular process—a "structure of record-keeping," for example—or to make visible assemblages that exceed the coordinates of any one repository—such as an "imperial archive" or an "archive of feelings."[4] Labeling such imagined assemblages as "an archive" is, as Kate Eichhorn argues, an "authorizing act" that gives analytical coherence to otherwise dislocated orders of meaning.[5]

This archival turn, however, has not fully attended to other discourses, both antecedent and contemporary, that attach to the term archives. Studies of "the archive" often begin with the etymology of *arkheion*—the place from which law emanates—as a brief nod to the history of ancient and modern archives.[6] But they largely bypass the body of knowledge that undergirds the operation of archival institutions since the eighteenth century, and which still shapes how humanistic information is organized. For archivists, archives represent an ongoing life cycle of record creation, retention, reuse, and destruction, and each of these concepts has been the subject of decades of professional debate. Humanities scholars who have adopted archive as a keyword without citing that historiography, Michelle Caswell argues, invoke a "hypothetical wonderland" but fail to acknowledge "the intellectual contribution of archival studies as a field of theory and praxis in its own right."[7] To what extent is that elision a casualty of the lexical ambiguity that attends interdisciplinarity, and in what ways does it represent an erasure—often gendered, Caswell suggests—of certain types of intellectual figures (the librarian, archivist, cataloger, or records manager) from the history of ideas? The metaphorical *archive*, Caswell says, is not an *archives*, that site where praxis and protocol are negotiated.

As such tensions suggest, while the conceptual openness of the term archive/s has productive qualities, it has also diluted the term's specificity. To name the keyword's grammatical politics, one might parse four ways in which it is frequently deployed—as singular and plural, literal and figurative—with contending stakes attending each instance:

> archive/s, n., *in sing. & in pl.*: sources, fonds, or repositories
> archives, n., *pl.*: praxis and theory for managing unique collections
> archive, n., *sing.*: metaphor for encoded records as memory
> archive, v.: to store, organize, or preserve, assigning enduring value to objects in anticipation of future (re)use

Can we name, and thus respect, the different traditions of practice and expertise these usages signal, while also maintaining the productive ambiguity of the plural/singular term "archives?" Addressing each of these grammatical propositions, this entry will identify major threads of contemporary archival theory, as well as the core archival principles—provenance, appraisal, arrangement, and description—that undergird any imagining or reimagining of the archive. It argues that if archive is to function as a useful keyword of the humanities, it should do so as a hinge between the metaphorical and material connotations of record-keeping. As a term that signals place, protocol, and theory, archive serves a reminder that the very terms of our conceptual engagement with historical presence or absence lean on specific legacies of archival inscription and institutions.

Archive/s

Since the professionalization of their discipline in the late nineteenth century, historians have understood archives as a primary research space, their corollary to the scientist's laboratory or the ethnographer's field. The question of how archival sources enable and constrain historical writing—by their abundance or paucity, the circumstances of their production, their accessibility or inaccessibility, and the institutions that mediate that access—has thus always been at the center of historians' work.[8] But for the most part, historians relegated their discussions of archives and archivists to paratext like acknowledgements, footnotes or a "note on sources." Rarely in historical prose did archives appear explicitly as an analytical object—with the exception of the genre of "archive stories," such as Arlette Farge's classic memoir of French judicial archives as a place where the historian revels in her "relationships to the documents and the people they might reveal."[9] As Natalie Zemon Davis notes in her introduction to Farge's work, historians have long known how to read "with and against the grain" of archives.[10] Scholars of the subaltern, especially, have perfected the art of reading against the grain: extracting from documents stories the document-creators did not intend to tell.[11] Ann Stoler, meanwhile, has called for scholars to read along the archival grain: to treat an archival document not as an object from which to extract information, but as itself a narrative about who has the power to archive and why.

This "archival turn" has reversed the historical axiom that archives are sources but rarely subjects. (To call it a "turn" may seem redundant, since historicist work is always already indebted to archives, but it signals a reflexive reexamination of the field's methodological apparatus.) Recent historical work has recognized that "the making of archives is frequently where knowledge production begins," not simply where it is stored and retrieved.[12] Colonial papers, notarial records, scrapbooks, slave ledgers: once understood as ground, collections are now figures in their own right, "elevated to new theoretical status."[13] This elevation has made visible the role of archives as sites that "convey authority and set the rules for credibility." This "archival power," Michel-Rolph Trouillot argues, is inscribed at four moments of record-keeping: creation, assembly, retrieval, and retrospection.[14] A growing body of work, especially in postcolonial studies, attends to each of these moments. Stoler mines archival documents, at the point of assembly, as artifacts whose bureaucratic "watermarks" catalog colonialism's "arts of governance" in the Netherlands Indies.[15] Kirsten Weld argues that the Guatemalan National Police records had "two distinct *archival* logics," the first, at their creation, a Cold War logic of surveillance and "ideological management," and the second, following the records' unexpected discovery and retrieval in the aftermath of civil war, a logic of "democratic opening."[16] In her work on the colonial archive in India, Anjali Arondekar questions the stakes of retrospection, the final stage of record-keeping.[17] Recognizing that "archives are untenable without readers," she argues that what they reveal is structured by our own desires for access and "discovery."

It is no accident that these works tell stories of surveillance, for, taken as a whole, the archival turn relies upon a default characterization of archives as a textual site of dominant discourse-making, usually imagined as a repository of the state.[18] Roberto Echevarría, Alice Yaeger Kaplan, and, most famously, Jacques Derrida, ground archival definitions in the etymology of *arkheion*, or *archē*, which refers to a physical dwelling synonymous with authority (the place from which law emanates). Derrida leans on this etymology to underscore how the term archive simultaneously connotes a sequential order, which marks a beginning, and a *jussive* order, which structures what *can* be said.[19] In other words, a Derridean notion of archive is about both origins and commandments: an archive does not simply hold documents, but also sanctifies the story the documents tell. It is perhaps the influence of this twinned emphasis on origin and edict that answers Gabrielle Dean's question about why the "archival turn" has in fact relied on "the term 'archive' all along, with its statist resonances, rather than the term 'collection,' which has institutional but also personal resonances."[20] The turn to archive as a keyword signals a concern with a range of functions, from preservation to classification, that are also central to many informational practices. But the term "archive," unlike its cognates "collection" or "memory," does extra epistemological work by encapsulating order and ordinance. (This statist emphasis is also the requisite foil for a theorization of "counter-archives.")[21] If, in Farge's account, an archive/s has sensory allure as a place of dust and revelation, in the archival turn it has conceptual allure as a keyword whose connotation is both mnemonic—pertaining to storage and recall—and bureaucratic—performing authority.

Archives

Such work on archival power draws attention to archival labor, or what Derrida calls the "signature of the archivists."[22] And yet, humanities scholarship of the archival turn—even when engaged with the history of archives in their plural form—remains largely removed from the professional literature of archivists themselves. Instead, it often borrows archival studies as a framing device without engaging directly with the historiography of the field. Stoler's useful formulation "archival genres," for example, refers to the handiwork of colonial records managers, not to the downstream navigational documents made by archivists (finding aids, container lists, catalog records) or to the body of theory underlying the organization of modern archives.[23] Here, the archival turn, for all its fluency across fields, meets the limits of interdisciplinarity. Archival history is imported as an intervention in the humanities, and, like many imports, finds itself disembodied from its place of production.

In the United States, archival practice as a modern profession began in the late nineteenth century and adopted a core theory from eighteenth-century France, *respect des fonds*. This principle, by which records are maintained in groups that reflect their original context of assembly, or provenance, fundamentally distinguishes archives from libraries and museums, which organize objects by subject or creator regardless of when and why they were acquired.[24] As unique materials generated through the operational life of an organization, records move along a continuum of use, retention, destruction, and preservation. Only some, appraised as having enduring value beyond short-term institutional memory, ever enter an archives.[25] Once archived, they remain attached to the creators and organizations that accumulated them. Take, for example, the story of Aima Ship, a Kentucky freedwoman. In 1866, in the aftermath of the Civil War, she corresponded with her daughters, Lethia and Adeline, as the family struggled to reunite after emancipation and to secure wages for their labor. These letters, which capture the mother's intimate admonitions to "come soon" and "write to your Brother," are filed at the National Archives in Record Group 105 alongside thousands of other cases handled by the Bureau of Refugees, Freedmen, and Abandoned Lands.[26] In traditional archival terms, they are not the Ship family's documents per se, but rather evidence of a government agency's bureaucracy.

The archives profession's founding theorems, which grew out of governmental and organizational records management, thus dovetail to a certain extent with the archival turn's emphasis on the juridical-administrative function of archives. But there was always another strand of archival practice, under the moniker "manuscripts" rather than "archives," that tended to a wider range of materials, including personal, communal, and ecclesiastical papers housed in specialized libraries or historical societies. A series of mid- and late twentieth-century shifts in informational practice brought together these two strands of professional record-keeping, and since that shift, the fundamentals of archival theory have undergone sustained revision.[27] Archivists who maintain literary papers, tribal repositories, community records, and ephemera collections, together with the state and federal archivists who began establishing protocols for digital archiving in the 1980s, have rethought core concepts like custodianship, creator, and record in light of a broader sense of what constitutes archives.[28] Theorists of a "postcustodial archive," for example, approach archives as praxis rather than place, redefining archival principles to deemphasize extraction and ownership. In a postcustodial model, record creators could maintain physical and legal possession of their materials but work with archival repositories to provide digital access.[29] Others have challenged the definition of creatorship to encompass a "records community" that accounts for how documenters *and* the documented shape records. This expansive approach also recognizes the cocreatorship of archivists, amanuenses, and users. While the novelist Margaret Atwood's papers, for example, contain the author's manuscripts, the collection was constructed by the "filing activities" of her personal assistants who chose what to keep and discard.[30]

This broader view of who creates archives lays bare the ethics of control and access. Indigenous archivists, for example, have challenged intellectual property structures that are the operable vestiges of settler colonialism.[31] Recent archival theory has also fueled experiments with making archives more explicitly collaborative spaces where many kinds of aesthetic or political practices could emerge.[32] To position archives not just as research spaces but also as artistic sites exemplifies Eric Ketelaar's argument that the "archive is an infinite activation of the record."[33] If the digital age has refigured the paradigm of archival time by shifting the burden of preservation from future archivists to present-day makers, so, too, has archival theory come to understand production and retrospection—two of Trouillot's once-discrete moments of archive-building—as "simultaneous and porous."[34] In this theory of archival chronology, repositories not only store past narratives but also continuously remake them through "reuse and reinterpretation."[35] The archivist, once imagined as passive custodian of an original order inscribed in records, is recognized as a contemporary interlocutor, alongside creators and users, who shapes what it means to access the past.[36]

Archive, the

If the keyword *archive* in its singular form rarely takes note of these conversations about post-custodianship or reuse in *archives*, it is, in part, because much of the metaphoric turn has concerned records that never were, and could never be, "in custody." Scholars have been touched by a *mal d'archive*, Derrida would say, but the fever is not site specific. *The* archive, as opposed to an archive*s*, can identify panoramic logics or social poetics that exceed the holdings of a physical place. Thomas Richards, for example, has read across literary texts to locate a British "imperial archive" that "pared the Empire down to file-cabinet size."[37] Ann Cvetkovich conjures an "archive of feelings" that indexes collective memories of queer trauma and pleasure recorded in ephemeral and experimental cultural productions that often resist preservation. For Cvetkovich, the archive reveals itself not only in curated forms but in "fantasy made material."[38] While Richards traces a state memory regime and Cvetkovich attends to modes of counterpublic memory that are, in fact, threats to such regimes, both scholars leverage the term archive to locate the diffuse "generative grammar" of encoded memory writ large—of what Stoler calls a "corpus of selective forgettings and collections."[39]

Once abstracted from materiality, the idea of the archive attends as closely to forgetting as to collecting. Indeed, among the archival turn's most influential texts are meditations on loss, where the archive is haunted by lives, objects, and affects unnamed, unremembered, or ineffable. These include Trouillot's foundational reflections on archival silences surrounding the Haitian Revolution and Saidiya Hartman's lament about the impossibility of narrating slavery's "unrecoverable past"—both responses to the "founding violence" of archives forged out of "New World black deracination, subjection, and exclusion."[40] This body of work did not invent the idea of archival absences; archivists have long understood the records they maintain as a "sliver of a sliver," and community documentarians have sought, in tandem and in tension with archivists, to counter this exclusion by collecting the uncollected.[41] But if the Afro-Puerto Rican bibliophile Arturo Schomburg expressed confidence in the 1920s that he could build an alternative archive, one that would "fill in the missing pages of world history," contemporary theorists have profoundly resisted the notion that such missing pages can be found.[42] While "it is tempting to fill in the gaps" of the archive, Hartman argues, history's violence "resides precisely in all the stories that we cannot know and that will never be recovered."[43] Such critiques recognize that archival encounters "do not simply reconnect us with what we have lost. Instead, they remind us ... of what we have never possessed in the first place."[44] The singular archive, then, has gained traction precisely because it conjures the idea of existing repositories as well as that which escapes inventory: the unrecorded. The archive, unlike *archives*, clearly signifies both erasure and memory.[45]

To be sure, the very terms in which we imagine archival loss are shaped by our sense of preservationist protocols, an imbrication that calls for the archival turn to attend more closely than it has to the theories that undergird archival praxis. And yet, while the dislocation of *the* archive from archives in their plural form represents a failure to fully enact the possibilities of interdisciplinarity, it has also posed a useful challenge to existing definitions of archives dependent on the fields of history and records management. Derrida's claim that the archive's penchant for positivist acquisition obscures its specter of dispossession and destruction has engendered lines of inquiry that begin in that negative space.[46] These queries traverse terrain difficult to ask of or within an archival institution: Is there an experimental archival imaginary that never resides in an archive and that cannot be cited as such, though it gives "language to strange and fragmentary pasts?"[47] If archives make possible certain "systems of statements," what statements can be made about what one wishes the archive held, but which it cannot?[48] As for those materials that *are* archived, what rises to the level of archival description and what escapes it, or, as Tina Campt has asked, what is the relationship between the "minute" and the "monumental?"[49] And what are the narrative (or, in M. NourbeSe Philip's terms, antinarrative) possibilities for contending with fragments— "stories caught halfway through"—that a cataloger must bracket as [undated], [unidentified], or [no place]?[50] A metaphorical archive, in other words, creates space for reimagining what has been kept or lost beyond the historian's notion of archive as place or the archivist's enactment of provenance and order.

Archive, to

If some scholars have bristled at appropriations of the term archive that seem to stray too far from their referent—used to invoke "nearly every means by which humans . . . leave traces of their existence"[51]—others have limited its reach by counterposing it to "repertoire," Diana Taylor's name for record-keeping forms that exceed the document. Foreshadowed by Luce Giard and Michel de Certeau's observation that "gestures are the true archives of the city," Taylor's repertoire destabilizes archives—so often imagined in terms of written inscriptions—as the privileged locus of memory.[52] And yet, while drawing attention to performance as a site of memory, this opposition can too narrowly define archives as that which "reduce gestures and embodied practices to narrative description."[53] Here, then, is an apparent contradiction of the archival turn: once unmoored from the literalness of existing archives, the idea of the archive can either vanish or harden; one moment the archive is fleeting (any memory trace), and the next moment static (only the document). In a useful reading of Taylor, however, Eichhorn suggests that the physical archive, seemingly the opposite of an embodied archive, is itself shaped by *acts*—of selection, storage, organization, and classification—that "arguably belong to the repertoire, not the archive."[54] Eichhorn's argument implies a shift from noun to verb, so that "archive" refers, each time it is deployed, to a specific instantiation of archiving.

Thinking about archival acts as themselves repertoire—or, in Achille Mbembe's formulation, as a set of "rituals"—pushes against abstractions of the archive that obscure archival labor.[55] Such labors, undertaken by collectors, keepers, and sorters, trained and self-taught alike, may be located within or outside of formal archives and may or may not produce a "record." In other words, there is no archive, singular, though there are innumerable acts that continuously refigure our idea of it. Encounters with archival forms may take shape as fidelity to archival protocols, efforts to rewrite those protocols, *and* as lamentation in the face of "research that positions us always on the brink of breakthrough and breakdown."[56] (Zora Neale Hurston made historical records through field recordings and transcriptions and retellings; she also declared, famously, that she would "turn her back on the past."[57] There is less contradiction between those two archival postures—turning her back or turning on the cylinder recorder—than one might assume.)

This view of archival *acts,* rather than archive as a discipline or metaphor, directs attention to how any record-keeping architecture—an archive, a catalog, a scrapbook, or a collection, whether analog or digital—is a space of "overlapping orders," some of which follow formal information theories, while others point elsewhere.[58] While positioning the modern archives profession as the literal standard-bearer of archival information practice, we can also underscore its proximity to other kinds of extra-institutional archival practice. Visible in these "overlapping orders," then, are potential kinships—and the forms of reciprocal estrangement kinship can imply—between professional, collective, and personal protocols of arrangement and description.[59] Rather than propose the archive as a singular entity, can we foreground how multiple modes of archiving—statist and experimental alike—constitute one another? Sara Grossman's work on the history of weather data, for example, considers the interplay of archival forms that range from haptic to documentary to "a million media," and traces how each form, situated in time, differently narrativizes the same phenomenon.[60] Such work builds on the metaphorical play of the archival turn while also maintaining the specificities of archival locations and moments. Or, in the words of Verne Harris, it traces the way archives "act through many conduits."[61]

Singular and plural, the keyword archive should evoke for humanities scholars the labor of the archivist, the paper and ephemeral protocols of record-keeping, and our imagined investments in archiving. In other words, archive, like the term information itself, encompasses practice, technology, and form. As the site of a specific information profession *and* a diffuse set of memory practices, archival studies offers an opportunity to think across the institutional contexts that define the work of scholars, record-keepers, artists, digital preservationists, and curators. Its continued salience as a keyword, however, depends on usages that attend carefully to cross-disciplinary unease, working along the grain of grammatical and citational incommensurability. It remains interesting as a keyword not in spite of its ambiguity, but precisely because it creates tension between those who make archives and those who use them, both notionally and notationally.

Notes

1. Lesley Brown, ed., *New Shorter Oxford English Dictionary*, vol. 1 (Oxford: Clarendon Press, 1993), 110.
2. The sequence of special issues devoted on archive/s *outside of* the core archival studies journals shows how the term has been taken up by nearly every discipline of the humanities. Since 1999, *History of the Human Sciences, Studies in the Literary Imagination, Visual Resources, Transgender Studies Quarterly, Social Text, History of the Present*, and *French Historical Studies*, among others, have dedicated full issues to the archive.
3. Paul J. Voss and Marta L. Werner, "Toward a Poetics of the Archive: Introduction," *Studies in the Literary Imagination* 32, no. 1 (1999), i. See also Marlene Manoff, "Theories of the Archive from Across the Disciplines," *Portal: Libraries and the Academy* 4, no. 1 (2004): 9–25.
4. Michel Foucault, *The Archaeology of Knowledge and the Discourse on Language*, trans. A. M. Sheridan Smith (New York: Pantheon Books, 1972), 128–129; Geoffrey Bowker, *Memory Practices in the Sciences* (Cambridge, MA: MIT Press, 2005), 10; Thomas Richards, *The Imperial Archive: Knowledge and the Fantasy of Empire* (London: Verso, 1996); Ann Cvetkovich, *An Archive of Feelings: Trauma, Sexuality, and Lesbian Public Cultures* (Durham, NC: Duke University Press, 2003).
5. Kate Eichhorn, *The Archival Turn in Feminism: Outrage in Order* (Philadelphia: Temple University Press, 2013), 15. See also Tom Nesmith, "Seeing Archives: Postmodernism and Changing Intellectual Place of Archives," *American Archivist* 65 (2002): 33–34.
6. Jacques Derrida, *Archive Fever: A Freudian Impression*, trans. Eric Prenowitz (Chicago: University of Chicago Press, 1995), 1–2.
7. Michelle Caswell, "'The Archive' Is Not an Archives: On Acknowledging the Intellectual Contributions of Archival Science," *Reconstruction* 16, no. 1 (2016).
8. Francis X. Blouin and William G. Rosenberg, *Processing the Past: Contesting Authority in History and the Archives* (New York: Oxford University Press, 2011), 16–30, 118–23.
9. Arlette Farge, *The Allure of the Archives*, trans. Thomas Scott-Railton (New Haven, CT: Yale University Press, 2013), 53.
10. Natalie Zemon Davis, foreword to *Allure of the Archives*, xi.
11. See, e.g., Jeannette Bastian, "Whispers in the Archives: Finding the Voices of the Colonized in the Records of the Colonizer," in Margaret Procter, Michael Cook, and Caroline Williams, eds., *Political Pressure and the Archival Record* (Chicago: Society of American Archivists, 2005); and, more recently, Marisa J. Fuentes, *Dispossessed Lives: Enslaved Women, Violence, and the Archive* (Philadelphia: University of Pennsylvania Press, 2016).

12. Eichhorn, *Archival Turn*, 3. See also Libbie Rifkin, "Association/Value: Creative Collaborations in the Library," *RBM* 2, no. 2 (2001): 123–39.
13. Ann Laura Stoler, "Colonial Archives and the Arts of Governance," *Archival Science* 2 (2002): 92.
14. Michel-Rolph Trouillot, *Silencing the Past: Power and the Production of History* (Boston: Beacon, 1995), 52, 55, 26. See also Randall C. Jimerson, *Archival Power: Memory, Accountability, and Social Justice* (Chicago: Society of American Archivists, 2009).
15. Stoler, "Colonial Archives"; Ann Stoler, *Along the Archival Grain: Epistemic Anxieties and Colonial Common Sense* (Princeton: Princeton University Press, 2009), 24.
16. Kirsten Weld, *Paper Cadavers: The Archives of Dictatorship in Guatemala* (Durham, NC: Duke University Press, 2014), 6. Italics in original.
17. Anjali Arondekar, *For the Record: On Sexuality and the Colonial Archive in India* (Durham, NC: Duke University Press, 2009), 20.
18. See, e.g., "The term archive refers to the place where government records are stored" in Mike Featherstone, "Archive," *Theory, Culture, and Society* 23, nos. 2–3 (2006): 591.
19. Derrida, *Archive Fever*, 1–3; Alice Yaeger Kaplan, "Working in the Archives," *Yale French Studies* 77 (1990): 103; Roberto González Echevarría, *Myth and Archive: A Theory of Latin American Narrative* (Cambridge: Cambridge University Press, 1990), 31–33.
20. Gabrielle Dean, "Disciplinarity and Disorder," *Archive Journal* 1, no. 1 (2011), http://www.archivejournal.net/issue/1/archives-remixed/.
21. See Deborah A. Thomas, "Caribbean Studies, Archive Building, and the Problem of Violence," *Small Axe* 17, no. 2 (2013): 27–42; Ann Cvetkovich, "The Queer Art of the Counterarchive," in *Cruising the Archive: Queer Art and Culture in Los Angeles, 1945–1980*, ed. David Frantz and Mia Locks (Los Angeles: ONE National Lesbian and Gay Archives, 2011): 32–35; and Stewart Motha and Honni van Rijswijk, eds., *Law, Memory, Violence: Uncovering the Counter-Archive* (London: Routledge, 2016).
22. Jacques Derrida, "An Archive," in Carolyn Hamilton, Verne Harris, Michèle Pickover et al., eds., *Refiguring the Archive* (Dordrecht: Kluwer Academic, 2002), 64.
23. Stoler, *Along the Archival Grain*, 52.
24. See David A. Bearman and Richard H. Lytle, "The Power of the Principle of Provenance," in *American Archival Studies: Readings in Theory and Practice*, ed. Randall C. Jimerson (Chicago: Society of American Archivists, 2000): 345–60; and Laura Millar, "The Death of the Fonds and the Resurrection of Provenance: Archival Context in Space and Time," *Archivaria* 53 (2002): 1–15.
25. Frank Boles and Julia Marks Young, "Exploring the Black Box: The Appraisal of University Administrative Records," in *American Archival Studies*, 279–300.
26. Freedmen and Southern Society Project, http://www.freedmen.umd.edu/Ship.html; Records of the Bureau of Refugees, Freedmen, and Abandoned Lands, Record Group 105, National Archives and Records Administration, https://www.archives.gov/research/guide-fed-records/groups/105.html. For a critique of this hierarchical approach, which does not capture "powerless transactions," see Luciana Duranti, *Diplomatics: New Uses for an Old Science* (Lanham, MD: Scarecrow, 1998), 177.
27. These shifts between the 1950s and 1980s include the development of the Modern Archives Institute, the National Union Catalog of Manuscript Collections, and machine-readable cataloging standards. James O'Toole, *Understanding Archives and Manuscripts* (Chicago: Society of American Archivists, 1990), 31, 35, 42–43. See Sue McKemmish and Michael Piggott, "Toward the Archival Multiverse: Challenging the Binary Opposition of the Personal and Corporate Archive in Modern Archival Theory and Practice," *Archivaria* 76 (2013): 111–44.

28. This rethinking has taken shape in interdisciplinary engagements with fields like critical race theory and human rights. See, e.g., Anne J. Gilliland, *Conceptualizing Twenty-first-Century Archives* (Chicago: Society of American Archivists, 2014); Bergis Jules, "Confronting Our Failure of Care Around the Legacies of Marginalized People in the Archives," Address at National Digital Stewardship Alliance, November 9, 2016, https://medium.com/on-archivy/confronting-our-failure-of-care-around-the-legacies-of-marginalized-people-in-the-archives-dc4180397280.
29. See Frank Upward, "Structuring the Records Continuum, Part One: Postcustodial Principles and Properties," *Archives and Manuscripts* 24, no. 2 (1996): 268–85; Hannah Alpert-Abrams, David A. Bliss, and Itza Carbajal, "Postcustodialism for the Common Good: Examining Neoliberalism in US–Latin American Archival Partnerships," *Journal of Critical Library and Information Studies* 2, no. 1 (2019).
30. Jennifer Douglas, "A Call to Rethink Archival Creation: Exploring Types of Creation in Personal Archives," *Archival Science* 18, no. 1 (2018): 29–49.
31. Livia Iacovino, "Rethinking Archival, Ethical and Legal Frameworks for Records of Indigenous Australian Communities: A Participant Relationship Model of Rights and Responsibilities," *Archival Science* 10 (2010): 353–72.
32. Collaborations between archives and artists include the University of Minnesota's partnership with Coffee House Press and the Interference Archive's model of an open-stacks archive. On archival themes in art, see Okwui Enwezor, *Archive Fever: Uses of the Document in Contemporary Art* (New York: ICP, 2008).
33. Eric Ketelaar, "Tacit Narratives: The Meanings of Archives," *Archival Science* 1 (2001): 137.
34. Margaret Hedstrom, *It's About Time: Research Challenges in Digital Archiving and Long-Term Preservation* (Washington, DC: National Science Foundation, 2003); Michelle Caswell, *Archiving the Unspeakable: Silence, Memory, and the Photographic Record in Cambodia* (Madison: University of Wisconsin Press, 2014), 21.
35. Caswell, *Archiving the Unspeakable*, 21.
36. Terry Cook, "What Is Past Is Prologue: A History of Archival Ideas Since 1898, and the Future Paradigm Shift," *Archivaria* 43 (1997): 17–63. This decentering of the archivist as the sole custodian of the archival record has expanded notions of "community archives" as well. See Gracen Brilmyer, Joyce Gabiola, Jimmy Zavala, and Michelle Caswell, "Reciprocal Archival Imaginaries: The Shifting Boundaries of 'Community' in Community Archives," *Archivaria* 88 (Fall 2019): 6–48.
37. Richards, *Imperial Archive*, 4.
38. Cvetkovich, *Archive of Feelings*, 268.
39. Stoler, "Colonial Archives," 94.
40. Saidiya Hartman, "Venus in Two Acts," *Small Axe*, no. 26 (2008): 10, 12; David Scott, "On the Archaeologies of Black Memory," *Small Axe*, no. 26 (2008): vi.
41. Verne Harris, "The Archival Sliver: Power, Memory, and Archives in South Africa," *Archival Science* 2, nos. 1–2 (2002): 65.
42. Schomburg paraphrased by John Henrik Clarke, "Remembering Arthur A. Schomburg," *Encore*, September 26, 1977, 3.
43. Hartman, "Venus," 8, 4.
44. Sven Spieker, *The Big Archive: Art from Bureaucracy* (Cambridge, MA: MIT Press, 2008), 4.
45. Ada Ferrer has encouraged scholars to move beyond the trope of silence and instead read archives for "traces of the conflicts between competing histories and their would-be tellers." "Talk about Haiti: The Archive and the Atlantic's Haitian Revolution," in

Tree of Liberty: Cultural Legacies of the Haitian Revolution in the Atlantic World, ed. Doris L. Garraway (Charlottesville: University of Virginia Press, 2008), 36.
46. Derrida, *Archive Fever*, 94.
47. Michel de Certeau, Luce Giard, and Pierre Mayol, *The Practice of Everyday Life*, vol. 2, trans. Timothy J. Tomasik (Minneapolis: University of Minnesota Press, 1998), 141.
48. Foucault, *Archaeology*, 128–29; Saidiya Hartman, "On Working with Archives," interviewed by Thora Siemsen, *Creative Independent*, April 18, 2018.
49. Tina Campt, *Other Germans: Black Germans and the Politics of Race, Gender and Memory in the Third Reich* (Ann Arbor: University of Michigan Press, 2004), 86–89.
50. M. NourbeSe Philip, *Zong* (Middletown: Wesleyan University Press, 2008), 204; Carolyn Steedman, *Dust: The Archive and Cultural History* (New Brunswick: Rutgers University Press), 45.
51. Richard J. Cox, review of *Archive Stories: Facts, Fictions, and the Writing of History*, ed. Antoinette Burton, *American Archivist* 69, no. 2 (2006): 535.
52. De Certeau, *Practice of Everyday Life*, 141.
53. Diana Taylor, *Archive and the Repertoire: Performing Cultural Memory in the Americas* (Durham, NC: Duke University Press, 2003), 16.
54. Kate Eichhorn, "Past Performance, Present Dilemma: A Poetics of Archiving Sound," *Mosaic* 42, no. 1 (2009), http://lion.chadwyck.com.
55. Achille Mbembe, "The Power of the Archive and Its Limits," in *Refiguring the Archive*, 19–20. The erasure of archival laborers is often grammatical; see, for example, Mbembe's repetition of passive voice: "the majority of documents deemed archivable . . . have to *be* coded and classified. They *are* then distributed according to the chronological, thematic or geographic criteria. Whatever criteria *are* used at the time of coding . . . these procedures *are* simply a matter of creating order" (emphasis added).
56. Jennifer L. Morgan, "Archives and Histories of Racial Capitalism," *Social Text* 33, no. 4 (2015), 154. See also Jennifer Douglas, Alexandra Alisauskas, and Devon Mordell, "'Treat Them with the Reverence of Archivists': Records Work, Grief Work, and Relationship Work in the Archives," *Archivaria* 88 (Fall 2019): 84–120.
57. Hurston quoted in Sharifa Rhodes-Pitts, *Harlem Is Nowhere: A Journey to the Mecca of Black America* (New York: Little, Brown, 2011), 106.
58. Henry Pisciotta, "The Library in Art's Crosshairs," *Art Documentation* 35 (2016): 24n51.
59. See Jarrett M. Drake, "#ArchivesForBlackLives: Building a Community Archives of Police Violence in Cleveland," talk delivered for panel titled "Uploading Black History: Archiving Blacks' Lived Experiences" at the Digital Blackness Conference, April 22, 2016, https://medium.com/on-archivy/archivesforblacklives-building-a-community-archives-of-police-violence-in-cleveland-93615d777289.
60. Sara Grossman, "Ugly Data in the Age of Weather Satellites," *American Literature* 88, no. 4 (2016): 815–37.
61. Harris, "Archival Sliver," 65.

BIOINFORMATICS

HAUN SAUSSY

Bioinformatics is the use of terms and concepts drawn from the study of information (including mathematics and computer science) to account for the origin and particularities of life. It began as a theoretical investigation into the conditions of possibility for such a discipline and has resulted in the prodigious growth of fields such as molecular biology, genomics, and artificial life.

What is life? As the saying goes: *If you have to ask...* When Erwin Schrödinger asked the question in a lecture-series of that name in 1943, he was, as if performatively, creating a situation in which an acceptable answer would have to be framed in a way that did not take the meaning of the word "life" to be self-evident.[1] What *kind of a thing* is life, then, where "thing" includes atoms, electrical charges, quantum states, wave functions, heat, motion, and so forth, but not consciousness, appetite, the soul, *élan vital*, or other apparent irreducibles? Framed as a problem of translation, the question becomes: Can the language of physics represent the language of biology without loss?

When asking the question, "What is life?", do we anticipate an answer with information-value, that is, something other than a tautology? It is not clear that the question can usefully be addressed to adherents of vitalism, who will take it as instead meaning "What is the essential property of life that necessarily and always transcends definition in merely physico-chemical terms?"—and answer it with words to the effect that "Life is life." Such answers assume that Schrödinger's question fails to be a question—that asking the question confirms the impertinence of any answer. The successful description of animate matter in terms devised for the description of inanimate matter becomes, then, a precondition for asking the question in a noncircular way. If "life" must be assumed as a property belonging to and known by any possible reader and respondent, then the question is merely rhetorical or heuristic, and means something like "Let's see how far we can get in the physics-based description of biology, and call a halt when we have to." Is a rhetorical question a good question?

Outside the realm of the natural sciences it is permissible to ask "bad questions," questions involving circularity or questions that repose on insufficiently clarified terms, and many such questions are eminently worth asking. Whether "What is life?" is a good question or a bad question is itself a question in need of clarification. But one way of making a better question out of the potentially bad question is to ask it again, but historically. What has it meant to ask the question "What is life?"

What Life Does

The characterization of life Schrödinger lays out in his lectures does not directly ask what life is. Instead, it asks what life *does*. Living creatures breathe and feed, they develop, they procreate. The sciences of matter and energy suggest descriptions for each of these activities. By taking nutrients from its surroundings, by sustaining homeostasis in its skin or bark, the plant or animal "feeds upon ... negative entropy."[2] Entropy, in thermodynamics, is a measure of the increase in disorder to which all physical systems are, in the long run, subject. Living creatures are islands of strenuously maintained "negative entropy"; they buck the trend of ever-increasing disorder common to inorganic matter. "Life seems to be orderly and lawful behavior of matter, not based exclusively on its tendency to go over from order to disorder, but based partly on existing order that is kept up."[3] This maintenance of internal order is accompanied by a speedier increase in disorder in the world around them: e.g., a sheep's digestive system breaks down the organized living matter in the grass it eats. A living creature is one that "succeeds in freeing itself from all the entropy it cannot help producing while alive."[4] And a creature that joins with others of its kind to beget new creatures will have succeeded in releasing, for at least one generation, some of its properties from the same wear, tear, and entropy. As long as life goes on, "the aperiodic crystal forming the hereditary substance [is] largely withdrawn from the disorder of heat motion."[5] Life is—or seems to be—an exception to the laws of inorganic nature.

Ideas of information creep into this account of physics and biology through a familiar metaphor. What makes possible the maintenance of life and identity over generations is imagined by Schrödinger to be a "pattern," a "codescript" in the form of an "aperiodic crystal" in the chromosome.[6] It is this "code-script," copied again and again on different media, that allows us living creatures, temporarily and locally, to reverse entropy. And chemistry is almost, says Schrödinger, at the point of reading the script: "With the molecular picture of the gene it is no longer inconceivable that the miniature code should precisely correspond with a highly complicated and specified plan of development and should somehow contain the means to put it into operation."[7] This, however, would have to wait for empirical confirmation in the following decade.

Storage and Manipulation

Open an introductory medical textbook and you will find passages like this one:

> Biological systems are particularly rich in information and in the ability to faithfully copy, transmit, decode, and act upon that information. The macromolecules chosen for this purpose through the course of evolution, such as DNA, RNA, and proteins, have features that are particularly well suited for storage and manipulation of information ... The information that specifies just about every feature that distinguishes us from each other—and from an armadillo or a jellyfish—is encoded in our genes in the form of specific sequences of relatively stable, double-stranded DNA. This information is expressed, first as the more labile and generally single-stranded RNA, and finally as proteins, the molecules that actually do the work that the information makes possible.[8]

No quotation marks, none of the signals—"like," "as if," "in a manner of speaking"—that might alert the reader to a metaphor occur in this passage written some sixty years after Schrödinger's anticipatory description of the genetic "code-script." The metaphor has been comprehensively naturalized—that is, it has sunk below the threshold of awareness and become the proper and the inevitable designation for what genes and cells do. The language of "code" and "information" permeates biology, and for good strategic reasons: DNA and RNA are active in every living thing, from bacteria to plants to animals, and in nearly every vital process, including the growth of cells and proteins to maintain the existence of any creature. But must their activity be represented as a process of communication? Against this vocabulary, the philosopher Peter Janich raises a rare objection, identifying "the myth of information as a natural object" as "a clearly identifiable intellectual and social failure.... Today, words like *coding, transcribing, translating, reading, speaking*, and so on, have become indispensable to the very representation of genetics. Their use is not a matter of the media finding figurative ways of explaining genetics to nonscientists but rather a reflection of the original language of the experts and of textbooks in the field."[9]

Janich contends that "the naturalization of information ... happened ... as the result of a single-minded, deliberate process whose goals make its ambitions clear: to reconstruct information as an objective, natural fact."[10] Talk of the genetic code is for him a "legacy of the mechanization of information ... a false imaginary of the mechanical apparatus itself, one that treats it as equivalent to human ability."[11] A reductive anthropomorphism of information acts to raise genes, amino acids, and markers to the status of the sorts of things that "send messages," "code for" this or that, "recognize" a corresponding base pair; and thus acts to lower humans to the status of mere operators of communication technologies. Against these canons of modeling, Janich holds that "no one has ever found a way to move from the description of material structures to the information they encode."[12] How did information become so pervasive as to dominate the very thought of our biological existences? Is it a delusion, or an inevitability? Can we still learn to do without the language of bioinformatics?

Lateral Thinkers

During the Second World War, moving from the description of material structures (sequences of letters and numbers) to the information they encoded was vital to the efforts of all combatants. For that is what it means to break a code; the code-writer emits "material structures" with the intention that their meaning remain hidden. The War Office's collection of prodigies and eccentrics at Bletchley Park included Alan Turing who was already known for the "Turing machine" (1936), a thought-experiment about a computer with unlimited memory but minimal analytic capacities, and would later be renowned for his proposal (1950) of the "Turing Test," a means of determining whether a machine could be said to "think." In the United States, communication theorists working at Bell Labs on Defense Department contracts sought to determine the constraints on any act of information exchange, by way of narrowing down the possible values to be churned through in seeking equivalents for an enemy cipher. Part of this work remained classified for decades; part of it was published in 1948, just at the moment that "information" was appearing to be the common key of several disciplines.[13]

When Shannon's 1944 paper was republished for wider circulation in 1949, it came introduced by an essay by Warren Weaver, which said in part:

> That information be measured by entropy is, after all, natural when we remember that information, in communication theory, is associated with the amount of freedom of choice we have in constructing messages. Thus for a communication source one can say, just as he would also say it of a thermodynamic

ensemble, "This situation is highly organized, it is not characterized by a large degree of randomness or of choice—that is to say, the information (or the entropy) is low."[14]

Let us consider a specific example. If we know that a submarine commander routinely ends communications with his superiors with the sign-off "Heil Hitler!," then we can use the nonrandom character of the closing formula of twelve characters (including the blank space and the exclamation point) to assign values to the Enigma cipher settings in use for any particular communication, and thus have a foothold for assigning letter-values to other parts of that message. That is, the entropy of the closing formula is low (it is predictable), and it permits the decipherer to reduce the randomness of the equivalents of the letters H, E, I, and so on, to zero—whereupon the Enigma settings are seriously breached; for we may know from statistical studies of the German language how often the letters E and I are likely to come up in written communication, and which letters are typically less frequent, so that a single piece of predictable behavior by a loyal submarine commander is apt to reveal the content of quite a few painstakingly coded messages. It is indeed possible to go from mere material structures to meaning, if only a few guesses about the probability of correlations between the two pay off.

References to "code" in scholarly or widely circulating texts before 1961 show no particular weighting toward the "genetic code" of our present common parlance, or of the "code-script" imagined by Schrödinger. Before 1961, the word most commonly designates either a secret code (a cipher) or a legal code. From 1961, however, references to "the genetic code" are ever more frequent, to the point of constituting the default meaning of the term "code" in many areas of publication.[15] The fact that a starting-point exists shows that later developments were not inevitable and permits us to historicize. Rather than allowing the language of "genetic information" to be naturalized, to be one of those things that is "naturally true," we should frame a question around it. How is it that people began talking, and continued talking, about the genetic code, the book of life, molecular signaling, and all the rest?

From Template to Code

The behavior of DNA and related molecules has been the central concern of biochemistry since Crick, Watson, and Franklin identified the structure of DNA in 1953. Their first published description observes drily that "This structure has novel features which are of considerable biological interest." It continues with details of the molecule, the subsequently famous double helix, and its atomic components, in particular the pairing of bases from opposite chains of the structure. Toward the end of the article, another dry observation: "It has not escaped our notice that the specific pairing we have postulated immediately suggests a possible copying mechanism for the genetic material."[16] *Copying.* The hint is one word of the six or seven hundred in the article, and not at all specific as to the "mechanism," for in addition to texts, many things in the world of objects can be copied: statues, paintings, coins, villas, for example. Crick and Watson's next publication, still mainly occupied with describing DNA's molecular structure, introduces the term "code." Here they conceive of the molecule's function as that of a "template," though it is a curiously active one, dividing itself into halves and generating a replica of the halves as a means of "self-duplication."

> The phosphate-sugar backbone of our model is completely regular, but any sequence of the pairs of bases can fit into the structure. It follows that in a long molecule many different permutations are possible, and it therefore seems likely that the precise sequence of the bases is the code which carries the genetical information. If the actual order of the bases on one of the pair of chains were given, one could write down the exact order of the bases on the other one, because of the specific pairing. This one chain is, as it were, the complement of the other, and it is this feature which suggests how the deoxyribonucleic acid molecule might duplicate itself.
>
> Previous discussions of self-duplication have usually involved the concept of a template, or mould. Either the template was supposed to copy itself directly or it was to produce a 'negative,' which in its turn was to act as a template and produce the original 'positive' once again. In no case has it been explained in detail how it would do this in term of atoms and molecules.
>
> Now our model for deoxyribonucleic acid is, in effect, a *pair* of templates, each of which is complementary to the other. We imagine that prior to duplication the hydrogen bonds are broken, and the two chains unwind and separate. Each chain then acts as a template for the formation onto itself of a new companion chain, so that eventually we shall have *two* pairs of chains, where we only had one before. Moreover, the sequence of the pairs of bases will have been duplicated exactly.[17]

Analogies to things and events at human scale are necessarily used to figure forth events and actions at the molecular scale. *How does it work? It works like this* . . . Among the metaphorical terms, "duplication" is the most abstract and general. "Template" could refer to many kinds of engineering solutions: stamping, cutting, imprinting, marking. "Positive" and "negative" refer to the specific duplicating technology of photography, and its ancestor, woodblock carving and printing. "Sequence," "permutation," and "code" occupy a recognizably linguistic or mathematical register, that of small elements that combine in larger series ruled by a syntax. But "code" is not yet the master term that organizes all the others: "template," with its connotations from the world of two- and three-dimensional engineering, returns and finishes the sequence of hypothetical actions. The same language—"capacity for self-duplication" and "a template for the formation" of complementary chains—appears in the longer article published the next year, "The Complementary Structure of Deoxyribonucleic Acid."[18] The form of the argument about duplication is analogue and physical, with the information vocabulary providing guidance to the human reader.

That would change as scientists in several interrelated labs began looking more closely at the operations of DNA and its fellow, RNA. Publications by Hoagland, Zamecnik, Pardee, Monod, and Jacob were conspicuous in resorting to informational terminology in trying to express how DNA generated proteins by means of various incompletely understood forms of RNA. In 1956, Crick sketched out what came to be called "the central dogma" of molecular biology: the direction of "transfer of information" goes always from DNA to RNA and thence to proteins, never the reverse. "Information here means the *sequence* of the amino acid residues," says Crick in 1957.[19] **[Figure 1]** Elements plus syntax: the structure begins to look less like a photographic negative and more like a language. But the scientific discussion was not yet conquered by the myth of the alphabet. Code and information metaphors were just one linguistic

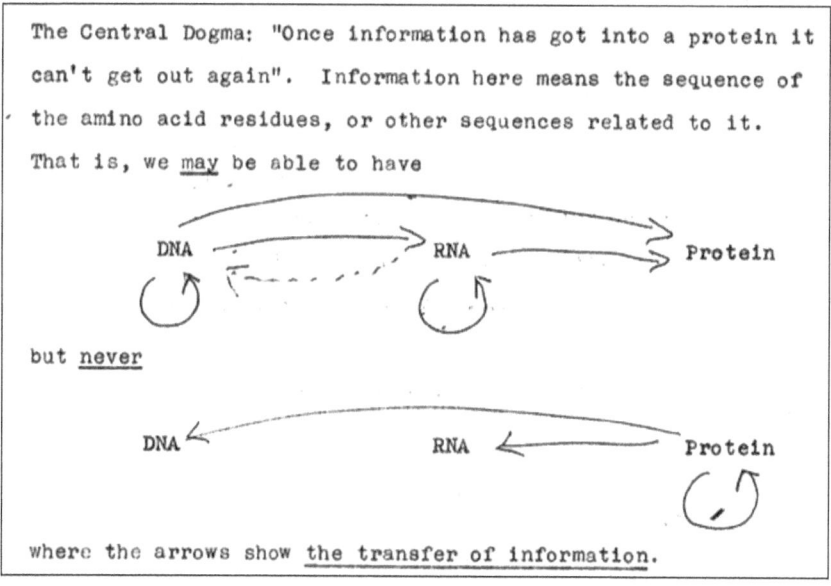

4.1 The Central Dogma, from Crick, "On Protein Synthesis" (1957).

device used in exploring the still-elusive behavior of molecules. Hans-Jörg Rheinberger's history of this moment in the study of protein synthesis frames it as a conflict of metaphorical vehicles:

> At the end of 1958 ... Zamecnik conjectures that "each RNA molecule *coded* in some fashion for a specific amino acid, and in turn perhaps *coded* for a specific, complementary site on the ribonucleic acid portion of the ribonucleoprotein particle which serves as a protein synthesizing *template*." "Coding" became the term for two different processes.... The soluble RNA was considered to carry the recognition signal for a specific amino acid; the ribonucleic acid of the microsome was considered to act as the template that specified the sequence of a particular protein. The language of molecular information transfer began to inscribe itself into the metabolic representation of protein synthesis. But it neither did nor could replace the biochemical framework immediately.[20]

The article to which Rheinberger refers bears out this observation: where its language is not strictly chemical, its domain of analogical reference is entirely three-dimensional, and physical, a language of "linkage," "attachment," and "incorporation," up to the last page, when "code" makes an appearance—but still in the company of the reassuringly physical term "template."[21] Rheinberger gives a precise account of the way analogies work in scientific language: they compete to "inscribe" themselves on the realities they purportedly "describe," and they must do so by "replacing" an earlier language. To restore the thought-processes that led to these analogies, we must scratch away the layers of palimpsestic reinscription. But that means temporarily forgetting what we "know" at later stages of the history. When there is still a lot of uncertainty about the validity of the descriptions, analogies compete for the best grip on the documented results. In a landscape of missing or ambiguous results, the eventually victorious language "neither did nor could replace" its predecessor. A splendid example of hesitation between the template and letterpress models for protein synthesis occurs in a 1959 publication by Hoagland: here the amino acids are depicted as binding to fragments of letters and conveying them to their destined places in order to compose the word TEMPLATE.[22] [**Figure 2**] This graphic compromise undoes the whole notion of a letter-like code, for a fragment of a letter is not a letter but an illegible mark. But it serves to show the condition of the debate at that moment: something is assembling the material structures into something that conveys a meaningful sequence, but it is unclear what directs the assemblage or what the items conveyed are. Arthur Pardee, François Jacob, and Jacques Monod, the team known under the abbreviation PaJaMo, first used the term "cytoplasmic messenger" in 1959, but as Matthew Cobb observes in his history of the mRNA concept, "how exactly the process worked, and above all what the messenger was made of, they could not say."[23]

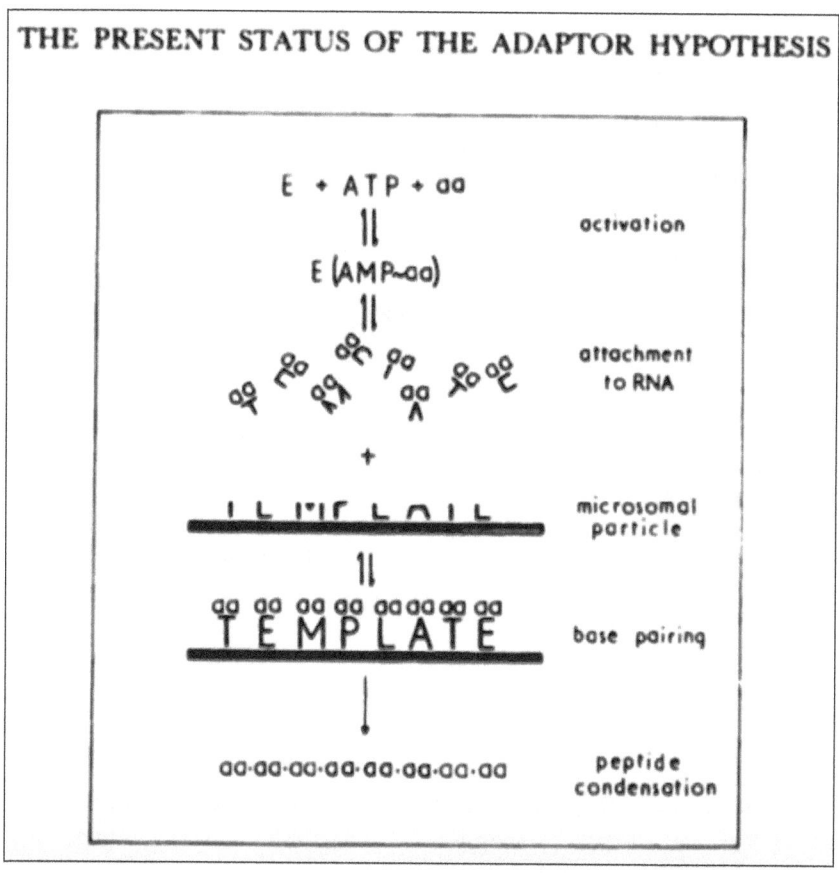

4.2 Hoagland, "The Present Status of the Adaptor Hypothesis," *Brookhaven Symposia in Biology* 12 (1959).

The decisive year for the term "genetic code" is 1961, when the series of events that must occur for the nucleotide sequences to be inscribed in protein form became clear through the conjoint operation of several labs. A famous and accidental 1961 meeting among the Cambridge group gathered around Crick and the Institut Pasteur group gathered around Monod and Jacob resulted in the elaboration of a new conceit, "messenger RNA," that Crick imagined "as a reading head, like in a tape recorder... Messenger RNA... was like a tape that copied information from DNA and then carried that information to the ribosome, which read it off and followed the instructions to make the appropriate protein." Now messenger RNA and its equipment of "code," "letters," "messages," and "instructions" was beginning to overwrite all the previous analogies. The code needed no longer to be "duplicated" but "regulated" by "operator" molecules.[24] "The use of the term 'messenger' is significant, as it indicated that Jacob and Monod were not thinking in terms of an analogue, template model, but rather were beginning to view the problem in informational terms. The form of the message was not the key point—the essence they were highlighting was its meaning, or function," Cobb assesses.[25]

A meeting at Cold Spring Harbor in 1961 consolidated the information-based model of DNA and RNA workings and sent workers back to their various labs with this new, powerful vocabulary.[26] From that point on, the status of "genetic information," as the most effective family of metaphors for evoking facts and explanations in relation to DNA, is secure. Although Crick in 1958 claimed that "informational talk" was just a way of making molecular biology accessible to "non-specialists," the success of the messenger-RNA hypothesis made such talk the dominant language among specialists.[27] François Jacob's history of the idea of heredity, *La Logique du Vivant*, published in 1970, is the triumph song of this informational biology, predicting its extension (with relevant adaptations) to social and cultural levels.[28]

In this way, in an involuntary interdisciplinary move, biology came to be saturated with terms taken from linguistics, philology, and communication. The language of information that we now find in biology was not necessarily there from start to finish. It has a history, an origin point, and rises to prominence through conflicts in argument. Had the "template" metaphor been a better vehicle for summarizing lab results, "code" and "message" talk would have faded away like a myth without believers; and it is still possible that investigation into other aspects of the genetic process, for example the folding of proteins, will one day demand a different vocabulary that will crowd out the language of genetic messaging, or confine it to a narrower domain within biology. Authoritative languages in science—what some would call "paradigms"—come and go, wax and wane, and are discarded with admirable ruthlessness by the researchers who find a new model to push.

Self-Generation

Strangely, however, a crucial part of information-based biology was already worked out (in sheer logical terms) before the structure of DNA had been identified and its function as "template" or "codebook" debated. The part of genetic theory thus elaborated, with no geneticists in the room, and no DNA theorists either, inasmuch as DNA was not yet understood, was precisely the part that anticipated Pardee, Jacob, and Monod's work on signaling in 1960–61 and the triumph of the informational vocabulary. It sketched the groundwork of what biochemistry would name the distinction between transcription and translation, or between the duplication of symbols and the representation of the content that they symbolize in the cell.

Claude Shannon's master's thesis at MIT included a demonstration of the feasibility of enacting Boolean logic in electric circuits.[29] This bit of engineering entered into the designs of the first stored-program electronic computer, the 1943–1955 ENIAC, like information theory a side-product of war work (the need to predict projectile trajectories and nuclear chain reactions).[30] The expansion of the practical capabilities of a "universal machine" like the one outlined by Turing suggested to the mathematician John von Neumann an investigation into the possibilities of artificial life.

In 1948, von Neumann gave a talk on "The General and Logical Theory of Automata" which was his variation on Schrödinger's "What Is Life?" lectures; only, where Schrödinger tried to formulate life as a problem for physics, von Neumann framed it as a logical problem. The starting point is the fact that organisms are able to reproduce themselves, generating new individuals that are no lower in complexity than the parent organism. In contrast, when dealing with machines that can build other machines, "there must be a decrease in complication as we go from the parent to the construct. That is, if A can produce B, then A in some way must have contained a complete description of B."[31] How can we account for the fact that in life there is no corresponding loss in complexity; indeed, that in the course of evolution we often see leaps and gains in complexity over time? And could that power of reproduction ever be simulated in a technological object? The main logical difficulty can be stated in the simple terms of von Neumann's earlier example. For A to produce a simpler object, B, A "must have contained a complete description of B." But if A is to produce another A, how can it "contain a complete description of" itself? In a variant of Russell's paradox, a self-reproducing A must both contain a complete description of itself and not contain such a description (since a complete description of A would have to include a description of the description of A, and so forth). The infinite regress of descriptions condemns the attempt to futility.

Von Neumann's solution is to split the operation of reproduction into two. Let us build, first, "Automaton A, which when furnished the description of any other automaton in terms of appropriate functions, will construct that entity."[32] Then "Automaton B . . . can make a copy of any instruction . . . that is furnished to it." Automaton A follows instructions to construct a copy of itself from which the working instructions are left out; Automaton B makes a copy of those instructions, and a control automaton, C, inserts the instructions into the new (and now complete) second-generation Automaton A. Circularity has been avoided. And a quite abstract model for biological reproduction has been proposed, for "it is quite clear that the [assembly] instruction . . . is roughly effecting the functions of a gene. It is also clear that the copying mechanism B performs . . . the duplication of the genetic material, which is clearly the fundamental operation in the multiplication of living cells,"[33] in von Neumann's prescient formulation.

This strange monogenesis or parthenogenesis does not attempt to duplicate sexual reproduction. "Male and female created he them," says the Book of Genesis (5:2), agreeing for once with ordinary experience; but the self-generating automaton corresponds to a far more primitive unicellular kind of organism. Heterogenesis is forced upon it by the need to separate data from instructions, a semiotic difference at the origins of what we might call, for this occasion, "life." The kind of life that we multicellular animals experience relies on many more levels and many more relays of what the medical textbook calls, once more, "communication": "Exploitation of the full potential of multicellular specialization required novel modes and increased sophistication of communication between cells.... Multicellular animals have evolved a number of modes of communication. The nervous system and the endocrine system are the best studied."[34] The single-celled automaton was the logical place to start for von Neumann, though biology, engaged with the analysis of complex wholes, took longer to work down to it.

In the language of post-1961 molecular biology, RNA when producing proteins carries out the work of von Neumann's Automaton A, namely a *translation* into new material of the information contained in the description furnished it; DNA, producing RNA, does the work of Automaton B, *transcribing* genetic information without interpreting it. Translation executes instructions; transliteration copies data. It takes both kinds of operation to synthesize a protein, as the researchers of 1961 realized. But the relationship between von Neumann's self-reproducing automata and the DNA-RNA complex outlined by molecular biologists came into view only ten years after von Neumann's death, when an expanded version of his lectures on the subject was published by his student Arthur Burks.[35]

Bringing together the two sides of this history—genetics as predicted by informatics and informatics as experimented with by biochemistry—is the task of theoretical bioinformatics, a field of investigation framed by an "as-if" scenario. As the chronology given above indicates, biosemiotics actually preceded the biochemistry of DNA, though their correlation was not recognized until long after the fact. Yet the relevance of semiotics to biochemistry is still debated, with such fields often being shunted off into the area of philosophy by practicing biologists and chemists.

Among the investigations that go under the heading of *bioinformatics*, one finds descriptive enterprises working from generally accepted understandings—for example cell biology or the modeling of biological processes by artificial means such as computers—and attempts to use the findings of semiotics or information theory in a more speculative and inductive fashion to redescribe such fundamental terms as "life," "organism," and "ecological milieu," using semiotics as the lever whereby to construct the general possibility of biology from physics.[36] Others take the "autopoietic" (self-maintaining) behavior of living systems as a clue to the nature of mind, or of society.[37] The broadened definition of "life" as a mode of externally observable behavior allows it to bridge the natural, social, and philological sciences, with some adjustment of the tolerances of the terms involved.

The history of the proliferation of models derived from communication should have something to teach those of us whose knowledge is about literary and cultural texts. How, without metaphor, can we describe the "life" of texts? Do they interbreed, scatter, become mutants, die? When our traces outlive us or outrun us (as when the confidentiality of genetic information is violated), is this a further demonstration of Plato's intuition that writing, with its propensity to "roll around and get into the wrong hands" exceeds and is at odds with what we usually know as life?[38] When terms such as translation and transcription are naturalized, that is, conceived of as material operations with their meaning held in suspense, do we find ourselves missing the point of artworks—or gaining a new perspective on them? Poems, symphonies, myths, novels, histories, nations, customs, and collective identities, we may say, are massively internally organized bodies of inscriptional matter, held together over generations by technological reproduction (transcription) and given new life in every generation or so by their translation into new situations. Once we consider cultural artifacts as a "form of life" epiphytic on human biological existence, we may find that the work of inscription takes precedence over that of interpretation, transcription over translation, inverting the usual hierarchy and teleology of the literary field, where understanding of meanings is thought to be the guiding aim.

What is life? To be sure of getting a noncircular answer, you may wish to ask an artificial life form.

Notes

1. Erwin Schrödinger, *What Is Life? With Mind and Matter and Autobiographical Sketches* (Cambridge: Cambridge University Press, 1992). Further references in the text. On the "strategic ambiguity" of Schrödinger's text, a property of its semantics and pragmatics that its later readings actualize, see Leah Ceccarelli, *Shaping Science with Rhetoric: The Cases of Dobzhansky, Schrödinger, and Wilson* (Chicago: University of Chicago Press, 2001), 97–110. Further citations of this work are given in the text.
2. Schrödinger, *What Is Life?*, 71.
3. Schrödinger, *What Is Life?*, 68.
4. Schrödinger, *What Is Life?*, 71.
5. Schrödinger, *What Is Life?*, 85.
6. Schrödinger, *What Is Life?*, 21, 25, 61.
7. Schrödinger, *What Is Life?*, 62.
8. Viswanath R. Lingappa and Krista Farey, *Physiological Medicine* (New York: McGraw-Hill, 2000), 42.

9. Peter Janich, *What Is Information?* trans. Eric Hayot and Lea Pao (Minneapolis: University of Minnesota Press, 2018), 4–5. Further citations of this work are given in the text.
10. Janich, *What Is Information?*, 54.
11. Janich, *What Is Information?*, 27.
12. Janich, *What Is Information?*, 91.
13. C. E. Shannon, "A Mathematical Theory of Communication," *Bell System Technical Journal* 27, no. 3 (1948): 379–423.
14. Warren Weaver, "Recent Contributions to the Mathematical Theory of Communication," in Claude E. Shannon and Warren Weaver, *The Mathematical Theory of Communication* (Urbana: University of Illinois Press, 1949), 13. The identification of information-theoretic entropy with thermodynamic entropy is one of the major points contested by Janich.
15. Searches conducted on the Hathi Trust database of scientific and scholarly texts using the terms "code," "transcription," "transliteration," and "genetic," singly and in combination, April 2018. The reader is invited to try with other such resources.
16. J. D. Watson and F. H. C. Crick, "A Structure for Deoxyribose Nucleic Acid," *Nature* 171 (April 25, 1953), 737–38. Watson and Crick based their hypothetical structure for DNA on crystallographic results attained by Rosalind Franklin, whose role in the discovery is insufficiently acknowledged. See R. E. Franklin and R. G. Gosling, "Molecular Configuration in Sodium Thymonucleate," *Nature* 171 (April 25, 1953): 740–41.
17. J. D. Watson and F. H. C. Crick, "Genetical Implications of the Structure of Deoxyribonucleic Acid," *Nature* 171 (May 30, 1953): 965–66.
18. F. H. C. Crick and J. D. Watson, "The Complementary Structure of Deoxyribonucleic Acid," *Proceedings of the Royal Society of London. Series A, Mathematical, Physical and Engineering Sciences*, 223 (1954): 95.
19. F. H. C. Crick, "On Protein Synthesis," *Symposia of the Society for Experimental Biology* 12 (1958): 138–63.
20. Hans-Jörg Rheinberger, *Toward a History of Epistemic Things: Synthesizing Proteins in the Test Tube* (Stanford: Stanford University Press, 1997), 175.
21. Liselotte I. Hecht, Mary L. Stephenson, and Paul C. Zamecnik, "Binding of Amino Acids to the End Group of a Soluble Ribonucleic Acid," *Proceedings of the NAS of the USA* 45: 505–18, referred to in Rheinberger, 269.
22. Mahlon B. Hoagland, "The Present Status of the Adaptor Hypothesis," *Brookhaven Symposia in Biology* 12 (1959): 40–46, at 45; also reproduced in Rheinberger, *Toward a History of Epistemic Things*, 193.
23. Matthew Cobb, "Who Discovered Messenger RNA?," *Current Biology* 25 (2015): R523–R48.
24. François Jacob and Jacques Monod, "Genetic Regulatory Mechanisms in the Synthesis of Proteins," *Journal of Molecular Biology* 3 (1961): 318–56.
25. Cobb, "Who Discovered Messenger RNA?," R529–30.
26. Jerard Hurwitz, "The Discovery of DNA Polymerase," *Journal of Biological Chemistry* 280.52 (December 30, 2005): 42477–85.
27. Predrag Šustar, "Crick's Notion of Genetic Information and the 'Central Dogma' of Molecular Biology," *British Journal of the Philosophy of Science* 58 (2007): 13–24.
28. François Jacob, *La Logique du vivant: Une histoire de l'hérédité* (Paris: Gallimard, 1970).
29. C. E. Shannon, "A Symbolic Analysis of Relay and Switching Circuits," *American Institute of Electrical Engineers Transactions* 57 (1938): 713–23.

30. Thomas Haigh, Mark Priestley, and Crispin Rope, *ENIAC in Action: Making and Remaking the Modern Computer* (Cambridge, MA: MIT Press, 2016).
31. John von Neumann, "The General and Logical Theory of Automata," in von Neumann, *Collected Works*, ed. A. H. Taub, 6 vols. (New York: Macmillan, 1961–63), 5:288–328; here 312. Further citations of this work are given in the text.
32. Von Neumann, "The General and Logical Theory of Automata," 316.
33. Von Neumann, "The General and Logical Theory of Automata," 317–318.
34. Lingappa and Farey, 114–15.
35. John von Neumann, *Theory of Self-Reproducing Automata*, ed. Arthur W. Burks (Urbana: University of Illinois Press, 1966).
36. See Luis Mateus Rocha, ed., *The Physics and Evolution of Symbols and Codes*, special number of *BioSystems* 60 (2001), https://www.informatics.indiana.edu/rocha/publications/pattee/index.html (accessed April 22, 2018); Marcello Barbieri, ed., *An Introduction to Biosemiotics: The New Biological Synthesis* (Dordrecht: Springer, 2008); Marcello Barbieri, "A Short History of Biosemiotics," *Biosemiotics* 2 (2009): 221–45.
37. See Evan Thompson, *Mind in Life: Biology, Phenomenology, and the Sciences of Mind* (Cambridge, MA: Harvard University Press, 2007); Niklas Luhmann, *Social Systems*, trans. John Bednarz Jr. and Dirk Baecker (Stanford: Stanford University Press, 1995).
38. Plato, *Plato in Twelve Volumes*, vol. 9, trans. Harold N. Fowler (Cambridge, MA: Harvard University Press, 1925), 275d.

COGNITION

N. KATHERINE HAYLES

Cognition and information are intimately entwined. Their relation is specified by a definition I proposed: *"cognition is a process that interprets information in contexts that connect it with meaning."*[1] This definition overcomes a major shortcoming of information as developed by the Shannon–Weaver theory; namely, its decontextualized and purely quantitative character. Not only does my definition explicitly include context, but it also makes clear that cognition includes interpretive acts that ground information, thereby connecting it with meaning. Broadening the scope of cognition beyond the anthropocentric bias toward "thinking," this framework invites explorations of the concept beyond the brain in humans, beyond the human species in nonhumans, and beyond biological lifeforms in computational media. It raises provocative questions about what constitutes "meaning," including how meaning-making practices may be understood outside the human realm and in media other than biological entities.

Human Cognition

An important step in going beyond "thought" is the realization that cognition in humans occurs in nonconscious as well as conscious neuronal processes, as indicated by the last two decades of research in neuroscience, cognitive science, and cognitive psychology.[2] Although these nonconscious processes are inaccessible to consciousness, they nevertheless perform functions essential for consciousness to operate. These include creating a coherent body image, processing information faster than consciousness, and recognizing patterns too noisy and subtle for consciousness to discern.[3] Unlike the Freudian unconscious (if one believes in it), which manifests through symptoms and dreams, nonconscious processes appear as subtle intuitions that consciousness can attend to if the context is appropriate. If these intuitions are not reinforced by "top-down" signals, the results of these processes die out within half a minute.[4] This timeline indicates that a primary contribution of nonconscious cognition is to keep consciousness that is operating relatively slowly and with limited processing power from being overwhelmed by the information flooding into sensory and neuronal systems every microsecond.

Recent research has made increasingly clear that the massive and complex feedback loops involved in conscious and nonconscious neuronal processes are thoroughly embodied, integrating information across different brain regions and connecting with sensing and information-processing performed by organs, glands, and tissues throughout the body.[5] Cognitive activities, including abstract symbol manipulation, are grounded in simulations of bodily actions.[6] Moreover, embodied and embedded cognitions also draw significantly on environmental resources to support and extend their reach.[7]

Animal Cognition

The study of animal cognition is a rapidly expanding area of inquiry that includes advances in biosemiotics; research into core consciousness in nonhuman mammalian species such as primates, dogs, cats, pigs, horses, and some cephalopods such as octopi; along with the study of the cognitive capacities of birds, reptiles, fish, bees, and species that do not have central nervous systems, such as mollusks. Around 1960, a "cognitive turn" opened the field to inferences about mental states from observed behaviors, representing a sharp departure from the constraints of behaviorism. Among the capacities that have been studied are navigational abilities in migrating species, spatial recognition in mammals and bees, tool use in primate species and ravens, allocation of attentional resources in pigeons and other species, and the ability among many species to form categories. Closely related to evolutionary psychology, animal cognition studies often invoke what an animal needs to know to survive to explain why a given species developed certain cognitive abilities rather than others.

That many nonhuman species possess consciousness, a historically contentious issue, is now accepted by many experts in the field. At a Cambridge conference in 2012 on "Consciousness in Human and Nonhuman Animals," the attending scientists signed this declaration:

> Convergent evidence indicates that non-human animals have the neuroanatomical, neurochemical, and neurophysiological substrates of conscious states along with the capacity to exhibit intentional behaviors... Non-human animals, including all mammals and birds, and many other creatures including octopuses, also possess these neurological substrates.[8]

The declaration shows an increasing awareness that species without neocortices may nevertheless demonstrate affective behaviors similar to humans:

> Systems associated with affect are concentrated in subcortical regions where neural homologies abound. Young humans and non-human animals without neocortices retain these brain-mind functions. Furthermore, neural circuits supporting behavior/electrophysiological states of attentiveness, sleep and decision making appear to have arisen in evolution as early as the invertebrate radiation, being evident in insects and cephalopod mollusks (e.g., octopus).

The conclusions extend beyond mammals as well:

> Birds appear to offer, in their behavior, neurophysiology, and neuroanatomy a striking case of parallel evolution of consciousness. Evidence of near human-like levels of consciousness has been most dramatically observed in African grey parrots. Mammalian and avian emotional networks and cognitive microcircuitries appear to be far more homologous than previously thought.

A notorious problem in the philosophy of thought, of course, has been the difficulty of proving that another creature, including another human, has awareness of mind comparable to oneself. It seems reasonable to conclude, however, that if similar neural architectures are present, so are the dynamics of neural processes identified with human consciousness. The declaration therefore does not speak of consciousness as such but rather the "substrates"—anatomical, chemical, physiological—associated with consciousness in humans. Unstated, yet fundamental to this research, is the assumption that these substrates work by creating, transmitting, receiving, storing, and processing information. This is the common framework that allows homologies to emerge across species while nevertheless emphasizing that each species has its distinctive sensory, affective, and neuronal capacities. The link between information and cognition forms the bridge that supports inferences about the ability of nonhuman species to grasp the world, interact with it, and understand it in their own terms and contexts. "Context" in this sense includes both the internal capabilities and constraints of the organism's biology as well as how they interact with the organism's environment.

With the concept of *Umwelt*, proposed in the 1920s and 1930s, Jakob von Uexküll recognized the importance of organismic specificity.[9] According to Uexküll, each organism constructs its own view of the world—its Umwelt— according to its sensing organs, neuronal processes, and the kinds of interactions in which it can engage. Opening the door to thinking about biological processes from an organism's viewpoint, Umwelt introduces a subjective component (in the sense of considering the organism as a subject), although, as Thomas Nagel famously pointed out, there remains an ineradicable difference between knowledge of an organism from the outside and the experience of *being* that organism.[10]

Subsequent commentators have observed that humans tend to be more sympathetic to lifeforms whose *Umwelten* are similar to our own. This anthropomorphic bias can be seen in the Cambridge declaration, which assumes that humans represent the standard for consciousness against which other lifeforms are measured. This makes sense from a certain perspective, since we (presumably) know that humans are conscious and the evidence for other species is indirect. Nevertheless, the anthropocentric bias continues to permeate discussions of cognition.

Plant Cognition

Plant intelligence research is an emerging area whose controversial status is reflected in the various names assigned to the field. The more controversial is "plant neurobiology"; the more conservative, "plant sensing and behavior." At issue is the extent to which plant behavior can be understood as adaptive, variable, and responsive to environmental contingencies rather than genetically programmed and inflexible. Plant research challenges notions of cognition based on human/animal neurobiologies and is thus especially important for understanding the full scope of what "cognition" may mean.

Anthony Trewavas, a plant biologist who has critically examined the question of plant cognition, makes three central claims in his book-length study: plant cells possess knowledge about themselves; they respond to environmental variations with changes in behavior; and their responses imply that they can assess their situation, anticipate environmental variations, and make decisions to optimize their survival—in brief, that they are at least minimally cognitive.[11] As early as 1880, Charles Darwin had suggested that plant roots act similarly to brains in animals: "the tip of the [root] radicle thus endowed [with sensitivity] and having the power of directing the movements of the adjoining parts, acts like the brain of one of the lower animals."[12] In plant neurobiology, this sensitive plant component is termed a "root-brain."

What is the evidence for a root-brain? The mechanisms for plant information-processing capacities include the presence of the phytohormone auxin, which acts similarly to neurotransmitters in animal brains. Brenner et al. explore long-distance electrical signaling through action potentials that travel through vascular bundles along the plant axis, a mechanism that allows roots to communicate with the upper portion of the plant as well as with others of the plant's roots.[13] Grazón and Keijzer emphasize the importance of the root apices, the area where roots converge just under the soil: root apices are "the forward command centers.... [It is] the distinctive decision-making capacities of the *transition zone* within the root-apex that led to the formulation of the root-brain concept."[14] They continue, "The transition zone is special. It is the one and only plant area where electrical activity is known to synchronize . . . and where—brain-like—decision-making takes place that controls phenotype changes by exchanging information vascularly all the way up from the roots themselves to the shoots and organs at the opposite end of the plant."[15] Research into these plant capacities indicates how a plant can achieve cognition even though it lacks neurons or a brain.

To distinguish between simple tropisms and more complex behaviors, researchers have focused on instances in which plants integrate competing signals to optimize their fitness. For example, Li and Zhang examined instances in which plants, which are normally gravitropic (preferentially growing downward), were faced with abnormal saline conditions.[16] The roots demonstrated phenotypic plasticity, exhibiting flexibility that went beyond a simple graviresponse, such as avoiding salty areas. Similar research has explored how plant parts preferentially expand and contract in response to changing environmental conditions, including chemical mechanisms that allow root tips to communicate with each other and with the above-ground parts. The stilt palm, for example, grows toward sunlight by extending its roots in that direction and allowing its shade-direction roots to diminish and die.[17] Other responses include root segregation (how the roots are distributed in space), which has been shown to respond to the amount of available soil, irrespective of nutrients and other variables.[18] In addition, roots can distinguish themselves from those of competing species, and also possess the ability to recognize themselves even from their clones, indicating that the mechanisms go beyond genotype discriminations.[19]

Cognitive plant behaviors that have been empirically verified include associative learning, memory (for example, habituation, off-line anticipation (as when a plant moves during the night to position itself for optimal light when the sun rises), territoriality, and perceptions of predators that initiate defensive responses.[20] Garzón emphasizes that these responses, particularly off-line competencies, "mark the borderline between reactive, noncognitive cases of covariation and the cognitive case of intentional systems."[21]

Since plants compose 80 percent of the world's biomass, the cognitive capacities of plants suggest the possibility of a planetary cognitive ecology in which humans, animals, and plants all participate. The next step in creating this kind of framework is to connect the cognitive capacities of the biosphere with meaning-making practices in humans, nonhuman animals, and plants. As defined above, cognition implies interpretation, and interpretation implies the possibility of choice or selection. Moreover, these meaning-making practices happen within contexts specific to organisms. To elucidate these issues, we turn next to biosemiotics and its emphasis on the biosphere as comprising interconnecting and interacting networks of signs.

Cognition and Meaning

Meaning making requires the sharing of information within parts or systems of an organism and between organisms, and this in turn requires the creation, transmission, and processing of signs. According to C. S. Peirce, a sign "is something which stands to somebody for something in some respect or capacity."[22] Dividing signs into the three categories of indexical (related to the object by cause and effect), iconic (related by morphology or form), and symbolic (related by abstract representation), Peirce opened semiotics to a much broader scope beyond symbol-dominated modes of communication, such as language, mathematics, and logic. Jesper Hoffmeyer, a biochemist, used Peirce's ideas to pioneer the study of biosemiotics. He argues that "life is based entirely on semiosis, on sign operations," starting with DNA code necessary for biological reproduction.[23] Other biosemiotic sign vehicles include chemicals, electrical signals, morphological formations (e.g., protein folding), as well as many kinds of indexical and iconic sign carriers.

Central to biosemiotics is Peirce's triadic logic of sign operations, in which the sign vehicle (for example, the genetic code) is related to the object (the organism) through the actions of an interpretant (genetic processes that read, transcribe, copy, and enact the code into the phenotype or organism). The interpretant, a feature not present in Saussurean linguistics, ensures that sign operations take place within specific contexts and that their meaning creation is relevant to these contexts. Building on Umwelt theory, Hoffmeyer illustrates the contextual qualities of sign relations using Uexküll's example of different lifeforms encountering a flower in a meadow: a bee that sips its nectar, an ant that crawls up its stem, a cow that eats it. Each, Uexküll writes, "imprints its meaning on the meaningless object, thereby turning it into a conveyor of meaning in each respective *umwelt*."[24] "As the two parts of a duet must be composed in harmony—note for note, point for point—so in nature the meaning-factors are related contrapuntally to the meaning-utilizers in its life."[25]

Philosophy has long insisted that cognition requires "aboutness," a sense of intentionality that implies purposeful, directed action. Hoffmeyer accepts this idea but argues that mental "aboutness" grows out of a preexisting bodily "aboutness," in particular behaviors necessary for an organism's survival and reproduction.[26] He suggests that this implies an *"evolutionary intentionality*, the anticipatory power inherent in all living things," thus re-positioning the mental activities of human intentionality within a more capacious context of what "intention" means in an evolutionary context.[27] Moreover, he turns the emphasis away from survival of the phenotype to survival in semiotic terms: organisms "survive semiotically inasmuch as they bequeath DNA self-referential messages to the next generation."[28] This emphasis on the inter-relationality of sign exchanges enables him to extrapolate beyond biological niches to niches occupied by specific kinds of sign relations; for example, the species-specific bird song that cooperates/competes with the many different kinds of birdsongs and other sign exchanges in a given territory.

Intentions, he continues, "presuppose temporality. If the present second were to last forever all our intentions would be to no purpose. Intentions are dependent upon being able to anticipate the future."[29] Each organism, even a unicellular one, has experiences that constitute its life history; this history conditions its responses and changes how it interacts with its environment. By reacting selectively, an organism carries the past into the present and anticipates the future, enacting a fold in time (an expression Bruno Latour uses in another context). This temporal fold exists on another level inasmuch as every organism carries within itself its self-representation, the DNA that enables the future to unfold out of the past. In this sense, all organisms not only exist in time but also manipulate temporalities, exhibiting "anticipatory power."[30]

Anticipation is also essential to learning. Hoffmeyer observes that "any process of selection presupposes an intention or ground rule that determines what will be selected," suggesting that the Umwelt concept provides such a theory.[31]

> The *umwelt* is the representation of the surrounding world within the creature. The *umwelt* could also be said to be the creature's way of opening up to the world around it, in that it allows selected aspects of that world to slip through in the form of signs. . . . [T]he specific character of its *umwelt* allows the creature to become part of the semiotic network found in that particular ecosystem.[32]

As noted above, organisms exist not only within ecological niches but also within semiotic niches, the specific flows of information coded into signs by the organism's senses and receptors, signs that are meaningful in that creature's specific Umwelt. Thus, it is not only organisms that survive, but also their "patterns of interpretation."[33]

The biosemiotic approach is essential, this observation implies, because it reveals these patterns in ways that other biological fields focusing on phenotypic survival may not. "It seems more appropriate and more satisfactory to speak of living creatures as messages rather than as vehicles for survival," Hoffmeyer suggests, although of course he recognizes that message and organism are inextricably bound together.[34] Similar to the competing/cooperating dynamics between different species that create an ecological niche, the flows of information and signs within and among creatures create a semiotic niche, and niches interact with one another to form a semiosphere, networks of signs and meanings, each specific to the Umwelten of the participating creatures.

A speculation emerging from this line of thought is whether evolutionary dynamics can be said to have directionality. Hoffmeyer believes so, suggesting that evolution in general proceeds toward greater complexity, a thesis that Stuart Kauffman has developed in another context (notwithstanding that many species, for example sharks, have not significantly changed for millennia). Complementing this physiological directionality is a corresponding increase in semiotic complexity, a tendency toward greater "logical depth" of biosemiotic networks. "Logical depth" is a term proposed by Charles Bennett, who defines it as the number of steps in an inferential process or chain of cause and effect linking something with its probable source.[35] Bennett developed the term as a measure of complexity in computer algorithms, but Hoffmeyer appropriates it for biosemiotics, suggesting that it corresponds to the "depth of meaning" that an individual or species is capable of communicating.[36] An evolutionary tendency toward greater semiotic complexity thus implies a tendency toward greater depth of meanings, each specific to the creature that converts information flows into signs meaningful to it.

The creation of meaning is also level-specific, operating not only within a species-specific context but also within the context at which an organismic unit creates and processes signs. In a multicellular organism, for example, the cell processes information according to receptors on its surface, for example proteins that lock together with specific molecules to perform operations such as self-other recognition essential to the operation of the organism's immune system. An advantage of a biosemiotic approach, Hoffmeyer suggests, is that "it leads us away from the standard 'chain of command models' of the brain-controlling-body or DNA-controls-embryogeny type. The whole essence of the sign process is that the decentralized units at tissue or cell level can interpret their own environment and act accordingly."[37] Thus, while causal reasoning leads to a top-down model of control and command, a model that Evelyn Keller critiqued decades ago, "semiotics paves the way for self-organized chaos."[38] "What emerges," Hoffmeyer writes, "when the authority for interpreting and making decisions is delegated to organs, tissues, and cells, is a hierarchical network of sign processes the accumulated output of which constitutes the coordinated actions of the organism. No single body controls this autonomous chaos, the efficacy of which can only by explained by its actual history throughout all the various stages of discoveries and conquests made by other life-forms."[39] Terrence Deacon points out that this modularity is essential to prevent what he calls a "complexity catastrophe," "too many components, needing to interact in a highly constrained manner in a finite time, despite vast possible degrees of freedom—setting an upper limit on the complexity of self."[40] Modularity also creates a finer-grained sense of contexts, extending not only down to organs and tissues but even to individual cells.

That distributed model of sign-processing and meaning creation leads to the issue of where the process ends, since the cell contains components such as mitochondria that also process information. "All my instincts," he writes, "tell me that the cell forms the boundary, the lowest level at which it is reasonable to talk about true sign processes. At the receptor level, on the other hand, we are dealing with proto-sign processes, which are covered quite perfectly by the term categorical perception."[41] While he justifies this intuition (somewhat problematically, in my view) by arguing that triadic sign-processes require the presence of a self-description within the unit, there are other good reasons to select the cell as the minimal level at which meaning creation occurs, since it is the smallest unit capable of living on its own.

Applied to organisms with consciousness, including humans, the biosemiotic approach leads to a "swarm" model, where hundreds or thousands of networks of sign-processors within the brain all interpret and make decisions, in a *"self-organizing chaos* of elements, cells, or pieces of tissue all working their way, more or less independently, to a plan of action that will work for the survival of the organism."[42] In this autonomous self-organized chaos, "consciousness acts . . . as a continuous means of taking stock . . . or an interpretation" within "a body which is at all times involved in one actual life, one true story. What I am trying to say," he concludes, "is that even though consciousness is a neurological phenomenon its unity is a function of the body's own historical oneness."[43] It is this historical trajectory that makes every cognizer distinct from every other, since no two trajectories will align exactly. "During every second of a human life, the body is effecting an *interpretation* of its situation vis-à-vis the biosemiotically rooted narrative which the individual sees him- or herself as being involved in at that moment. This interpretation is what we experience as consciousness."[44] Consciousness, in this view, then, is built on top of, and is a result of, all the myriad sign-processes and relations within the body and between the body and the environment. The enormous mistake that has dogged centuries of commentary about consciousness is to envision it as a self-contained faculty independent of all the bodily processes that coconstitute it. Citing Hoffmeyer, Wendy Wheeler observes that mental "aboutness" grows out of bodily "aboutness," and bodily "aboutness" in turn grows out of all the sign processes enacted within organs, tissues, glands and cells.[45]

Considered as a whole, what do these multi-level networks of sign processes interpret? "The total sensory input in which the organism is immersed at any given moment," both from within (endosemiosis), via communications between body components, and from without (exosemiosis), via the sensory receptors through the peripheral nervous system to the central nervous system to the brain and back again. The distinctive advantage of focusing on sign-exchanges rather than, say, energy or matter exchanges, is that it provides an opening to understanding how meanings are created, exchanged and interpreted between all living organisms and not simply between humans.

This view of meaning creation provides a compelling alternative to a traditional view of meaning as associated solely with consciousness, an anthropocentric orientation that inevitably tends to privilege humans above all other organisms. "How could it have come about," Hoffmeyer asks, "that this self-consciousness could glorify itself to such an extent that it could eventually imagine that nothing else in this world had any real meaning."[46] Acknowledging that he is leaving this question to others, he summarizes, "What I wanted to demonstrate is simply that this idea and all of its destructive side effects are an illusion. We did not invent meaning. This world has always meant something. It just did not know it."[47] The territory toward which he gestures here is now being extensively explored in the environmental humanities, commentaries on the anthropocene, and myriad other areas connecting the dots between massive environmental damage, neoliberal capitalism, and ideologies of human dominion over the earth.

Returning now to the initial definition of cognition, we can understand what the key terms "information," "interpret," and "meaning" imply from a biosemiotic perspective. Unlike the computationalist view of meaning and interpretation, which postulates that the brain operates through symbols in a way similar to the computer, the biosemiotic approach works through biological processes such as neurotransmitters, immune responses, and many other chemical, electrical, and physiological dynamics that have already been extensively researched in humans, nonhuman animals, and plants, without needing to postulate representations (symbols in the brain) that have not been shown to exist. The key move is to connect information flows with sign-creations through an organism's specific responses and actions within its environment. The result is a view of cognition that is embodied and embedded both within the dynamics of a creature's Umwelt and within the networks of signs that comprise a semiotic niche, which combine with other niches to form the semiosphere.

The next challenge this entry undertakes is to relate the biological realm of meaning creation to artificially created networks of sign-creation generated by computational and programmable media. The path will not be through a computationalist view that leaves out embodiment ("the brain operates like a computer"), but rather through a critical and close examination of how computational media, with their profoundly different embodiments, nevertheless also engage in meaning-making practices.

Machine Cognition

A persistent heresy haunting biology has been the impression that organisms evolve toward some purpose: the dolphin's sleek body for fast swimming, the giraffe's long neck for eating tall vegetation, the lion's fierce canines for tearing flesh. No, biologists keep saying, that's an illusion created by the imperative to survive and reproduce, a second-order effect of the fitness criteria matching an organism to its environment. Computational media, by contrast, are designed precisely for human-assigned purposes. They have no imperative to survive and reproduce (except in special cases when programs give them that purpose); rather, they make choices, interpret information, and create meanings in the contexts defined by their assigned purposes and enacted through their specific embodiments. This situation suggests that machine cognition stands in relation to biological cognition like those equivocal figures that can be seen either as a young or old woman, depending on the observer's perceptual orientation: is it purpose and design or survival and reproduction? If purpose, then it leans toward machine cognition; if survival, toward the biological. This kind of perceptual flip has led to important developments in computational design, such as evolutionary and genetic algorithms, neural network programs, and artificial life, all of which use design parameters geared toward selection and reproduction. For our purposes here, the equivocal relation between machine and biological cognition suggests that crucial aspects of biosemiotics may have inverse equivalents in machine cognition, especially the specificity of an organism's Umwelt, the multi-level hierarchy of sign interpretations, and the importance of context and embodiment for connecting those interpretations with meanings, now understood in the overall framework of purpose and design rather than survival and reproduction as the overarching imperative.

Machine cognition in general includes mechanical calculation as well as computational media. For the purposes of this essay, however, "machine cognition" will be taken to refer to networked and programmable machines and systems, because they demonstrate the potential for increasingly complex choices and decisions, and also because, in the contemporary world, they are connected to a very large variety of sensors and actuators to perform myriad tasks, from data mining to satellite imaging to controlling pacemakers and insulin pumps.

To connect a computer's selection procedures with the kinds of selections or choices made by biological organisms, we need a theory of meaning that emphasizes the connection of meaning with consequences. John Dewey developed such a theory in the context of his work as a pragmatist, aimed at overcoming (paraphrasing Mark Twain) "the luminous fog that passes for clarity" in linguistically oriented philosophical discourses. Many of the problems that philosophers ponder, Dewey believed, disappear when the focus shifts to the consequences of decisions. Dewey thought that language, and hence meaning making, evolved in social contexts of use and relied on a set of expectations or anticipations based on past experiences. Although Dewey was specifically concerned with language, his usage-focused approach accords well with the kind of learning that biological systems undergo; for example, when an immune system learns to recognize foreign bacteria and develops antibodies to attack them. "The very conception of cognitive meaning," he wrote in *Experience and Nature*, "... is that things in their immediacy are subordinated to what they portend and give evidence of. An intellectual sign denotes that a thing is not taken immediately but is referred to something that may come in consequence of it ... the character of intellectual meaning is instrumental."[48] In terms of computer programs, this focus is exemplified by the family of branching conditional commands, such as "if/else," which in addition to providing for choice or selection also specify consequences depending on whether the test expression is evaluated as true or false. If true, then statements inside the body of IF are executed; if false, then those statements are skipped. The advantage of this approach for meaning making is that it does not depend on consciousness and therefore can be extended to nonhuman lifeforms; by the same token, it can also be extended to computational cognition.

The biosemiotic framework discussed above provides a springboard to launch a parallel exploration into machine cognition. As we have seen, the key move in biosemiotics is to connect biological processes to meaning through the creation, interpretation, and transmission of signs. With computational cognition, signs are explicitly present. The issue, then, is how sign operations work in the contexts of embodied machines and real-world interactions to create interpretations and decisions meaningful first to the machine and then to human designers and users as well. These parallels are as follows.

1) The Umwelt. Media archeology, as articulated by Wolfgang Ernst (2012), Jussi Parikka (2012), Ian Bogost (2012), and others, emphasizes the specificities of computational devices, the sensors through which they know their environments and the actuators that enable them to interact with it.[49] Similar to an organism developing an Umwelt, a computational device senses its surroundings, which may be a set of data, sub-routines nested within functions, or other internal (endosemiotic) systems. Many computational systems also have sensors that reach out into the world (exosemiosis), including sensors for vision,

motion, location, temperature, pressure, and many other parameters. Actuators may include such devices as stepper motors, traffic lights, controllers that open or close valves, and myriad other kinds of capabilities.

2) Multileveled interpretations and decisions. Similar to the multiple levels at which decisions are made in biological organisms, computers also have multiple levels of codes, starting from the electronics that sense whether an incoming signal counts as 0 or 1, through logic gates, to machines, on up to high-level languages such as C++, Java, and Python, developed because they are easy (or easier) for humans to understand. Every command, however, must ultimately be translated into machine code, for that is all the computer's CPU (central processing unit) understands. The software that carries out these translations, conventionally called the compiler and/or interpreter, interprets the high-level commands in its contexts, which include equivalent statements for the lower-level code. Nested loops, functions, and subroutines may make decision trees extremely complex, as for example when some commands wait on others to be evaluated before they can proceed. The degree to which flexibility is built into the program varies with the complexity and logical depth of the algorithms. Even at the level of logic gates, however, selection may be emphasized through such architectures as programmable gate arrays, which enable the computer to configure the logic gates itself through evolutionary trial and error to determine the most efficient way to solve a problem. When a computer is networked with other programmable systems and interfaced with a wide variety of sensors and actuators, the possibilities for choice and interpretation increase still more, resulting in deeper and more complex cognitions.

3) Context and embodiment. Although it is common in computer science departments to regard computers as abstract schemas based on formal logic, computers, like biological organisms, must be instantiated in physical form to exist in the world, and the details of this embodiment matter. Each CPU and each computer architecture has distinctive characteristics that define the specific contexts in which programs are read, interpreted, executed, and understood. Additionally, the emerging areas of context-aware computation and tangible computing, in which everyday objects such as tabletops, vases, chairs, and walls are invested with sensors and computational capabilities, emphasize the physical interfaces through which humans can interact with computational devices through everyday activities rather than through space-restricted devices such as screens and cursors. Paul Dourish, among others, suggests that such capabilities connect human embodied and embedded cognition with homologous capacities in the computational realm.[50]

4) Cognition as anticipation and learning. Many computer programs anticipate and learn; examples are the auto-complete features of text processing, or, on a more complex level, dictation programs, such as Dragon Dictate, that learn

to recognize the distinctive pronunciations of a specific user and become more accurate as the user provides inputs and corrections. The development of deep learning algorithms has taken this aspect of computer cognition much further. Inspired by the neurological features of biological cognition, deep learning programs typically employ a cascade of multiple layers of nonlinear processing units, each layer of which uses the output from a previous layer for input. Multiple levels of representations are also used, moving from less to more abstract and arranged in a hierarchy of concepts, much as a cell in a multicellular organism communicates with larger systems and, in species with brains and central nervous systems, with brain neurons in complex systems of feedforward and feedback loops.

The potential of neural net architecture is exemplified in the development of AlphaGo by DeepMind, recently acquired by Google. Go is considered a more "intuitive" game than chess because the possible combinations of moves are exponentially greater. Employing neural net architecture, AlphaGo used cascading levels of input/output feedback, training on human-played games. It became progressively better until it beat the human Go champions, Lee Sedol in 2016 and Ke Jie in 2017. Now DeepMind has developed a new version that "learns from scratch," AlphaGoZero, that uses no human input at all, starting only with the basic rules of the game.[51] Combining neural net architecture with a powerful search algorithm, it plays against itself and learns strategies through trial and error. At three hours, AlphaGoZero was at the level of a beginning player, focusing on immediate advances rather than long-term strategies; at 19 hours, it had advanced to an intermediate level, able to evolve and pursue long-term goals; and at 70 hours, it was playing at a superhuman level, able to beat AlphaGo 100 games to 0, and arguably becoming the best Go player on the planet.

Cognitive Planetary Ecologies

The belief that evolution has directionality, that it is moving to create more complex organisms and consequently a deeper and more complex semiosphere, is frankly speculative and would have to be carefully evaluated in view of the huge diversity of lifeforms. Furthermore, special caution would be necessary to avoid anthropocentric bias and to take into account, for example, bacteria and insects as well as more complex animals. It is beyond question, however, that the depth and complexity of human-originated signs are expanding exponentially, primarily through the myriad technological devices that are generating, processing, storing, and interpreting signals of all types. Since "semiosphere" was developed specifically to describe sign-exchanges between biological organisms, I am reluctant to appropriate it to describe this expanding complexity. To avoid confusion, I prefer "cognisphere," which explicitly includes technological as well as biological cognitions.[52]

From a bird's-eye view, the expanding cognisphere looks like this: in its tendency toward greater complexity, evolution produced *Homo sapiens*, the first species to find ways to exteriorize cognition. Progress was understandably slow at first: imagine the effort it took to produce the first tools, technically defined as artifacts that create other artifacts. Their creation was tedious because, by definition, there were no other tools to aid in their construction, only natural objects such as rocks and plant materials. But, as the depth and complexity of the tool-world increased, each layer made it possible to accelerate the development of further layers. Sometime in the early twentieth century, a qualitative leap occurred with the development of computational media. Embodied and embedded in very different ways than human cognition, computational cognition nevertheless performed many of the same functions, including (and especially) the creation and interpretation of signs within contexts that connected them with meaning.

The result is nothing less than a planetary cognitive ecology that includes, for the first time, artificial cognizers more numerous than the human population (Cisco estimates that by 2020, devices connected to the internet will exceed 50 billion, compared to a human population of 7.8 billion). It remains to be seen, of course, whether this exponential expansion will continue, or whether countervailing forces, such as environmental degradation, nuclear war, or other human-caused disasters, will change the dynamics catastrophically. What is certain is that cognitive activities across the bio-techno-spectrum have never been as deep, complex, and pervasive as they are at present.

Notes

1. N. Katherine Hayles, *Unthought: The Power of the Cognitive Nonconscious* (Chicago: University of Chicago Press, 2017), 22.
2. Antonio Damasio, *The Feeling of What Happens: Body and Emotion in the Making of Consciousness* (New York: Mariner Books, 2000); Gerald M. Edelman and Giulio Tononi, *A Universe of Consciousness: How Matter Becomes Imagination* (New York: Basic Books, 2000); Stanislas Dehaene, "Conscious and Nonconscious Processes: Distinct Forms of Evidence Accumulation?," *Séminaire Poincaré* XII (2009): 99–114; Birgitta Dresp-Langley, "Why the Brain Knows More Than We Do: Non-Conscious Representations and Their Role in the Construction of Conscious Experience," *Brain Science* 2, no. 1 (March 2012): 1–21; Sid Kouider and Stanislaw Dehaene, "Levels of Processing During Non-conscious Perception: A Critical Review of Visual Masking," *Philosophical Transactions of the Royal Society B* 362 (2007): 857–75.
3. Pawel Lewicki, Thomas Hill, and Maria Czyzewska, "Nonconscious Acquisition of Information," *American Psychology* 47, no. 6 (June 1992): 796–801.

4. Stanislas Dehaene, *Consciousness and the Brain: Deciphering How the Brain Codes Our Thoughts* (New York: Penguin, 2014).
5. Edelman and Tononi, *A Universe of Consciousness*.
6. Lawrence W. Barsalou, "Grounded Cognition," *Annual Review of Psychology* 59 (2008): 617–45; Francisco Varela, Evan Thompson, and Eleanor Rosch, *The Embodied Mind: Cognitive Science and the Human Experience*, revised ed. (Cambridge, MA: MIT Press, 2017).
7. Andy Clark, *Supersizing the Mind: Embodiment, Action, and Cognitive Extension* (London: Oxford University Press, 2008).
8. N.a., "The Cambridge Declaration on Consciousness," 2012, http://fcmconference.org/img/CambridgeDeclarationOnConsciousness.pdf (accessed January 20, 2018).
9. Jakob von Uexküll, *A Foray Into the Worlds of Animals and Humans: With a Theory of Meaning*, trans. Joseph O'Neill (Minneapolis: University of Minnesota Press, 2010).
10. Thomas Nagel, "What Is It Like to Be a Bat?" *Philosophical Review* 83, no. 4 (October 1974): 435–50.
11. Anthony Trewavas, "Aspects of Plant Intelligence," *Annals of Botany* 92 (2003): 1–20; Anthony Trewavas, "Green Plants as Intelligent Organisms," *Trends in Plant Science* 10 (2005): 413–19; Anthony Trewavas, *Plant Behavior and Intelligence* (Oxford: Oxford University Press, 2014).
12. Charles Darwin and Francis Darwin, *The Power of Movement in Plants* (London: John Murray, 1980), 574.
13. E. D. Brenner, R. Stahlberg, S. Mancuso, J. Vivanco, F. Baluška, and E. Van Volkenburgh, "Plant Neurobiology: An Integrated View of Plant Signaling," *Trends in Plant Science* 11 (2006): 413–19.
14. Francisco Calvo Grazón and Fred Keijzer, "Plants: Adaptive Behavior, Root-Brains, and Minimal Cognition," *Adaptive Behavior* 19, no. 3 (2011):155–71.
15. Grazón and Keijzer, "Plants," 161.
16. X. Li and W. S. Zhang, "Salt-Avoidance Tropism in *Arabidopsis thalania*," *Plant Signaling and Behavior* 3 (2008): 351–53.
17. Trewavas, "Aspects of Plant Intelligence."
18. D. Koller, "Plants in Search of Sunlight," *Advances in Botanical Research* 33 (2000): 35–131.
19. Michal Gruntman and Ariel Novoplansky, "Physiologically Mediated Self/Nonself Discrimination in Roots," *Proceedings of the National Academy of Sciences USA*, 101 (2004): 3863–67.
20. Sarah Laskow, "The Hidden Memories of Plants," *Atlas Obscura* (September 5, 2017), http://www.atlasobscura.com/articles/plant-memory-vernalization. Accessed October 20, 2018.
21. Francisco Calvo Garzón, "The Quest for Cognition in Plant Neurobiology," *Plant Signaling and Behavior* 2 (2007): 208–11, 211.
22. Charles S. Peirce, *The Collected Papers of C. S. Peirce*, vols. 1 and 2: *Principles of Philosophy and Elements of Logic*, ed. Charles Hartshorne and Paul Weiss (Cambridge, MA: Belknap Press, 1932), 2.228.
23. Jesper Hoffmeyer, *Signs of Meaning in the Universe*, trans. Barbara J. Haveland (Bloomington: Indiana University Press, 1996), 24.
24. Quoted in Hoffmeyer, *Signs of Meaning in the Universe*, 54.
25. Quoted in Hoffmeyer, *Signs of Meaning in the Universe*, 55.
26. Hoffmeyer, *Signs of Meaning in the Universe*, 47.
27. Hoffmeyer, *Signs of Meaning in the Universe*, 47.

28. Hoffmeyer, *Signs of Meaning in the Universe*, 48.
29. Hoffmeyer, *Signs of Meaning in the Universe*, 48.
30. Hoffmeyer, *Signs of Meaning in the Universe*, 47.
31. Hoffmeyer, *Signs of Meaning in the Universe*, 57.
32. Hoffmeyer, *Signs of Meaning in the Universe*, 58.
33. Hoffmeyer, *Signs of Meaning in the Universe*, 58.
34. Hoffmeyer, *Signs of Meaning in the Universe*, 46.
35. Bennett H Charles, "Logical Depth and Physical Complexity," in Rolf Herken, ed. *The Universal Turning Machine: A Half-Century Survey* (Oxford: Oxford University Press, 1988), 227–57.
36. Hoffmeyer, *Signs of Meaning in the Universe*, 62.
37. Hoffmeyer, *Signs of Meaning in the Universe*, 94.
38. Hoffmeyer, *Signs of Meaning in the Universe*, 94.
39. Hoffmeyer, *Signs of Meaning in the Universe*, 95.
40. Terrence W. Deacon, *Incomplete Nature: How Mind Emerged from Matter* (New York: Norton, 2011), 473.
41. Hoffmeyer, *Signs of Meaning in the Universe*, 78.
42. Hoffmeyer, *Signs of Meaning in the Universe*, 113.
43. Hoffmeyer, *Signs of Meaning in the Universe*, 120.
44. Hoffmeyer, *Signs of Meaning in the Universe*, 120–21.
45. Wendy Wheeler, *Expecting the Earth: Life|Culture|Biosemiotics* (London: Lawrence and Wishart, 2016), 159.
46. Hoffmeyer, *Signs of Meaning in the Universe*, 146.
47. Hoffmeyer, *Signs of Meaning in the Universe*, 146.
48. John Dewey, *Experience and Nature* (New York: Dover, 1958), 128.
49. Wolfgang Ernst, *Memory and the Digital Archive* (Minneapolis: University of Minnesota Press, 2012); Jussi Parikka, *What Is Media Archaeology?* (Cambridge: Polity, 2012); Ian Bogost, *Alien Phenomenology, or What It's Like to Be a Thing* (Minneapolis: University of Minnesota Press, 2012).
50. Paul Dourish, *Where the Action Is: The Foundation of Embodied Interaction* (Cambridge, MA: MIT Press, 2004).
51. DeepMind, "Learning from Scratch," 2017. https://deepmind.com/blog/alphago-zero-learning-scratch/.
52. Hayles, N. Katherine, "Unfinished Work: From Cyborg to Cognisphere," *Theory, Culture, and Society* 23 (2006): 159–66.

GOSSIP

ELIZABETH HORODOWICH

Gossip has always performed myriad functions: it is a pastime, a means of entertainment, a form of sociability, a tool of education, and a source of information. It captures our attention, rationalizes or justifies worries, and, like modern forms of social media, which frequently relay gossip these days, often makes us feel better about ourselves, at least when it's not about us. Though often equated with aimless chatter, gossip is rarely just background noise. It may begin in private settings or informal conversations, but it often manages to work its way up food chains of linguistic exchange and networks of information to wield tangible influence over social life and political culture, and acquires a variety of prerogatives and expressions of power. How does this happen, and what are the mechanics at work?

Gossip is necessarily linked to a variety of other speech acts, and an attempt to parse their differences helps us better understand what exactly gossip is. Dictionaries often define gossip as "idle talk," but, more accurately, gossip is talk about people or passing on talk about others when they are not present.[1] In this way, the same statement or information could be gossip or not gossip, depending on who communicates it to whom. Gossip is, in effect, a kind of metacommunication, or a form of exchange about interaction itself. It typically tends to occupy private spaces, building on and implicitly articulating the shared values of intimates. At its most basic level, it implies the absence of persons discussed, implicit and shared beliefs between speakers and listeners, and a loose adherence to accuracy of fact.

If gossip is intimate speech, it becomes rumor when its volume increases, when it reaches a larger audience, and has a greater impact on a wider stage (and, in turn, often becomes less substantiated as it moves further afield from its original source). Gossip and rumor are almost indistinguishable, and serve almost identical functions, though those who gossip may be motivated to enhance their own social standing, whereas those that spread rumor may reveal a greater desire for truth and information. In addition, the content of rumor is sometimes about events, whereas that of gossip is relentlessly people. These shades of meaning are made clear in Vergil's *Aeneid*, where in the Roman poet's justly famous passage, rumor amounts to a kind of blazon where the poem catalogues its physical attributes. In the wake of Dido and Aeneas's potential marriage,

> Now in no time at all
> Through all the African cities Rumor goes
> Nimble as quicksilver among evils. Rumor
> Thrives on motion, stronger for the running
> Lowly at first through fear, then rearing high
> She treads the land and hides her head in cloud.
> As people fable it, the Earth, her mother . . .
> Giving her speed on foot and on the wing
> Monstrous, deformed, titanic. Pinioned, with
> An eye beneath for every body feather
> And, strange to say, as many tongues and buzzing
> Mouths as eyes, as many pricked-up ears
> By night she flies between the earth and heaven
> Shrieking through darkness, and she never turns
> Her eye-lids down to sleep. By day she broods
> On the alert, on rooftops or on towers
> Bringing great cities fear, harping on lies
> And slander evenhandedly with truth.
> In those days Rumor took an evil joy
> At filling countrysides with whispers, whispers
> Gossip of what was done, and never done.[2]

Vergil reveals to us how the power of networks of information is timeless, hardly exclusive to the contemporary world or exclusively wedded to the technologies of modernity. With mouths under every feather and tongues placed anywhere and everywhere on Rumor's body, in Vergil's first century CE rendition, rumor and gossip become both revolting and alarming. Vergil notes that unlike the Owl of Minerva that flies at dusk (implying that we gain wisdom from history and philosophy through hindsight), Rumor flies by night, indicating perhaps the inherently hidden nature of these forms of talk. Indeed, hearsay tends to defy quantitative analysis, compared to the study of wages or commercial exchanges or even to other types of communication such as blasphemy, insults, or slander, whose incidents could be named or counted. Perhaps it evades quantitative analysis since it is ubiquitous; what people talk about most, in reality, is other people. Gossip also naturally elides with a host of other subjects and categories of information, including reputation, defamation, slander, news, and public opinion.

As the *Aeneid* indicates, gossip has long been personified as female. The apostle Paul, for instance, counseled his followers to be wary of the talk of widows, who "get into the habit of being idle and going about from house to house. And not only do they become idlers, but also busybodies who talk nonsense, saying things they ought not to," revealing how men told stories, but women gossiped.[3] The verb "to gossip" dates from the early seventeenth century, derived from the Old English "godsibb," meaning a baptismal sponsor or, more directly, in medieval Europe, a close friend. The spinning of wool was, in the late medieval world, both women's work and a common metaphor for gossiping. We might easily visualize gossip in a group of heavily powdered *mademoiselles* whispering behind a wall of fans at Versailles, at the early eighteenth-century court of the Sun King. Gossip is typically voiced in soft murmurs, shared informally and in private, and operates as a foil to what are otherwise official, formal, or public expressions. In this way, gossip and hearsay appear, at first, as the provinces of women, compared to oratory and rhetoric, the verbal arenas of men. Because it originates with women, the information it carries is often assumed to be inaccurate (or, more precisely, to have a crucial shred of accuracy embedded in it), and as such is always neatly linked to its sisters, hearsay and rumor. Gossip is shifty, evanescent, and changeable; it represents a fluid reality and moves rapidly and unpredictably like mercury, in stark contrast to the reliability, stability, and fixity of print. (Of course, gossip can also be printed, but printed gossip always smacks of the oral.) Despite its historic gendering, neither men nor women possess a monopoly on gossip or its powers, and while it is often considered in a negative light, it is never inherently good or evil.

What is the relationship between gossip and "the truth?" As Vergil points out, gossip conveys both truths and untruths, what was done as well as what was never done. In *Being and Time* (1927) Martin Heidegger makes these concerns central to his discussion of *Gerede*, or hearsay/idle talk. He wonders about our ability to winnow out "the truth" from pointless chatter, and about the ways in which people employ gossip or idle talk as a means of distraction from "the truths" of death and nothingness. Heidegger understood gossip as something that interfered with or got in the way of what was otherwise important or real. Intrigued by the relationship between gossip and truth, the journalist Blythe Holbrook attempted to understand their correlation scientifically (albeit somewhat with her tongue in her cheek) by proposing the Law of Inverse Accuracy: $C = (TI)^v - t$, in which the possibility of gossip's circulation (C) equals its timeliness (T) times its interest (I) to the power of its unverifiability (v) minus a speaker's hesitancy to repeat the piece of gossip (t).[4] Such witticisms aside, many observers, from medieval chroniclers to society journalists, have regularly scoffed at passing expressions they label as "mere gossip," suggesting that gossip perverts, ignores, or corrupts the truth. On the contrary, it can be argued that gossip is, in fact, highly productive and constitutive in the way that it allows for fantasy to supplement or even supplant fact and generate new narratives that have the potential to displace old ideas or storylines. Nevertheless, such chroniclers and reporters usually still report pieces of gossip, which implies that gossip continues to be perceived as containing a thread or core of truth, and that the challenge remains for the savvy reader or listener to weed it out. While hearsay implies information that cannot be verified, gossip and rumor posit the potential existence of at least a grain of truth amidst their content. Even the most reputable newspapers, engaged in reporting "the truth," have regularly employed gossip columnists to expose the titillating intimacies and misdeeds of others, transmitting and mediating insider knowledge to the larger world (here settling gossip into the fixity of print). Tellingly, the income of these writers occasionally exceeds that of other columnists or editors, pointing to a capacious public appetite for otherwise private or not clearly truthful information.[5] Often, in the end, gossip need not worry about "the truth," since it has a slippery means of confirming itself: when everyone repeats something, its truthfulness is at once constructed and affirmed in that very repetition.

Gossip implies mischief, scandal, and immorality; however, sociologists, anthropologists, linguists, historians, and psychologists have regularly argued for its positive social functions. At the most basic, if not primordial level, gossip has long worked to regulate and police community behavior, whether it be in Paleolithic communities of early hominids, medieval cities, or modern workplaces.[6] In all these settings, gossip has functioned as a form of group problem-solving. Anthropologists, for instance, have argued that paleolithic peoples were among the most inveterate and persistent of gossips; these scholars have speculated that gossip serves as a bonding mechanism that promotes unity by working to maintain the morals and values of groups. The psychologist Robin Dunbar has argued that language evolved from social grooming, and that, for our primate ancestors, grooming was less about hygiene than it was about cementing relationships, influencing other primates, and helping all members of the group become more aware of their environment. That is to say, for Dunbar, primate language did not develop during the hunt, but instead, formed in response to a need to develop and maintain social bonds within a family or group.[7] Social units constructed and defined themselves through community talk, and gossip then reinforced and policed their chosen values. In other words, if a given group of early modern Catholics valued eating fish on Fridays, gossiping about a neighbor who had been seen eating meat could potentially correct this behavior. When word of his transgression got back to him through the grapevine, the offender could decide to recant and re-enter the community fold. (It should not seem surprising that historically, many accusations of witchcraft came to the fore through the force of gossip.) In this way, we might argue that gossip is a form of bullying; or, that it has the potential to reform bullying, encourage social cooperation, and even promote political stability by encouraging the maintenance of shared values and practices. It is a means of ensuring that no individual comes to preside over, or take advantage of, a group, and may even go so far as to ensure a group's survival. Gossip patrols community conduct and disciplines community misbehavior. Those who hear gossip might use that information to improve, promote, or protect themselves, employing gossip about others to evaluate their own habits, ideas, and actions. It helps to maintain social norms and, in effect, to keep people in line. Indeed, even the threat of gossip has the power to alter individual and group behavior, and to establish and maintain a community's moral and political ideas. In these ways, gossip has clear social effects; it validates and crystallizes shared beliefs.[8]

Perhaps because of the powerful role of gossip in social life, a subset or facet of gossip, *vox populi* and *fama*, public opinion or hearsay, has a long history in Roman and western law, and hearsay, or what people thought, heard, and said to others traditionally played a large role in western legal proceedings.[9] *Fama*, or "reputation" in the western legal tradition, did not prove guilt or innocence, but could lend strength to accusations. Legal compendia frequently prescribed investigating someone's fama—that is, exploring what people said about someone—as a means of gathering information. In this context, to be clear, fama is not the same as gossip; it was more formal and official, since it carried legal weight in arbitration and litigation. Public opinion is not the same as rumor but is related to it in the way that it forms through networks of community talk. That is to say, fama represented more than gossip; it also referred to the legal status of people and groups, as well as their wealth, power, and general prestige. The relationship between the two is always somewhat ambiguous, and there was no direct connection between social fama and legal fama. Nevertheless, the western legal tradition offers a sense of the intimate connections between community, law, and the subtle play of legal purposes on the one side and social actions on the other. The *Corpus Juris Secundum*, a standard encyclopedia of American federal and state law, named after the Byzantine Emperor Justinian's sixth-century *Corpus Juris Civilis*, defines rumor as "common talk ... passing from one person to another without any known authority for the truth of it," indicating the persistence of rumor as a category in legal culture today.

Judges and court officials knew that gossip was slippery, requiring that, when used as evidence, it had to be checked and qualified. Nevertheless, litigation up through the nineteenth century often functioned as an extension of gossip into the courtroom, codifying "what people heard" and giving it weight in arbitration and litigation: a sign of gossip's transformation and transubstantiation from the world of the feminine, private, and/or mobile into the realm of the public and the masculine, as it became codified and ossified in public, written records. Litigation and exchanges in the courtroom in much of the history of the West, in turn, were a test of what was known. In this way, trials in court effectively functioned as an extension of gossip into the realm of the law, validating gossip as a means of establishing honor, trust, and credit. In this way, gossip often worked historically as a kind of well or bank of community voices, a reserve or archive of verbal knowledge, or an unofficial realm of potency, where circuits of information were constantly being made and re-made amidst a variety of people and relationships. This resource then could be called upon and manipulated to different ends, to vouch for or vindicate someone's good name or to condemn someone who had abused community norms. Rumors had the power to spread and reach the ears of authorities. They provoked those in power to respond and tested their ability to control their circulation or manage their effects. In addition, rumors imply a fantasy about secrecy: that someone maintains a certain secret, and by keeping it, places him or herself at a remove from those in power. We are often, on the one hand, suspicious of gossip, while on the other hand simultaneously in need of extracting knowledge and information from it, since gossip is always both an activity, a resource, and an allegation. We might even say that gossip represents a kind of broadcast technology of power and control, or a tool for the creation and distribution of knowledge.

Along similar lines, gossip has been implicit in the establishment of reputation in countless societies. It functions as an invaluable commodity in marketplaces of social exchange, serving in effect as the means by which public reputations are decided, built, or destroyed. Indeed, the relationship between gossip and reputation reveals the positive and productive workings of gossip, when we understand how verbal networks of talk shape reputations and alter behaviors without confrontation or recourse to violence. It can contribute to the selection of leaders, or to other political processes with relatively less hostility, embarrassment, or loss of face.

Gossip certainly did not need to enter a courtroom for it to be able to wield real power; nevertheless, the idea of legal systems tapping into networks of gossip gives us a real sense of the various ways in which, historically in particular, gossip was a powerful tool of the underclasses. The shared economy of those relatively impoverished arguably depended on reliable social networks. Exchanging information was crucial in establishing and maintaining such relationships, and important for people seeking any kind of social or professional advancement. For those too poor, or who perceived themselves as too isolated from official mechanisms of justice, speaking negatively about a community member and encouraging such talk to spread functioned as a means of enacting a more personal and local form of justice, by humiliating, scapegoating, or outcasting one who had misbehaved or broken community rules.[10] Gossip is, in this way, a classic example of the weapons of the weak, or what the political scientist and anthropologist James Scott calls the "hidden transcript" that critiques power and contests subordination.[11] Gossip is a subversive speech act, and was especially so in the urban societies of the premodern world that were decidedly oral cultures. Of course, this power can cut both ways, since gossip can also be used as a weapon of the powerful and by those who consider themselves higher in status to keep those beneath them in their so-called proper place. In whichever way it flows, up or down, it transforms communities into testing grounds for claims to political and social authority.

In this way, gossip has the potential to impact official politics, and often becomes more than just a casual force in history. Early modern rulers often likened gossip and rumor among the underclasses to plague and contagion—especially rumors of war or insurrection—and political elites regularly feared "bad tongues" more than swords. The spoken word is full of power, and, by implication, danger. It is naturally embedded in political life, since libel and gossip can define or question the relationship between rulers and their subjects. Verbalizing and sharing subversive thoughts is an essential element of political culture, and for much of the history of the West, rumor counted among the best available forms of media with which people could complain about politics. With great regularity historical actors have resisted corrupt rulers who spent more on private affairs than the public good, misused taxes, or participated in fraud and corruption as much through gossip as through physical violence. That is to say, people used gossip as a way of constructing an agreed upon image of the past, or of how things should be. Gossip was the medium in (or the platform on) which such images were built, a means of communicating political discontent. Within the circles of ruling classes and politicians, too, it has always played a role, either as a means of subversion, or as a part of lobbying for votes and jostling for political position, which necessarily entails the likes of rumor mongering and/or recourse to gossip.

Much like economies of exchange, gossip benefits both the speaker and listener, who in the practice of gossip enter into an interlocking relationship of power. What is offered and what is received in this exchange? As we have noted, gossip tends to occur in spaces of intimacy, and in addition, it deepens intimacy, bonding, and feelings of belonging, often among otherwise disparate groups or individuals. It both reflects and generates closeness. In this way, both or all participants benefit, so to speak, from the generation of community and a sense of inclusion. Additionally, gossip also mirrors the rules of patron-client relationships, or even commercial exchange, as it is inherently transactional in nature. It corresponds to the consumption of goods and services, and there are notable similarities between the practice of gossip and the principles of the market.[12] An individual who regularly supplies good information provides a valuable commodity, especially when information is scarce, which it often is. Apart from scarcity, gossip is also much like other goods or services in that it is something that is consumed, and often conspicuously. The original speaker of gossip enhances their self-image by demonstrating their knowledge, and perhaps also by assisting others in addressing threats or fears. Negative or critical gossip in particular generates intimacy and promotes the speaker by elevating their comparative status.[13] Listeners, by contrast, receive information, and perhaps also a guide to behavior. In this way, perhaps somewhat surprisingly, the most negative gossip at times can serve the speaker and listener much more than it injures its target. Speakers earn prestige as patrons of knowledge, and listeners benefit from the knowledge of privileged information, though overall in this market of exchange, profits tilt in favor of the producer.

If we follow these ideas to their logical conclusion, we can think of gossip as an endeavor to lend a certain syntax to events by converting unexpected or surprising occurrences into narratives that can move among talkers and listeners. Rumor and gossip involve networks of communication, including cycles of receiving and then passing on something that came from someone else.[14] Indeed, Vergil's sense of both fascination and alarm is fundamentally linked to the growing scope of Rumor's circulation. For psychologists, these networks tend to be linear, formed through a model of serial chains or connecting links, whereas for sociologists, these networks are more lattice-like. In either model, passing on rumors necessarily places both speakers and listeners in the midst of a circuit and makes them relays or nodes in networks of communiqués, often unauthorized or semi-grounded. Considering gossip as a network allows us to see how gossip defines and distinguishes groups. It marks one group from another since outsiders can't participate in gossip, and gossip is a hallmark of membership. Networks of gossip are systems of interconnectivity, composed of parts held in endless and distributed relation. In this way, those who gossip represent neither the origin nor the destination of information, but instead function as transmitting conduits or the netting of a web, so that authorship usually involves becoming part of a chain rather than creating or inventing a narrative (though this could also be the case). Rumors tend to be expressed by "someone," or by "no one in particular," or get attached to names, origins, or sources with only shadowy identities, and necessarily lack the sanction, systematization, or official qualities of laws, sermons, or even folk tales.

That said, however, gossip and rumor certainly go through certain stages or patterns of evolution and disintegration. They have lifespans, at least traditionally. A rumor can arise spontaneously—we have noted that it is often impossible to identify a moment of creation for gossip or rumor, one of their inherent traits—or, instead, a rumor can be carefully calculated and constructed on the part of individual actors or propagandists. While remaining shadowy in its origins, gossip usually comes to the fore surrounding exciting, mysterious, or unexplained events. During its lifecycle, it typically undergoes distortion and aberration. It can die when refuted, evaporate, or undergo a process of distillation to become part of legend, folklore, or the belief structures of cultures at large, as we might describe the great quantity of rumors surrounding Kennedy's assassination. Indeed, conspiracy theories today are one of the most virulent forms of rumor.

A consideration of the lifespan of such talk helps us understand how the forces of gossip and rumor are both timeless and historically contingent. In the twenty-first century, an age drenched with data that can spread with incredible efficiency and power, gossip and rumor continue to inhabit their old haunts, and have additionally migrated to the internet and have become increasingly implicated with questions of privacy and free speech as they pose larger threats to control over *vox pupuli et fama*. While the press, television, and radio long facilitated the transmission, and sometimes the origin, of these forms of talk, the internet has indelibly reshaped, amplified, and heightened the effects of gossip. That is to say, if the western legal tradition often codified the language of gossip in courtroom documents, then the internet has attached a new degree of permanence to the talk about other people and the practice of sharing and spreading information. In historical societies, gossip traveled more slowly and typically was contained in relatively smaller social circles. The digital age, however, has impacted the forces of gossip and rumor in ways that the journalist Malcolm Gladwell might describe as a "tipping point," by generating the exponential proliferation of talk and information in ways that are now, as he puts it, "contagious" and easily spreadable to the globe, like an epidemic.[15] Electronic networks now amplify personal networks, allowing gossip to not only become codified, but also to cross more easily the boundaries between different social groups and networks. In historic societies, gossip tended to remain relatively fleeting and localized, and most likely was shared in a specific spatial and social context; modern technologies, however, have made gossip both more permanent and far-reaching, and increasingly removed from its original context.[16] Historically, most rumors were born, existed for a time, and then died out because they were judged untruthful or because they became irrelevant. They were contextualized by proximity and relevance, which determined their patterns of movement, when rumors spread most quickly in areas where they started. In the digital age, the patterns and evolution of gossip are different; there is faster growth, an untethering from local contexts, and often a longer half-life. Here, considerations of gossip and rumor necessarily merge with the realm of media studies as they overlap with questions of communication, cybernetics, exchange, networks, and systems more broadly.

Perhaps most fundamentally, in both historical and contemporary societies, gossip represents a rhetoric of constitution. That is to say, it both reflects and constructs social reality and posits the ways in which we should interpret the world. It does not merely echo or mirror values, but also functions productively to construct, confirm, and maintain the identity, membership, and vision of a group.

Notes

1. See Max Gluckman, "Gossip and Scandal," *Current Anthropology* 4 (1963): 307–26; Patricia Meyer Spacks, *Gossip* (New York: Knopf Doubleday, 1985); Chris Wickham, "Gossip and Resistance Among the Medieval Peasantry," *Past and Present* 160 (1998): 3–24; Joseph Epstein, *Gossip: The Untrivial Pursuit* (Boston: Houghton Mifflin Harcourt, 2011).
2. Virgil (also Vergil), *The Aeneid*, trans. Robert Fitzgerald (New York: Penguin, 1990), 101–2, book 4, 239–61.
3. 1 Timothy 5:13. See Marianne Bjelland Kartzow, *Gossip and Gender: Othering of Speech in the Pastoral Epistles* (Berlin: de Gruyter, 2009), 32; Elizabeth Horodowich, "The Gossiping Tongue: Oral Networks, Public Life, and Political Culture in Early Modern Venice," *Renaissance Studies* 19 (2005): 22–45; Heather Kerr and Claire Walker, eds., *"Fama" and Her Sisters: Gossip and Rumour in Early Modern Europe* (Turnhout: Brepols, 2015).
4. Blythe Holbrooke, *Gossip: How to Get It Before It Gets You, And Other Suggestions for Social Survival* (New York: St. Martin's, 1983).
5. Robert D. McFadden, "Liz Smith, Longtime Queen of Tabloid Gossip Columns, Dies at 94," *New York Times*, November 12, 2017.
6. Bianca Beersma and Gerben A. Van Kleef, "How the Grapevine Keeps You in Line: Gossip Increases Contributions to the Group," *Social Psychological and Personality Science* 2 (2011): 642–49.
7. Robin Dunbar, *Grooming, Gossip, and the Evolution of Language* (Cambridge, MA: Harvard University Press, 1996).
8. See Elena Martinescu, Onne Janssen, and Bernard A. Nijstad, "Tell Me the Gossip: The Self-Evaluative Function of Receiving Gossip About Others," *Personality and Social Psychology Bulletin* 40 (2014): 1668–80.
9. See Thelma S. Fenster and Daniel Lord Smail, introduction to *Fama: The Politics of Talk and Reputation in Medieval Europe*, ed. Thelma S. Fenster and Daniel Lord Smail (Ithaca: Cornell University Press, 2003), 1–11.
10. See Roy Baumeister, Liqing Zhang, and Kathleen D. Vohs, "Gossip as Cultural Learning," *Review of General Psychology* 8 (2004): 111–21.
11. James C. Scott, *Domination and the Arts of Resistance—Hidden Transcripts* (New Haven, CT: Yale University Press, 1990), ix–xiii.
12. Ralph L. Rosnow and Gary Alan Fine, *Rumor and Gossip: The Social Psychology of Hearsay* (New York: Elsevier, 1976), 77–80.

13. See Jennifer K. Bosson, Amber B. Johnson, Kate Niederhoffer, and William B. Swann Jr., "Interpersonal Chemistry Through Negativity: Bonding by Sharing Negative Attitudes About Others," *Personal Relationships* 13 (2006): 135–50.
14. See Alexander R. Galloway, "Networks," In *Critical Terms for Media Studies*, ed. W. J. T. Mitchell and Mark B. N. Hansen (Chicago: University of Chicago Press, 2010), 280–96.
15. Malcolm Gladwell, *The Tipping Point: How Little Things Can Make a Big Difference* (New York: Little, Brown, 2000), 25.
16. Daniel J. Solove, *The Future of Reputation: Gossip, Rumor, and Privacy on the Internet* (New Haven, CT: Yale University Press, 2007), 50–75.

INDEX

DENNIS DUNCAN

J. G. Ballard's short story "The Index" (1977) begins with a brief editor's note: "the text printed below is the index to the unpublished and perhaps suppressed autobiography of a man who may well have been one of the most remarkable figures of the twentieth century. . . . Incarcerated within an unspecified government institution, he presumably spent his last years writing his autobiography of which this index is the only surviving fragment."[1] The rest of the story—the rise and fall of one Henry Rhodes Hamilton—comes in the form of an alphabetical index, from which the reader must piece together a narrative using only keywords, brief subheadings, and the sense of chronology that the page numbers provide. This oblique approach to storytelling offers plenty of opportunities for wry euphemism. We are left to guess, for instance, at Hamilton's true ancestry from the following early entries:

Avignon, birthplace of HRH, 9–13.
George V, secret visits to Chatsworth, 3, 4–6; rumoured liaison with
    Mrs. Alexander Hamilton, 7; suppresses court circular, 9.
Hamilton, Alexander, British Consul, Marseilles, . . . depression after birth of
    HRH, 6; surprise recall to London, 12; first nervous breakdown, 16;
    transfer to Tsingtao, 43.

Further entries reveal Hamilton to have been foremost among the twentieth century's alpha males:

D-Day, HRH ashore on Juno Beach, 223; decorated, 242.
Hamilton, Marcelline (formerly Marcelline Renault), abandons industrialist husband, 177; accompanies HRH to Angkor, 189; marries HRH, 191.
Hemingway, Ernest, . . . portrays HRH in *The Old Man and the Sea*, 453.
Inchon, Korea, HRH observes landings with Gen. MacArthur, 348.
Jesus Christ, HRH compared to by Malraux, 476.
Nobel Prize, HRH nominated for, 220, 267, 342, 375, 459, 611.

Meanwhile, the pattern of entries relating to statesmen and religious figures—initial friendships followed by denouncements—suggests the story's clearest plot line, concerning Hamilton's world-conquering megalomania:

Churchill, Winston, conversations with HRH, 221; at Chequers with HRH, 235; spinal tap performed by HRH, 247; at Yalta with HRH, 298; "iron curtain" speech, Fulton, Missouri, suggested by HRH, 312; attacks HRH in Commons debate, 367.
Dalai Lama, grants audience to HRH, 321; supports HRH's initiatives with Mao Tse-tung, 325; refuses to receive HRH, 381.
Gandhi, Mahatma, visited in prison by HRH, 251; discusses *Bhagavadgita* with HRH, 253; has dhoti washed by HRH, 254; denounces HRH, 256.
Paul VI, Pope, praises Perfect Light Movement, 462; receives HRH, 464; attacked by HRH, 471; deplores messianic pretentions of HRH, 487; criticises Avignon counter-papacy established by HRH, 498; excommunicates HRH, 533.

For the story of Hamilton's downfall, Ballard picks up the pace of the action by clustering the events sequentially around the last letters of the alphabet. HRH forms a cult, the Perfect Light Movement, which proclaims his divinity and seizes the UN Assembly, calling for a world war on the U.S. and USSR; he is arrested and incarcerated, but then disappears, with the Lord Chancellor raising questions about his true identity. The final entry concerns the mysterious indexer himself: "Zielinski, Bronislaw, suggests autobiography to HRH, 742; commissioned to prepare index, 748; warns of suppression threats, 752; disappears, 761."

Ballard's conceit with "The Index" is a rather brilliant one, playing to a number of Ballardian touchstones: the fragmentation of narrative, a mordant wit (brevity, after all, is the soul of the subheading). Nevertheless, on one key level, "The Index" doesn't quite *get* indexes, and perhaps no readable narrative really can. Ballard knows we'll read his index from start to finish—from A to Z—and so he pegs the chronology of his story, albeit loosely, to the order of the alphabet. Keywords to the front of the alphabet tell of HRH's early years; his hubris becomes pathological in the Ts through Vs; his comeuppance is told among the

Ws and Ys. The story's two ordering systems, alphabetical (form) and chronological (content), are actually largely congruent. This is not what indexes are about at all.

This might be a good time to differentiate the index from its older sibling, the table of contents. The two paratexts have much in common, of course. Both take the form of a list of labels accompanied by locators. But in following the order of the main text, the table of contents has a structural relationship to the text it supports, revealing its architecture, presenting the argument in summary. The index, by contrast, does no such thing. Its principal innovation is in severing the relationship between the structure of the work and the structure of the table. The ordering of an index is reader-oriented, rather than text-oriented: if you know what you're looking for, the letters of the alphabet provide a universal, text-independent system in which to look it up. The chief mechanism of the index is its arbitrariness in relation to the work. We might even say that most indexes are doubly arbitrary since the commonest locator—the page number—bears no intrinsic relationship to the work or its subject matter, being linked only to its medium.

These factors have a bearing on the index's history. While the table of contents can be found in antiquity, the index by comparison is a rather late arrival.[2] "The Middle Ages," write Mary and Richard Rouse, "did not like alphabetical order, which it considered to be the antithesis of reason."[3] The universe had been created harmoniously, rationally, and the scholar's responsibility was to discern and reflect this order, and not to abdicate this duty by deferring to the arbitrary ordering of the letters of the alphabet. In the mid-eleventh century, the lexicographer Papias the Lombard compiled his great Latin dictionary, *Elementarium Doctrinae Rudimentum*, arranging the entries alphabetically by the first three letters of each headword. The principle, however, did not catch on.

If we jump forward another hundred years, however, we find a new literary genre, the collection of *distinctiones*, beginning to flourish in the late twelfth century. The English theologian William de Montibus (d. 1213), for example, produced a work entitled *Distinctiones Theologicae* that takes terms found in the Scriptures and analyzes all the different ways they might be used. As de Montibus's biographer, Joseph Goering, explains, the method is to "begin with a Scripture passage, such as 'Asperges me hyssopo, et mundabor; lavabis me, et super niuem dealbabor' ['Purge me with hyssop, and I shall be clean: wash me, and I shall be whiter than snow' (Psalms 51:7)], and then to proceed ... listing the various ways one is 'washed' and explicating each."[4] The *distinctiones* of the title, therefore, are not divisions of narrative; rather, they are the semantic distinctions between the different ways a term can be used. The preacher, or teacher, wishing to arrange a sermon or class around this passage, or around the different spiritual meanings of being washed, has de Montibus's text as a handy basis, with a ready-made set of references to draw from.

De Montibus's *Distinctiones* have another important quality that makes them especially easy to use: they are organized alphabetically in order of their keywords, starting with *arcus* (bow) and running through to *zona* (belt or girdle). Typically, the entry for *arcus* runs through a variety of meanings, beginning with a summary which looks rather like a dictionary entry:

ARCUS dicitur Christus, et propitiatio Dei, scriptura, iudicium, robur, intentio, insidie, et dolus.

[The bow represents Christ, and God's forgiveness, Scripture, judgment, strength, intention, plotting, and deceit]

The paragraphs that follow flesh out these meanings, quoting more than a dozen Bible passages in which the term *arcus* is used, from the visible rainbow signifying God's covenant with humankind (Genesis 9:13), through the bow as a metaphor for God's wrath (Psalms 7: 11–12), to the bow as weapon of choice for enemies of the righteous (Psalms 11: 2).

The text of the *Distinctiones* cannot be said to resemble an index in a form we would be familiar with today. Each entry is discursive, more like an encyclopedia entry, with locators commonly hived off into the margin. Nevertheless, we are clearly somewhere on the approach to the streamlined, tabular index, and the elements—headwords, locators, alphabetical order—are in place. It is not possible to identify precisely what the first index was, but the middle of the thirteenth century would see perhaps the signal achievement of medieval information technology: the concordance to the Bible produced by the Dominican friars of St. Jacques.

On the left bank of the Seine in Paris, just beside where the Panthéon now stands, was the Dominican priory of St. Jacques. In 1230, a new prior was appointed, a young man named Hugh, or Hugo, from the town of Saint-Cher in what is now the southeast of France. Hugh's ecclesiastical career would be a distinguished one: he had the confidence of a succession of popes and served as papal legate on several diplomatic missions. As a scholar he would produce a monumental commentary on the Bible, the *Postillae in Sacram Scripturam*, which would endure well into the early modern period, along with a monumental corrected text of the Scriptures, the *Correctio Biblie*, which would not. But it was another of Hugh's great projects that would have the most lasting and far-reaching impact, and it is that which will concern us here. It was at St. Jacques, during Hugh's time as prior (1230–1235), that the first verbal concordance to the Bible was undertaken.[5]

At the beginning of the thirteenth century, two significant new arrivals—the universities (at Bologna, Paris, and Oxford) and the mendicant orders (the Dominicans and the Franciscans)—were bringing about a new set of requirements for the way that books were read. The twin demands of preaching and teaching necessitated a closer, swifter analysis of biblical material than had hitherto been available. As Lloyd Daly puts it, "[a]ll of this critical effort demanded more than even intimate knowledge of the Scriptures could provide; it demanded the ability to bring to bear on any one word or passage a knowledge of all similar words or passages in the Bible."[6] The St. Jacques Concordance—a word-by-word index—identifies over 10,000 terms in the Latin Bible, and lists them in alphabetical order, beginning with the exclamation *A, a, a* (usually translated as *ah!* or *alas*) and ending with *Zorobabel*. As well as names and exclamations, the concordance includes the ordinary language of the Bible—common nouns, verbs, adjectives—and for each term it lists every instance of its occurrence, giving the book, chapter, and chapter section in which it appears.

While the division of the Bible into chapters had been undertaken by the English scholar Stephen Langton (later Archbishop of Canterbury) in around 1200, the system of verses which we know today was still centuries away, first appearing in Robert Estienne's Greek, French and Latin texts of the 1550s. The monks of St. Jacques therefore developed an innovation of their own: a subdivision of Langton's chapters which would become widely adopted during the thirteenth century. Each chapter is imagined as being composed of seven equal parts, labeled *a-g*. Thus, a passage appearing at the start of a chapter would be referenced as *a*; passages from near the middle would be *d*; passages from the end, *g*.

Taking the first entry, then, the concordance gives us the following information:

A, a, a. Je.i.c. xiiii.d. eze.iiii.f Joel.i.f.

Expanding the abbreviations, this is telling us that our search term appears in Jeremiah 1 at position *c* (i.e., just before the middle of the chapter), as well as Jeremiah 14*d*, Ezekiel 4*f* and Joel 1*f*. Following these up, sure enough we find, for example,

Jer. 1:6 Et dixi: A, a, a, Domine Deus, ecce nescio loqui, quia puer ego sum.
[Then said I, Ah, Lord God! behold, I cannot speak: for I am a child.]

That tight half-line of text contains everything we need to lead us to the passages we want, while the alphabetical arrangement means that any search term can be located within seconds. One extraordinary feature of the St. Jacques Concordance is its size. Despite the vast amount of referencing information it contains, thanks to its five-column format and heavy use of abbreviation, it can be produced as a single small volume. One surviving example, in the Bodleian Library in Oxford, is about the size (fractionally shorter, slightly wider) of an index card, or a smartphone at the bulkier end of the market.[7]

Nevertheless, if portability was an advantage, it brought with it a significant drawback. If we take another term from the first page, we can get a sense of the problem. Here are the first few entries for the term *abire*, to depart:

Abire, Gen. xiiii.d. xviii.e.g. xxi.c. xxii.b. xxiii.a. xxv.b.g xxvii.a. xxx.c. xxxi.b.c xxxv.f. xxxvi.a. xliiii.c.d

That's sixteen separate references in the book of Genesis alone. The full list runs to hundreds of entries across several columns. In cases like these, and they are not uncommon, the concordance is little use in locating a passage one might be looking for since the amount of work still left to do—all that page-turning and locating the term within those broad chapter divisions—is still impracticable.

As a device that can bring about a new type of reading, the promise of the index relies on its allowing a reader to locate a passage within a timeframe that is reasonable. Where the reader is presented with an undifferentiated list running to dozens of entries, the index fails in its basic function as a finding aid. To take a modern example, here is a sample entry from the index to Ian Ker's biography of Cardinal Newman: "Wiseman, Nicholas 69, 118–19, 129, 133–4, 135, 158, 182–3, 187, 192, 198, 213, 225, 232, 234, 317–18, 321, 325, 328, 330, 331–2, 339, 341, 342, 345, 352, 360, 372–4, 382, 400, 405, 418, 419, 420, 424–7, 435–6, 437, 446–7, 463, 464, 466–8, 469, 470, 471, 472, 474–5, 476–7, 486–9, 499, 506, 507, 512, 515–17, 521, 526, 535, 540, 565, 567, 568, 569–72, 574, 597, 598, 608, 662, 694, 709."[8] A mass of locators without the structuring of subheadings, leading one critic to vituperate in *The Times*: "What is the point of wasting space on idiocy of that order? What conceivable purpose could it serve? How *dare* the publishers print it under the noble and meaningful heading 'Index'?"[9]

It was this same failing in the St. Jacques Concordance that led to an innovation, and the creation of a second version, the so-called *Concordantiae Anglicanae* or English Concordance. The title of the work comes from the fact that it was compiled, once again at St. Jacques in Paris, by one or more English Dominicans, among them Richard of Stavensby. The innovation of the English Concordance is to add a passage of contextual quotation for each reference— what we would now call a keyword-in-context or KWIC index of the type seen in, for instance, the "snippet view" of Google Books. Here's how the first few entries for *regnum* [kingdom] appear in one of the English Concordance fragments held in the Bodleian Library:

Regnum
    Gen. x.c. fuit autem principium .R. eius Babilon et arach
    [And the beginning of his kingdom was Babylon, and Arach];
      xx.e. quid peccavimus in te quia induxisti super me et super .R. meum peccatum grande

[what have we offended thee in, that thou hast brought on me and my kingdom a great sin?];

xxxvi.g. cumque et hic obiisset successit in .R. balaam filius achobor
[And when he also was dead, Balanan the son of Achobor succeeded to the kingdom];

xli.e. uno tantum .R. solio te precedam
[only in the kingly throne will I be above thee].[10]

As we can see, with the new concordance, as well as being told the book, chapter, and chapter section, we can see at a glance the sentence in which it appears.

The English Concordance was not without its drawbacks, chiefly that with so much contextual quotation, the work had now swelled to a vast, multivolume size, cumbersome enough to compromise its usefulness. A third version, therefore, was produced, which kept the snippet view, but shrank it to three or four words, and it is this format which would become the standard for centuries to come.

The index had entered the mainstream, and in a monumental form, such that by the middle of the next century, Thomas Waleys, a Dominican Master of Theology at Oxford, could write that "this mode of preaching, that is, by bundles of the authorities [of Holy Scripture], is very easy, because it is easy to have the authorities, since Concordances of the Bible have been made ... in alphabetical order, so that the authorities can be easily found."[11] But the Bible represents something of a special case for indexing. In one sense, the history of the index is the history of the locator. Early tables of contents, such as the one Pliny the Elder provided for his *Naturalis historia*, for example, divide the text into *libri*, i.e., "bookrolls," and although these are considerably shorter than what we might think of as a book ("chapter" is closer as a conceptual unit), this is still rather a blunt instrument for navigation. Langton's chapter divisions for the Bible provide a relatively fine-grained unit, but not every work was so well provided.

Returning to de Montibus's *Distinctiones*, the British Library holds a copy, produced in the mid-thirteenth century, which includes a bonus feature, added in the fourteenth: an index, keyed to the manuscript's folio numbers (i.e., each whole leaf, front and back, gets a number, rather than the modern practice of numbering both sides).[12] In the bottom right corner of each leaf, the later scribe has written the folio number, while the front flyleaf includes a table showing which entries appear on each page. The already-alphabetical arrangement of de Montibus's work was clearly not enough: the scribe here thought it would save labor if, knowing what entry you wanted to read, you could refer to a listing and then flip only the corners of the leaves until you found the page you wanted. Readers had discovered that the book, rather than the text, could offer a locator of sufficient granularity to be useful in almost every case. The trouble was that in an age when every copy of a work was exactly that—a *copy*, written out in full, by hand, by a scribe with an earlier version of the same text in front of them to work from—books would very rarely retain the exact pagination of their exemplars. It would not be until the arrival of print, in the mid-fifteenth century, and the widespread adoption of page numbers some fifty or sixty years later, that the index would become a booksellers' staple, a consideration, across many genres, at the point of production.[13] These, then, are the index's origins, a coming together of three essential features: the abridgement of the primary material into useful heads (i.e., keywords); the re-arrangement of these heads into an order that is easily searchable; and a locator of sufficient granularity that the reference can be followed up swiftly. There is, of course, no requirement that such an instrument should limit itself to a single book, or indeed to books at all.

* * *

On October 2, 1877, representatives from a hundred and forty of the world's great libraries descended on London for a Conference of Librarians. The conference, running across four days, addressed the full gamut of matters important for a long-lasting, smooth-running library, and for the survival of knowledge, effectively: cataloguing methods, durable book bindings, the selection of books for acquisition. On the evening of the second day, however, J. Ashton Cross, former librarian of the Oxford Union Society, delivered a paper that had something rather grander in mind. Cross's lecture was entitled, "A Universal Index of Subjects," and in it he would propose a vast, international project to come up with a grand, joined-up index to every branch of knowledge. In case this should sound hopelessly quixotic, he reminded his audience that the work was already being done every time a student indexed a book for their own use, but that this effort was being wasted, and repeated, since there was no system to collect and publish these results: "Hundreds of librarians and students are now . . . indexing over and over again the very same books."[14] Besides, in many fields valuable general indexes had already been made available, albeit in a piecemeal fashion: "The literature . . . of many miscellaneous subjects, such as Printing, Shorthand, Chess, Wine, Tobacco, Angling, the Gypsies, Slang, Mountains, Cyclones, Earthquakes and Volcanos, the Drama, Romanticism, Mesmerism, Darwinism, the Devil, the Doctrine of a Future Life, has been indexed by individual effort."[15] What was needed now, asserted Cross, was a regulated drive. Different libraries, he proposed, would have their own specialisms, indexing the major works and journals in that field, and feeding up to a clearinghouse that could join these myriad sub-indexes together, along with an international committee to oversee what was required. There would need to be money, of course. In the discussion after Cross had delivered his paper, the librarian of the London Library apologized for throwing "a damper on the project" but declared that he had "no great faith in the plan of employing gratuitous labour."[16] Of course, responded Cross, nobody wanted librarians to work for nothing, but the division of labor between libraries might free up time that was already being spent in cataloguing.

Whatever the financial arrangements, Cross's idea had proved a stimulating one. When *The Athenaeum* reported on the conference the following week, it was his suggestion that received the most attention. Financing, surely, could be found; after all, other projects of less obvious value—a swipe at the Palestine Exploration Fund—were being funded: "Find the labourers, or the money that will pay a competent staff of labourers for a series of years, and the thing may be done. If funds were found for the execution of a task so remote from most men's business as the exploration of Palestine, a purse ought soon to be made for the erection of so mighty an instrument of education as a Universal Index of Knowledge."[17] A Universal Index of Knowledge? In this context, it sounds improbably grand, Borgesian even; but in our own time, of course, it is something we take for granted. When Cross foresaw his index in 1877, he confidently stated: "The question . . . ought to be, not whether a Universal Index shall be made, but only in what way it can best be made."[18] The solution would turn out not to be an army of students and librarians filling in slips and passing them up to a clearing committee. Document scanning, character recognition software, the ability—for better or for worse—of anyone with a smartphone to publish their contribution to knowledge without first submitting it for the approval of an international committee of librarians: all of these would play their part. Most of all, however, today's Universal Index is the result of the microelectronic revolution and the enormous, distributed processing power by which storing and searching an unthinkably large index is made possible. In the age of the search engine, Cross's prediction has come, palpably, utterly, to pass. As Google put it, "Crawling and Indexing" are the methods that underpin their search product, crawling the web in a bid for universality, then indexing it—via headwords, locators, order—to make it functional: "It's like the index in the back of a book—with an entry for every word seen on every web page we index. When we index a web page, we add it to the entries for all of the words it contains."[19] Whether the Universal Index has been achieved in a manner that would satisfy or horrify the Conference of Librarians is a moot point. What should be beyond question, however, is that we are living in the age of the index. The Oxford English Dictionary dates the first use of the phrase "to look something up"—as in, to search for a piece of information in a table or index—to 1692. It is hard, now, to imagine a time when this was not a linguistic essential.

Notes

1. J. G. Ballard, "The Index," *Bananas* 8 (Summer 1977): 24–25, 24. The story is also anthologized in *War Fever* (London: Collins, 1990), 171–76, and *Complete Short Stories* (London: Flamingo, 2001), 940–45.

2. At least four classical Latin works are known to have been provided with tables by their authors (as opposed to by later scribes). See Andrew M. Riggsby, "Ordering Knowledge in the Roman Empire," in *Guides to the Wor(l)d*, ed. Jason König and Tim Whitmarsh (Cambridge: Cambridge University Press, 2007), 88–107.
3. ['Le Moyen Âge n'aimait pas l'ordre alphabétique qu'il considérait comme une antithèse de la raison']. Mary A. Rouse and Richard H. Rouse, 'La Naissance des index,' in vol. 1, *Histoire de l'édition française*, 4 vols., ed. Henri-Jean Martin and Roger Chartier (Paris: Promodis, 1983), 77–85, 80.
4. Joseph Goering, *William de Montibus (c. 1140–1213): The Schools and the Literature of Pastoral Care* (Toronto: Pontifical Institute of Mediaeval Studies, 1992), 262.
5. As Rouse and Rouse have shown, much of the detail surrounding the composition of the first concordances is based on assertions from much later that have circulated without corroboration. One such detail is the dating for the completion of the St. Jacques Concordance, commonly given as 1230, although this is almost certainly too early. All we can state with certainty is that it was begun during Hugh's time at St. Jacques (i.e., by 1235) and completed by 1247, by which date a copy had been made at Jumièges in Normandy. See Richard H. Rouse and Mary A. Rouse, "The Verbal Concordance to the Scriptures," *Archivum Fratrum Praedicatorum* 44 (1974): 5–30, 6–8.
6. Lloyd W. Daly, *Contributions to a History of Alphabetization in Antiquity and the Middle Ages* (Brussels: Collection Latomus, 1967), 74.
7. Oxford, Bodleian Library, MS Canon Pat. lat. 7.
8. Ian Ker, *John Henry Newman: A Biography* (Oxford: Clarendon, 1988), 762.
9. Bernard Levin, "Don't Come to Me for a Reference," *Times* #63548 (November 10, 1989), 16; reprinted as "The Index Finger Points," *Now Read On* (London: Jonathan Cape, 1990), 159.
10. Oxford, Bodleian Library MS Lat. misc. b. 18 f. 61. Translations are from the corresponding passages in the Douay-Rheims Version.
11. ["iste modus praedicandi, scilicet per colligationes auctoritatum, est multum facilis, quia facile est auctoritates habere, ex eo quod factae sunt Concordantiae super Bibliam . . . secundum ordinem alphabeti, ut auctoritates possint faciliter inveniri."] Thomas Waleys, "De modo componendi sermones," in *Artes praedicandi: Contribution à l'histoire de la rhétorique au moyen âge*, ed. Thomas-Marie Charland (Paris: Vrin, 1936), 390.
12. London, British Library, Royal MS 8 G ii.
13. For more detail on the rise of the printed page number in the latter part of the fifteenth century, see Margaret M. Smith, "Printed Foliation: Forerunner to Printed Page-numbers?" *Gutenberg-Jahrbuch* 63 (1988): 54–70.
14. J. Ashton Cross, "A Universal Index of Subjects," in *Transactions and Proceedings of the Conference of Librarians Held in London, October 1877*, ed. Edward B. Nicholson and Henry R. Tedder (London: Chiswick, 1878), 104–7, 107.
15. Ashton Cross, "Universal Index," 105.
16. "Proceedings of the Conference of Librarians, Fourth Sitting," in Nicholson and Tedder, 159–64, 163.
17. "The Conference of Librarians," *Athenaeum*, no. 2607 (October 13, 1877): 467–68 (467).
18. Ashton Cross, "Universal Index," 107.
19. "How Search Organizes Information: Crawling and Indexing," Google, https://www.google.com/search/howsearchworks/crawling-indexing/ (accessed April 13, 2018).

INTEL

GEOFFREY WINTHROP-YOUNG

Information is a concept with an extraordinarily broad reach. It is also extraordinarily well defended. Think of information as a large, low-lying coastal area wrested from the sea. Extracted from an ocean of noise, it is a mass of data ready for further processing, in the course of which it will acquire a peculiar quality known as *meaning*. In order to guarantee its safety and fertility, it is surrounded by a number of dikes, the most formidable of which is the modern theory of communication associated with the work of Claude Shannon. Like any good dike, it does not present a frontal area of attack to the pounding waters. Instead, the many critical, hermeneutic, or politically engaged waves that insist on the meaning, context, and social impact of information lose their momentum and peter out on the mathematically calculated flat slopes that configure information primarily in terms of statistics and probability. In other words, information can be mapped as a cultural technique: rather than presupposing a clear distinction between the meaningful and the meaningless, it appears to provide the ground on which that distinction can operate.

This assumed prehermeneutic quality endows information with a certain *neutrality*, and this neutrality is precisely what renders information so hospitable to subsequent impositions of meaning. Neutrality is a stance vigorously dissected by those who dislike it; and few disliked it more than Carl Schmitt. In "The Age of Neutralizations and Depoliticizations," an addendum to his *Concept of the Political*, Schmitt offered a crudely effective analysis of the basic dynamics of western history since the sixteenth century.[1] Time and again, a central sphere that had become too conflict-ridden was replaced by an ostensibly neutral alternative. By the late seventeenth century, theology was entangled in so many devastating conflicts that it was pushed aside by metaphysics, an allegedly more neutral way of involving the transcendental in the here and now. Towards the end of the nineteenth century, the seemingly neutral sphere of the economy (which had supplanted metaphysics) had accumulated such bellicose potential that it was replaced by "neutral" technology. Today, only the most blinkered partisans of pragmatic technocracy still believe that technology is a neutral affair. Theology, metaphysics, economy, technology—in the end, *enmity* will reassert itself and render all "neutral" spheres political. Technology, too, will come to be determined by a fundamental us-versus-them structure that, as Schmitt would have it, is indispensable for the identity, coherence, and purpose of any viable political body. With this in mind, it may be helpful to summon the dubious spirit of Schmitt and recognize the modern concept of information as another grand neutralization, a Swiss social sphere, as it were, which promises us a respite from the forever wars of meaning. But just as Swiss neutrality fundamentally depends on the storage of money and the productions of arms, both of which inevitably find their way to wars abroad, there is a century's worth of irony to the fact that information, a concept firmly rooted in business and war (that is, in attempts to gain advantages in economic and military competition), should have been so successful in marketing its alleged neutrality as well as its ability to share and connect. The following remarks propose to analyze intelligence as the *martial aggregate state of information*. Information passes through many such states. Secret information obtained by surveillance, interception, espionage or treason is known as intelligence or "intel." As it crosses boundaries of secrecy, enmity, and public accessibility, some formerly classified intel may be converted into news while other portions end up as archival material. Within this sequence, the spy obtaining intelligence occupies a position symmetrical to that of the archivist (or, increasingly, the artist) retrieving archived material. Against the background of the classic communication model, the sender assumes the guise of an extractor processing the source in the service of the receiver or handler. Reversing the flow of communication does not affect the structure itself, but those who were the receivers are now the senders, and vice versa. If spies are "turned" and begin to communicate false intelligence or "chicken feed" to their (former) masters, the basic structure of the treacherous transaction remains the same, but the formerly duped party is now the beneficiary.

It appears, then, that the conditions under which we speak of information in terms of intel involve conflict, subterfuge, secrecy, betrayal, treason, and espionage. The master signifier is clearly in sight: "Intelligence is thus a knowledge suffused by the danger and cunning of its origin: war."[2] This rather bleak outlook, however, is crucial for the purposes of this volume. For if its goal is indeed to (re)articulate information as a humanistic concept, we have to go beyond the traditional confines of humanism. We cannot restrict ourselves to articulating information in terms of an ideology of "real" communication that, ideally, culminates in consensus or even communion as a merging of minds and souls. We also have to articulate information, and the human factors involved in its procurement and further processing, with a view toward enmity and war. In short, if communication gestures toward the social nature of information, we have to use intel to grasp its predatory nature.

A second, no less important aspect is the recourse to fiction. This goes beyond the trivial reminder of the extensive commuter traffic that connects espionage to literature. From William Somerset Maugham to John le Carré, are there any noteworthy modern male British authors *not* involved in the intelligence business? It goes beyond the hollow (yet defensible) claim that literature—and the novel in particular—has always been a form of intelligence. Indeed, what is the nineteenth-century novel from Balzac to Zola, from Turgenev to Tolstoy, from Austen to Eliot, other than a pile of early intelligence reports? (Think of *Middlemarch*, *Germinal*, and *The Possessed* as internal security dossiers that escaped redaction.) What is at stake is the far more complex issue of evaluating information, that is, of projecting plausible structures of meaning onto data extracted from hostile waters. As we shall see, the conversion of data into actionable intelligence depends on techniques that are uncannily similar to the production of fiction.

But what is intelligence? It is something that prompts definitions to dissolve into descriptions: "Intelligence is the umbrella term referring to the range of activities—from planning and information collection to analysis and dissemination—conducted in secret, and aimed at maintaining or enhancing relative security by providing forewarning of threats or potential threats in a manner that allows for the timely implementation of a preventive policy or strategy, including, where deemed desirable, covert activities."[3] Intel is an initial condition, a set of operations, and an outcome. To quote a founding theorist of the intelligence business, it is "a kind of knowledge; the kind of organization which produces this knowledge; the activity pursued by this intelligence organization."[4] This is as much a list of key features as a recursive sequence. Intelligence worth its name depends on multi-layered observations and subsequent systemic self-adjustments. The outcome of any operation (from clandestine surveillance to destabilizing interventions) must be fed back into the system, which is under constant pressure to catch up with its own observations. Over the course of the last century, this sequence has been subject to increased professionalization. Organizations like the CIA have emerged as *epistepolemological* institutions, that is, operationally closed systems dedicated to conflict-focused knowledge processing. This operational closure involves crucial functional differentiations in the areas of intelligence procurement and evaluation, some of which affect the treatment and very existence of external and internal human operators. It is necessary to ground this abstract analysis in historical realities in order to show how the human factor exits and enters intelligence.

The recognition of the importance of intel—to be precise, the understanding that procuring secret information by means of covert activities is indispensable for the successful completion of key governmental and military operations—precedes its twentieth-century institutionalized professionalization by well over twenty centuries. Kautilya's *Arthashastra*, the oldest parts of which date back to the second century BCE, already describes something that resembles North Korea or the Stasi-run German Democratic Republic, an "untrammeled espionage state where surveillance and provocation are as essential to the work of government as coinage and road building."[5] The Old Testament has its share of informers, codes, and spies, some of them with a license to kill. But first, and still unsurpassed, is Sun Tzu's *Art of War*. While some sections may sound dated—"generally, operations of war require one thousand fast four-horse chariots"—all that deals with deception and espionage, especially the concluding section on the "Employment of Secret Agents," with its description of proper spy handling practices and the use of "native, inside, doubled, expendable, and living" agents, reads like a mixture of a KGB manual and the summary of a 1950s Cold War think tank session.[6] *The Art of War* is the first systematic expression of trust in an intelligence machinery of almost cybernetic perfection capable of skillfully deploying well-oiled human operators. It manifests a palpable disdain for any kind of improvisation, military or otherwise, no matter how impressive. For Sun Tzu, the opportunity to display genius in battle merely signals a lack of preparation. The true art of war reveals itself less in actual combat than in creating a situation in which you know for certain that you will win should you choose to fight: "To subdue the enemy without fighting is the acme of skill."[7] Victory rests on utilizing "foreknowledge" that will enable you to dictate the time and terrain of engagement.[8] "Therefore only the enlightened sovereign and the worthy general who are able to use the most intelligent people as agents are certain to achieve great things. Secret operations are essential in war, upon them the army relies to make its every move."[9] It is almost as if Sun Tzu had anticipated by two and a half millennia the unwinnable war of the thermonuclear age. Even if the generals of his time had had one million rather than one thousand chariots at their disposal, they could not have laid waste to the entire world, which is precisely what became possible in the 1950s. *The Art of War* says a lot about fighting, but in its most interesting parts it is a manual for avoiding combat by means of intelligence. In times when weapons no longer discriminate between handlers and targets, the intelligence war—from spy wars to war games—comes to replace real war.[10]

Historically, the human factor—the soiling of the intelligence machinery by human imperfection—emerges as a key problem in the wake of the modern professionalization and subsequent internal differentiation of the intelligence machinery. The first formative event was the transition to administrative independence. Of course, spies and informal spy networks have been around much longer, but there was no separate bureaucracy to speak of prior to the establishment of the British Secret Service in 1909. Its creation, incidentally, was the result of fake news: namely, the widespread belief that Britain had been overrun by German spies. In the eyes of its critics, the wayward perception of reality that prompted its creation has been inherited by the institution itself. In John le Carré's novels (an indispensable literary outpost when it comes to reconnoitering the murkier depths of the business), intelligence professionals like to refer to their workplace as "The Circus." This name not only ironically acknowledges the paranoid acrobatics of their trade and the zoo-like atmosphere of intel work, but also hints at its constitutive self-immuration. A circus, like a Roman arena, consists of a circular arrangement that has the audience turn its back on the outside world in order to focus, frequently with a high degree of involvement and obsession, on a distorted and questionable representation of said outside world. In more theoretical terms, intelligence agencies are operationally closed systems that process incoming data according to their own systemic properties. In itself this is nothing new; the same can be said of a taxation office. The obvious problem is that we are on a different level of relevance and impact. To stick to le Carré's image, the circus rotunda aspires to be both God's eye (ideally, it wants to observe and judge everything) and God's gun sight (it targets and potentially disrupts or destroys everything).

External professional differentiation was followed by a no less crucial internal functional differentiation, when the distinction between the agency ("Circus") and the outside world was re-entered within the agency. In a nutshell, obtaining, evaluating, and (if need be) responding to intelligence are assigned to separate operators. We are familiar with the literary glorification of pristine intelligence heroics in which all three functions are carried out by one and the same person. Rudyard Kipling's eponymous Kim or Sandy Arbuthnot, the master of disguise in John Buchan's Richard Hannay novels, are self-guided protean operators blessed with such powers of initiative, adaptability, and chameleon-like mimicry that they can fully blend into, and at times even assume leadership over, a native population, no matter how racially different. At this point, intelligence is a conspicuously thespian affair. To be a spy is to play a part in front of people who do not know they are an audience. Maybe it is no coincidence that acting became a respectable profession at the same time it was deemed a necessary skill for state security. Likewise, it may be no coincidence that the two most incisive and disturbing texts about role-playing in the intelligence domain—T. E. Lawrence's *Seven Pillars of Wisdom* and Bertolt Brecht's *The Measures Taken*—address the ethical and, ultimately, lethal fallacies of method acting under revolutionary circumstances.

The days of Kim and Arbuthnot soon passed—if they ever really existed outside of book covers at all. Spies are no longer inserted from the outside but recruited within. As Stephen Grey has shown, this functional (and national) differentiation into agent and handler, spy and spymaster, comes with a new set of problems.[11] The troubling possibility that a spy may "go native" and migrate to the other side is replaced by the troubling prospect that a native could "go foreign." Trust is put in someone who has broken trust: "At the root of spying . . . was a grubby act of betrayal. . . . [T]he shift from spying to hiring others had made spying synonymous with treachery and far less glorious. Spies could be liked but never fully trusted. Fundamentally, spies were not *our* people."[12] As a result, intelligence operatives are burdened with the double task of evaluating messenger and message. Is the former dependable? Is the latter correct? What is the relationship between dubious source and uncertain message? By foregrounding questions of meaning, intention, and response, the quandaries of intelligence exacerbate the very problems which classic information theory had tried to remove from the center. The human factor heats up the "neutral" analysis of communication, which may well turn out to be the historically last form of humanism. What Shannon and others had described in the dry formulas of probability and redundancy is scrutinized with an additional layer of expectation and distrust. The historical record, however, as illustrated in the story of Richard Sorge below, indicates that intel failures are bound to increase the more quantitative and qualitative assessments of human intelligence (HUMINT) confirm each other. It is more likely that we consider messages with a very high quantum of information value too good to be true when we perceive the quality of the source not to be true in the old, moral sense of word.

If the greatness of spies is determined by the importance of their intel, then Richard Sorge was the greatest spy of World War II, since he was able to inform his Moscow contacts not only of the date of the planned German attack on the Soviet Union, but also of the Japanese decision not to open a second front in the East. Yet it took a long time before Stalin and his minions put any trust in him. Sorge was, after all, a German residing in Japan, betraying both his home and his host country. No wonder the careful handling of those who handle information becomes such an important topic, both within the intelligence business and its fictional mirrorworld. As handlers struggle to develop the most appropriate routines when interacting with their coveted deplorables, the problems of acting are joined by those of mentoring. Sun Tzu knew this well: "He who is not sage and wise, humane and just, cannot use secret agents. And he who is not delicate and subtle cannot get the truth out of them."[13]

Obviously, one straightforward way of eliminating the troublesome human factor on the procurement side is to downgrade HUMINT and rely more on SIGINT (signals intelligence): dispense with prefashioned narratives and biased accounts furnished by human sources and instead focus on so-called raw, unprocessed data, from intercepted communication to the spikes and lulls of signals analysis. In other words, replace the shady human factor with trustworthy machines. Despite repeated reminders over the past three decades of how necessary it is to infiltrate terrorist networks with human agents and to entrust the collection of local information to native operators familiar with terrain, customs, and history, this downgrading of human media in favor of allegedly less biased and more predictable nonhuman technologies has been the overall global trend. There are, no doubt, several good reasons for this shift, just as there are several revealing problems and consequences. To begin with, it appears that the increasingly technologized routines of intel procurement allow us to isolate and retire that "most feared creature of our contemporary world: [the] solitary decider."[14] But the more independent human operators are downgraded, the more artificial intelligence technologies are, in turn, entrusted with these human decision-making capabilities. Initiative and sovereignty cross over from synapses to CPUs. As James Bond exits, drones with licenses to observe, evaluate, and kill enter. Such machine trust (which is a variation of the initially described retreat into neutrality) creates machine envy, or what the philosopher Günther Anders memorably described as "Promethean shame."[15] It is the feeling of ontological inferiority that arises when we compare the malaise of our human uniqueness to the standardized mechanical perfection of our artifices; and it compels us to mimic our creations as fervently as we once tried to imitate our divine creators. First gods and now machines—they think so much faster and kill so much better than we do; how can we not aspire to be like them? This human envy plays into le Carré's novels, several of which depict human beings within the "Circus" engaged in reverse Turing tests, constantly trying to convince each other that they are fully functioning machines.

Yet who would doubt that machine trust in the intelligence business is justified? The interception range and storage capabilities of digital surveillance technologies are increasing by leaps and bounds, reaching a panoramic breadth old master criminals from Moriarity to Mabuse never dreamed of. Modern intelligence operators have come to look at society the way Romantic poets looked at nature: every nook, cranny, and crevice is worthy of attention because each harbors potential messages. Nothing in creation escapes the burden of meaning. This plenitude of significance, however, is not an ontological given but an effect of media. The possible range of meaning is determined by the factual range of media technology. The medium can only become the message because the medium determines *that* something can be a message in the first place. As Friedrich Kittler has argued, it took the arrival of the hermeneutically supercharged "Discourse Network 1800" with all its revised linguistic practices and protocols to make language appear as a homogeneous, transparent, and infinitely hospitable medium with virtually infinite reach and carrying capacity.[16] As a result, language became the unquestioned natural means of recording, storing, and transmitting nature, truth, and everything that occurs within hearts and heads. There is, no doubt, a religious residue at work here. The new presupposition of inescapable meaningfulness inherits the old presupposition of inescapable divinity in nature. First, there was a time when God hid tongues and voices all over creation, and then humans grew ears to hear them all. This basic notion that there is nothing not worth listening to moves from language to signals. But once this presupposition is inherited and repurposed by digital technologies, and once the latter are employed by the war-bred intel business, they give rise to the *presupposition of planetary enmity*. The realization that intelligence operations will become ever more important as climate change leads to global turmoil is related to the fact that Gaia herself has moved into the crosshairs of le Carré's Circus. The intelligence paradigm suggests that we monitor the alleged deviations and anomalies of nature (from water levels and heat waves to increases of atmospheric turbulence) as if they were terrorist activities.

On a more positive note, intelligence infrastructures may offer a form of redemption and final justice. With this in mind, the always-quotable William Gibson has sounded a note of warning to those in power: "In the age of the leak and the blog, of evidence extraction and link discovery, truths will either out or be outed, later if not sooner. This is something I would bring to the attention of every diplomat, politician and corporate leader. The future, eventually, will find you out. The future, wielding unimaginable tools of transparency, will have its way with you. In the end, you will be seen to have done that which you did."[17] At a certain point storage capacity takes on religious dimensions: total capture is divine (whereas total leakage is the devil's work). As data plants with yottabyte deepnet processing capabilities inaugurate a digital regime of unprecedented traceability, the Book of Judgment, to be opened at the end of times to judge the living and the dead, is being compiled in NSA supercomputers. While the so-called Great Game, the thespian spycraft of Kim and Lawrence of Arabia, served to define us as *Homo ludens* ("Man the Player"), omnipresent surveillance technologies now redefine us as *Homo vestigia faciens* ("Man the Trace-maker"), a leaking being determined by inscription surfaces, recording devices, and storage facilities able to capture far more of our signs and traces than we are willing to divulge.

But of course, it is not that easy. To continue Gibson's quote:

> Regardless of the number and power of the tools used to extract patterns from information, any sense of meaning depends on context, with interpretation coming along in support of one agenda or another. A world of informational transparency will necessarily be one of deliriously multiple viewpoints, shot through with misinformation, disinformation, conspiracy theories and a

quotidian degree of madness. We may be able to see what's going on more quickly, but that doesn't mean we'll agree about it more readily.[18]

Where everything can be seen, nothing can be discerned; where everything is in sight, nothing is in focus. Increase of information does not necessarily terminate in certainty; it can just as well result in an increase of ignorance, because the more we know about something, the more we know that we can (and maybe should) know more. Indeed, the human-factor hermeneutics of suspicion innate to the intelligence paradigm compel us to conduct constant alterations, since there is always the possibility that a given definite reading may be precisely what the hostile source wants us to believe. The quandaries of intelligence assessment, then, recall the literary theory wars fueled by the permanent revolution of interpretation: conclusion versus deconstruction, the need to arrive at a conclusive meaning versus the need to constantly defer any such closure.

At this point we have reached a core problem of intelligence evaluation tied to the uncanny resemblance between intelligence and fiction. Following Eva Horn's lead, a good place to start is Sydney Pollack's classic 1975 CIA movie *Three Days of the Condor*.[19] Robert Redford plays Joe Turner, a CIA operative holed up in a New York office that bills itself as the "American Literary Historical Society." This is both a flimsy cover and perfectly accurate, for Turner spends his time reading "everything that's published in the world" in search of material for historically important intelligence analyses. He scours "adventures," "novels," and "journals" for fictional codes, leaks, and dirty tricks, all of which are fed into a computer to be checked against actual CIA plans and operations. Because he stumbles upon a fictional narrative that resembles a plot hatched by a renegade unit within the CIA, a professional assassin—the great Max von Sydow in his most memorable non-Bergman performance—is hired to clean out Turner's outfit. Turner, played by Redford as a wide-eyed Parsifal of open source intelligence, is dumbstruck by the fact that some of his less bookish colleagues go around killing people, including members of their own team. "I work for the CIA. I am not a spy," he explains to an incredulous Faye Dunaway (standing in for an equally skeptical audience), "I just read books." Indeed he does: he is a thoroughly modern reader, that is, the human precursor to a Google search engine. He just fails to realize the chiasmus that connects literature to espionage: readers spy on texts the way spies read the world. In the final encounter, a player from the bad side of the CIA explains their modus operandi: "We play games. What if? How many men? What would it take? Is there a cheaper way to destabilize a regime?" When fictional plots on the outside too closely resemble plotted games on the inside, the result is murder.

But what, or rather where, is the real? Where exactly is the boundary between fiction and reality? Between real games and "gamed" realities? It is important to remind the more committed advocates of "indisputable reality" that the difference between reality and fiction is not simply the difference between a real thing and a fake or artifice. It is not the difference between a real house and a mock-up building in a studio back lot. Rather, it is the difference between a real house people live in and a no less real house that is up for sale and that has been prepared by home stagers. The function of the carefully arranged furniture is not to be used but to provide a guiding suggestion as to how the house could be furnished and lived in. Sometimes the clients may purchase the furniture, in which case a mere suggestion turns into the reality of a chosen option. This is where the worlds of authors and intelligence operatives intersect: both are engaged in the *staging of information*. A piece of fiction and an intelligence report are highly complex arrangements of sequential events that keep signaling the contingent decisions on which their assumptions of causality are based. Intelligence involves the communication of various, occasionally mutually exclusive interpretations of information, while simultaneously advocating and relativizing one particular interpretation. Those who write for pleasure and those who write as a possible inducement to kill thus face

> the difficulty of writing a text that can be read in many different ways but that nonetheless will and must result in one particular reading, a text whose meaning is so clear that it cannot be obscured by any changes from above. A text, in other words, that is both one and many. The reader—the political decision maker—is to be offered the full range of possible hypotheses but is then supposed to arrive at one decisive conclusion. In short, [it is] . . . a text that cannot be. It exists only in the head of an author who does not yet know which words he will use, and in the head of a reader who has either missed or already forgotten the many possibilities of reading.[20]

To rephrase this in terms that come more easily to literary theorists: fiction is, on the one hand, a selection of information that by virtue of its selection is invested with significance. On the other hand, literature—large parts of our education system would collapse if we did not believe this—is a meaningful reduction of reality's complexity. Fiction is a technique that paradoxically and self-consciously manages to present one particular selection rather than another against the background of those not selected.

This is, once again and in conclusion, the binary of terminal definition versus ongoing deferral. To sum up, in our bleak estrangement operation we looked at intelligence as the martial aggregate state of information. We witnessed its administrative autonomization followed by crucial functional differentiations. We saw how the human factor enters and exits this increasingly complex feedback of procurement, evaluation, and response. And we saw how the evaluation stage employs techniques also on display in a domain intelligence is keen to separate itself from, but which it can never fully escape: the production of literary fiction. Most importantly, we saw how the dynamics of closure and deferral condemn intelligence to pursue itself in widening gyres, a vast Midgard snake of martial information threatening the world as it devours its own tail. It is difficult not to see once more the unwelcome spirit of Carl Schmitt, for the binary of closure and deferral (or satiated meaning and deconstructive urge) resembles his categories of sovereign and *katechon* (the ambiguous figure who holds back the arrival of the Antichrist). On the one hand, we have the sovereign's ability to suspend the processing of information and act outside of the laws that usually govern the former; on the other hand, fear of what might happen when the processing is suspended compels us to continue the latter. If we look at information under the auspices of polemogenic intelligence, humans are beings always going to war.

Notes

1. Carl Schmitt, *The Concept of the Political*, trans. George Schwab (Chicago: University of Chicago Press, 2007).
2. Eva Horn, *The Secret War: Treason, Espionage, and Modern Fiction*, trans. Geoffrey Winthrop-Young (Evanston, IL: Northwestern University Press, 2013), 101.
3. Peter Gill and Mark Phythian, *Intelligence in an Insecure World* (Cambridge: Polity, 2006), 7.
4. Sheldon Kent, *Strategic Intelligence for American World Policy* (Hamden, UK: Archon, 1965), xxiii.
5. Philip H. J. Davies, "The Original Surveillance State: Kautilya's *Arthashastra* and Government by Espionage in Classical India," in *Intelligence Elsewhere: Spies and Espionage Outside the Anglosphere*, ed. Philip H. J. Davies and Kristian C. Gustafson (Washington, DC: Georgetown University Press), 49–66, 50.
6. Sun Tzu, *The Art of War*, trans. Samuel B. Griffith (London: Oxford University Press, 1971). 72, 144–49, 145.
7. Sun Tzu, *The Art of War*, 77.
8. Sun Tzu, *The Art of War*, 145
9. Sun Tzu, *The Art of War*, 149.
10. Horn, *The Secret War*, 229–35.
11. Stephen Grey, *The New Spymasters: Inside the Modern World of Espionage from the Cold War to Global Terror* (New York: St. Martin's, 2015), 38–81.
12. Grey, *The New Spymaster*, 34–35; emphasis in the original.
13. Sun Tzu, *The Art of War*, 147.
14. John le Carré, *A Delicate Truth* (Toronto: Viking, 2013), 47.
15. Günther Anders, *Die Antiquiertheit des Menschen*, 2 vols. (Munich: Beck, 1988).
16. Friedrich Kittler, *Discourse Networks*, trans. Michael Metteer and Chris Cullens (Stanford: Stanford University Press, 1990).
17. William Gibson, *Distrust That Particular Flavor* (New York: Putnam, 2012), 170.
18. Gibson, *Distrust That Particular Flavor*, 170.
19. Horn, *The Secret War*, 235–37.
20. Horn, *The Secret War*, 113.

KEYWORD

DANIEL ROSENBERG

There may be no word more emblematic of our information age than *keyword* itself. Try Googling it. The result of your search (as of today) is the definition, *a word or concept of great significance*, and a line graph showing the increasing use of the term in the second half of the twentieth century. As Google offers it to us, the keyword *keyword* appears not only to *mean* a word or concept of great significance but also to *be* of great significance from the perspective of the modern history of words.

In fact, there are two contrasting notions of *keyword* that underlie the impressive ascent of the term represented in the Google graph. The first we already know from Google's main definition. For the other, we need to refer to the secondary definition, *an informative word used in an information retrieval system to indicate the content of a document*. The ways in which these two formulations relate to each other is not transparent. Which, after all, should lead? Viewed one way, the second definition is a subcategory of the first, since to be an informative word in a document is one type of significance. Yet, viewed another way, especially in light of the Google curve, the first may equally be seen as a subcategory of the second: in our era, to be of great significance, arguably a word or concept must first be informative in precisely the way suggested by the second definition. What makes *keyword* such a powerful idea is precisely the ambiguity of the relationship that it mediates between what is informative and what is significant, a conundrum of our time if ever there was one.

In its modern formulation, *keyword* has been with us for about six decades. This may be demonstrated straightforwardly through a quantitative analysis

Dictionary

Search for a word

🔊 **key·word**
/ˈkēˌwərd/

noun
noun: **keyword**; plural noun: **keywords**; noun: **key word**; plural noun: **key words**

a word or concept of great significance.
"homes and jobs are the keywords in the campaign"
- a word that acts as the key to a cipher or code.
- an informative word used in an information retrieval system to indicate the content of a document.
- a significant word mentioned in an index.

Translate keyword to   Choose language

Use over time for: keyword

1800   1850   1900   1950   2010

Show less

9.1 Google search for *keyword*. July 2018.

of usage. As the Google ngram referenced above shows, between 1950 and 2000 the relative frequency of usage of the term *keyword* in English increased by two orders of magnitude. One can find the character string *k-e-y-w-o-r-d* in publications before the late 1950s, but its occurrence then was very uncommon and, in relation to the ideas with which we reflexively associate the term today, tentative. This remains the case even if we consider the phrase *key word* as well. Indeed, a graph of the changing relative frequencies of the two-word phrase and the compound term in the Google Books corpus neatly expresses both the growing prevalence of the new word and the timing of its emergence. As late as 1980, a word could still be *key* without being a *keyword*. After that point, the notion of the *keyword* increasingly captured both the idea of the important word and of the word of present interest.

Beginning about 1958, *keyword* mattered in English, but, from the start, it mattered in two different ways and in two very different areas: literary and

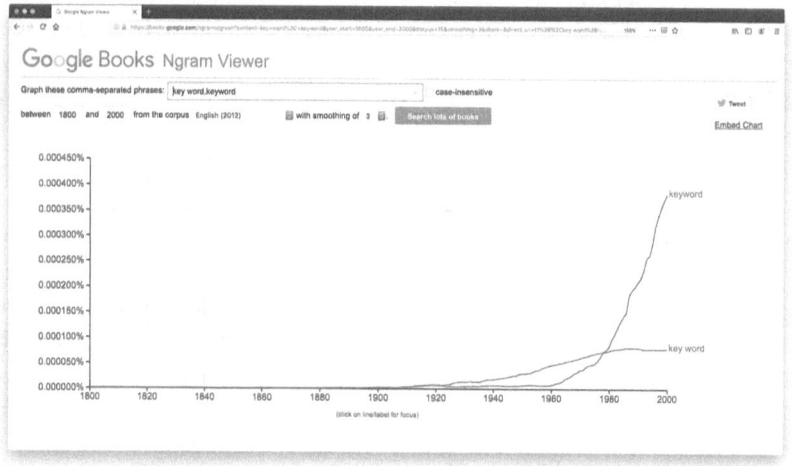

9.2 Google Books Ngram Viewer search for *key word* and *keyword*, 1800–2000. July 2018.

cultural theory, on the one hand, and computer and information theory, on the other. Yet, during the late twentieth century, these two senses came eventually not only to interact but also to reinforce and invigorate each other in ways that tell us a great deal about the emerging epistemological environment.

Early on, the sense of *keyword* in the literary domain, that of a word of special social and cultural importance, was both typified and driven by the work of the Welsh critic Raymond Williams in his 1958 book *Culture & Society, 1780–1850* and its sequel *Keywords: A Vocabulary of Culture & Society* from 1976.[1] Of the terms discussed in these works, Williams writes, "I called these ... Keywords in two connected senses: they are significant, binding words in certain activities and their interpretation; they are significant, indicative words in certain forms of thought."[2] Though any word might in principle be studied using something like Williams's historical semantic approach, the words he was interested in were not just any words, they were always and only words of "an especially problematical kind" embodying both historical "continuity and discontinuity, and also deep conflicts of value and belief."[3]

The sense of the term *keyword* in the domain of computer and information theory was another thing entirely. Here, the key writer is the IBM engineer, Hans Peter Luhn, innovator of important contemporary information devices ranging from the optical scanner to the algorithm that governs the generation of credit card numbers, and the key texts, a series of articles Luhn published between 1958 and 1962 including the information studies classic, "Keyword-in-Context Index for Technical Literature" from 1960.[4] Evidently, the context of information retrieval is very different from that of literary criticism, but the contrast between the usages of Williams and Luhn is even stronger than the difference between their fields would suggest. When Luhn talked about *keywords*, he did not assume, as did Williams, that these ought to be either problematical or deep; by *keyword*, he meant any word that characterized a document because it occurred in it in statistically notable ways, or conversely any word provided in an information query used to search that same document. The Keyword-in-Context (KWIC) index discussed in Luhn's 1960 article is essentially a machine-generated concordance. It breaks a document down into an alphabetized list of words, displaying for each occurrence of each word in that document a *context*, that is, the small group of words that appear before and after it in the original. In contrast to the carefully curated *keyword* lists in Raymond Williams's books, with the exception of certain words determined by either a statistical or an editorial procedure to be noninforming, KWIC is an index to *every* word in a document.[5]

In the beginning, the usages of Williams and Luhn were sharply distinct from, and even antagonistic to, one another. Luhn's KWIC index was designed to speed up the kind of work that Williams was engaged in by placing every instance of a given term immediately at a reader's fingertips, but also, by the same mechanism, to reduce the authority of the textual analyst or scholar, allowing readers to select their own terms of importance and to easily discover their contextual uses. In any system which preselects terms of interest, Luhn wrote, "the inquirer has to adjust himself to the point of view" of a prior reader. In his own system, the inquirer "has complete freedom in reflecting his own view of the present."[6]

The phenomenon of a powerful new term emerging through what appears to be contrasting uses is not at all unique to *keyword*. Indeed, it is precisely this sort of collaborative contradiction that got Raymond Williams interested in the keyword problem in the first place, and it is at the heart of the argument of his 1958 *Culture & Society*. At that time, the principal word that concerned Williams was *culture*. As he shows, before the nineteenth century, the word *culture* performed very different work from what it soon began to do. Before the nineteenth century, he writes, *culture* meant,

> the tending of natural growth, and then, by analogy a process of human training. But this latter use, which had usually been a culture *of* something, was changed, in the nineteenth century, to *culture* as such, a thing in itself. It came to mean, first, "a general state or habit of mind," having close relations with the idea of human perfection. Second, it came to mean "the general state of intellectual development, in a society as a whole." Third, it came to mean "the general body of the arts." Fourth, later in the century, it came to mean "a whole way of life, material, intellectual and spiritual." It came also, as we know, to be a word which often provoked either hostility or embarrassment.[7]

In *Culture & Society*, Williams discusses at length four other keywords that he thought crucial to characterizing the period 1780–1950. These are *industry, democracy, class,* and *art,* words that could either be considered "new" in this period or as having "acquired new and important meanings."[8] These words, Williams argues, not only *changed* during this period but also, in their own contrasting uses, exemplified a "general *pattern* of change" in life and thought.[9] He writes,

> The development of *culture* is perhaps the most striking among all the words named. It might be said, indeed, that the question now concentrated in the meanings of the word *culture* are questions directly raised by the great historical changes which the changes in *industry, democracy* and *class,* in their own way, represent, and to which the changes in *art* are a closely related response. The development of the word *culture* is a record of a number of important and continuing reactions to these changes in our social, economic and political life, and may be seen, in itself, as a special kind of map by means of which the nature of the changes can be explored.[10]

In *Culture & Society*, then, Williams strives not just to unearth the history of several important words in the language but to map an entire cultural landscape as well. The possibility that, for our own period, a history of the keyword *keyword* might serve a similar function is, to say the least, tantalizing.

Williams argued that in order to understand the cultural as opposed to only the intellectual importance of keywords such as *culture,* one needed to examine a range of texts that put the term into play in strongly contrasting ways. This, in part, reflects the inherent complexity of culturally important terms, but more fundamentally, it reflects the dialectical character of the historical processes of industrialization and modernization themselves. "The mood of England in the Industrial Revolution is a mood of contrasts," writes Williams.[11] And yet these contrasts are produced and articulated through a common language. "Edmund Burke has been called 'the first modern Conservative'; William Cobbett 'the first great tribune of the industrial proletariat.'"[12] Williams continues, "Yet to put together the names of Burke and Cobbett is important, not only as contrast, but because we can only understand this tradition of criticism of the new industrial society if we recognize that it is compounded of very different and at times even directly contradictory elements."[13] True, Burke and Cobbett were opposed in their views and commitments, yet, from the perspective of language, their works resonate strongly with one another. Each represents a crucial dimension of a historical and conceptual situation that is contradictory at its core, and in this respect, they are inseparably linked. "The growth of the new society," writes Williams, was so confusing, even to the best minds, that positions were drawn up in terms of inherited categories, which then revealed unsuspected and even opposing implications. There was much overlapping even in the opposing positions of a Cobbett and a Burke, and the continuing attack on utilitarianism, and on the driving philosophy of the new industrialism, was to make many more strange affiliations: Marx, for instance, was to attack capitalism, in his early writings, in very much the same language of Coleridge, of Burke, and—of Cobbett.[14]

The contradictory senses of a word such as *culture* at the beginning of the industrial age were both possible and necessary because in that time the idea of culture expressed real social contradictions and because changes in the idea of culture reflected powerful ongoing social change.

From the perspective of history, Williams explains, the particular agreements and disagreements of writers from the period are now "less interesting" than their common identification of a locus of social and cultural concern: "those first apprehensions of the social significance of the Industrial Revolution which all felt and none revoked."[15] Indeed, an important claim in Williams's books is not only that no contemporary of Coleridge, Burke, or Cobbett "revoked" these terms, but that none since has either. To the contrary, in Williams's view, over the course of two centuries through the very processes that have *changed* them, these key terms have accumulated new meanings that together make up a kind of moving portrait of the industrial period in both its conflict and its continuity.

In 1958, Williams thought that he could best capture the dimensions of this emergent industrial world through an account of several powerful terms essential to the arguments of opposing figures from the time; *five* culturally important terms, to be precise. But, in point of fact, already then, Williams was gathering other words worth accounting for, and to this end, he composed a "vocabulary" containing dozens to appear as an appendix to his book. His publisher demurred, however, and so his glossary remained unpublished for two decades until it appeared as its own book, *Keywords: A Vocabulary of Culture & Society*, augmented to include one hundred ten terms, many more than the five with which he began.[16] In 1983, a second edition of *Keywords* added twenty-one more terms.[17] A 2005 book, *New Keywords*, by continuers of Williams, offered a further one hundred twenty-one.[18] While it is hard to assail any of the choices made later by Williams or by the editors of *New Keywords*—characteristic additions include entries such as *desire, diaspora, emotion, everyday, fashion,* and *home*—it is also hard not to notice, along with an ever-lengthening list, a shift in the sensibility of the *keyword* itself away from the *keyword* as a word of rare importance to something more like a word of current interest.

Keyword is everywhere today, and, like so much of the furniture of everyday life, its complexity is easy to overlook, but to any reader of Williams, the sorts of issues raised by the keyword *keyword* will be familiar. Do the same Google search that we started out with again, the one that produced the knowledge graph containing the definitions of *keyword* and the word-frequency diagram showing the use of *keyword* shooting up in the later twentieth century. When I do this search, my first nine results refer neither to Williams nor to Luhn nor to the problems considered by either but to the business of advertising and more specifically to the area of advertising that most relies upon keyword research, search engine optimization or SEO, and, in a striking twist, to the use of keywords for advertising on the Google search engine itself.

SEO attempts to discover how to optimize a web page for search engine hits and especially for hits that produce multiple clicks, return views, and sometimes sales, largely by choosing which words to put on the page. From the point of view of SEO, a word matters because it produces certain effects, not because it *means* one thing or another to a reader. Indeed, in many cases, the words that a search engine responds to on a web page are hidden in code, invisible in the standard browser view. The hits produced by our own keyword search for *keyword* are the product of this same process. The businesses behind the links we generate when we search on *keyword* are *customers* of Google, paying for the hits we are giving them. And every one of these businesses is a *vendor* selling insights into that same Google enterprise in the form of *lists of keywords* for other Google customers to use to achieve a similar effect. Without going into more detail, it is enough here to point out that the commodification of the word is a crucial vector in the larger story of the keyword, and it is certainly one for which we could take some direction from Williams, for whom the problem of capitalism was directly implied by any analysis of the modern history of culture.

To appreciate *keyword* newly, it may be useful to go back about a half century to that key year, 1958, when, according to a Google search on the character string *1-9-5-8*, Sputnik fell into the ocean, Nikita Khrushchev became Soviet Premier, fourteen-year-old Bobby Fischer won the United States Chess Championship, Momofuku Ando first sold instant *Chikin Ramen* in Japan, and what is said to be the first video game, Tennis for Two, was introduced at the Visitors' Day Exhibit at the Brookhaven National Laboratory on Long Island. This was also the year that Williams published *Culture & Society* and that Luhn published the first in the series of articles in which he proposed a process for "deriving key words for encoding documents for mechanical information retrieval" by automatic techniques.[19] Together, these set in motion a series of developments foundational for our contemporary uses of the term *keyword*.

This was a crucial year and a crucial new word, but these things would have been hard to perceive at the time. In 1958, Williams himself still didn't appreciate the term's salience. *Culture & Society* lays out a well-articulated theory of keywords; it offers a compelling model for their study; but it never gets around to giving the concept a name. In that book, Williams mostly just talks about *words* of great (and sometimes *capital*) importance.[20] Remarkably, even when Williams published the book, *Keywords*, two decades later, he had still not fully settled in with his neologism. Though the word *keyword* appears in its title, the book *Keywords: A Vocabulary of Culture & Society* is itself surprisingly indecisive in its use of the term. In most places in the book where today we would reflexively employ the term *keyword*, Williams simply uses *word*. There are exceptions to this rule. The book's entries on the terms *alienation, dialect, improve, masses, mediation, originality, psychological, sensibility*, and *utilitarian* all use a two-word phrase, *key word* or *key term*. In the entry *unconscious*, we find the compound word *keyword* all by itself and, in the entry for the term *structural*, we find *both* the phrase *key word* and the compound *keyword*. It is of course tempting to suggest that there is something unconscious and structural about those variations occurring in those two particular entries.

In fact, Williams does not seem to have really become committed to his own neologism for several more years during which time the impact of his book *Keywords* itself greatly contributed to the currency of the term. At the same time, part of what was happening during these years, both linguistically and epistemologically, is that the principles of importance and complexity behind Williams's approach in 1958 were in fact eroding. In many ways, Williams's book *Keywords* could be successful in 1976 because *keyword* was becoming something that it was not and could not yet be in 1958.

This brings us back to Hans Peter Luhn. In the late 1950s and early 1960s, while Williams, in England, was still only flirting with the term *keyword*, across the Atlantic, on the IBM campus in New York, Luhn was making a strong case for a different notion of what a keyword was and might be good for. And by 1960, he was making the case using the neologism *keyword* itself. During this period, Luhn produced that burst of influential articles on electronic full-text search, automatic indexing, optical scanning, and selective dissemination of information, which are foundational to our contemporary experience of electronic text.

Like Williams in his contemporaneous publications, Luhn didn't get to *keyword* immediately. In his early publications, he tried out a variety of formulations (*significant, important, key*) before settling on the phrase and eventually the compound, *keyword*. The parallelism is important. From the point of view of approach, there is little that Williams and Luhn share. But, as Williams argues in the cases of Burke and Cobbett on *democracy* and Coleridge and Southey on *culture*, this very difference is what makes their common linguistic choice so significant: together their works functioned to delineate a new semantic field.

How different were they? In his 1960 article on KWIC, Luhn takes one of his most radical stances on the anywordness of the *keyword*, proposing not only that measures of significance could be made statistical rather than semantic but also that the best way of determining the significance of words in a text is negatively, by identifying and eliminating nonsignificant words, rather than seeking out important ones. He writes, "Keywords need only be defined as those which characterize a subject more than others. To derive them, rules have to be established for differentiating that which is significant from the nonsignificant. Since significance is difficult to predict, it is more practicable to isolate it by rejecting all obviously non-significant or 'common' words."[21] In this and several other articles, Luhn proposes a variety of ways of achieving such a result. Among these, one of the most enduring is a test that eliminates terms that occur too frequently or too infrequently in a document as represented on a bell curve. Though Luhn's approach is no longer commonly applied in this simple form, later variations such as TFIDF (term frequency inverse document frequency) continue to be widely employed.

All of this makes a very striking contrast. For Williams, significance is a matter of importance. For Luhn, it is a ratio of signal to noise.

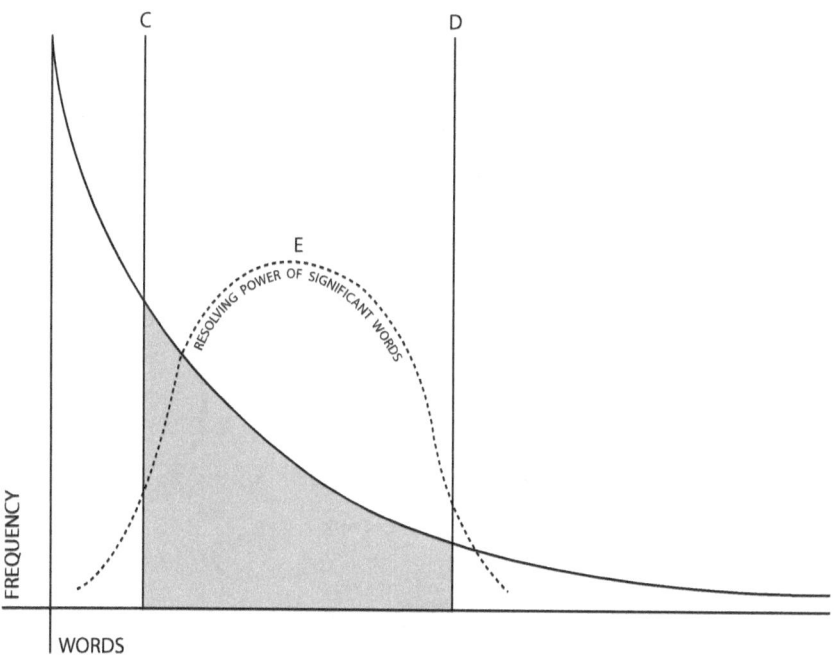

9.3 Word-frequency diagram from Hans Peter Luhn, "The Automatic Creation of Literature Abstracts," *IBM Journal* (April 1958): 161.

In contrast to Williams, Luhn strongly resisted the notion that *keywords* ought to be preselected. To Luhn, *a priori* taxonomies were by their nature alien to the documents to which they were applied. His own method was, as he put it, "native" to the document. In a wonderfully poetic turn, he expresses its advantage as follows: "Since it is born of the collection, it reflects most naturally the spirit of the collection."[22]

Luhn's aim was to set aside preformed assumptions about what made a text meaningful or interesting and to leave that to a mediated negotiation between reader and text. Characteristic of this approach is the system for the "selective dissemination of information" that Luhn proposed in another important article from 1958, "A Business Intelligence System." The system Luhn sketched there sought to automatically direct new technical literature to appropriate readers within an organization. To do so, it would assign keywords to both texts *and* readers and then use matching algorithms to determine which subscribers should get which articles. As readers selected articles that were useful to them, the system would refine its profiles. In the logic of the business intelligence

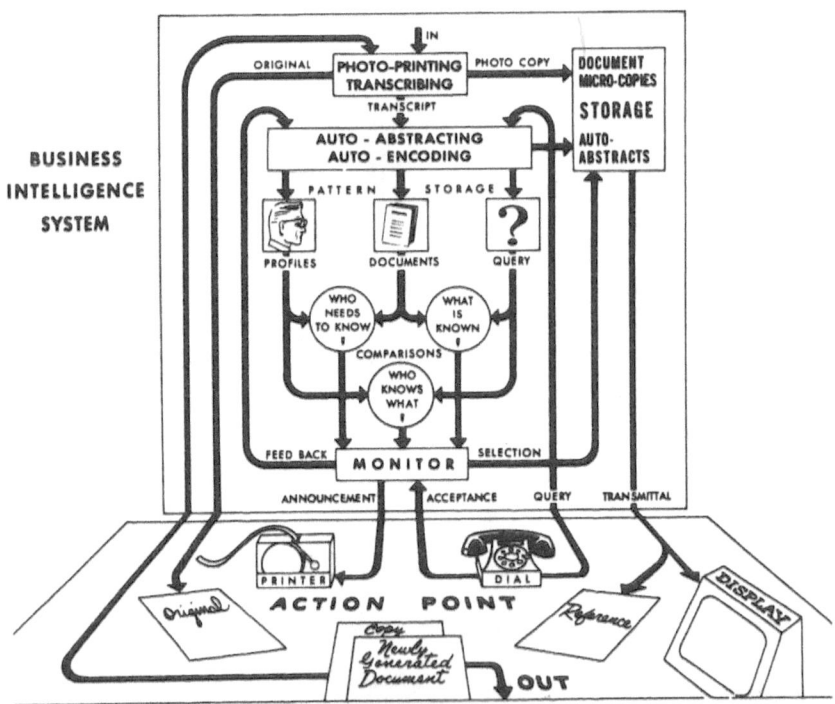

9.4 Diagram of the "business intelligence system," from Hans Peter Luhn, "Automated Intelligence Systems—Some Basic Problems and Prerequisites for Their Solution," IBM Corporation, Yorktown Heights, NY (April 1, 1961): 3.

system, nonhuman and human system nodes would *both* be characterized by keyword lists, a suggestion with enduring resonance.

The contrast between Williams and Luhn is sharp. Williams comes from literary studies; Luhn from engineering. Williams's *keywords* are words of great cultural importance; Luhn's are words characteristic only of a given document or query. Williams's *keywords* are derived by closely reading texts; Luhn's, if they may be said to come from *reading* at all, come from reading of a most distant sort. What is remarkable, then, from a historical point of view, is that these two approaches and ideas came to be so thoroughly intertwined in both idea and practice that today they are entirely hard to distinguish from one another. Consider, for example, the first image in this essay, that graph of the relative frequency of *keyword* in Google Books in the nineteenth and twentieth centuries. On its basis, I made what I take to be a highly intuitive claim: we ought to think of *keyword* as a keyword for our time, and to subject it to the same kind of hermeneutic and historical scrutiny to which Williams subjected the terms *culture, industry, democracy, class,* and *art* in *Society & Culture* in 1958. In an assertion such as this, which sense of the term am I employing, that of Williams or that of Luhn? If the question is hard to answer, there is a good reason for it: like it or not, today, in some way, the answer must always be *both*.

Notes

1. Raymond Williams, *Culture and Society, 1780–1850* (Garden City, NY: Doubleday, 1960); Raymond Williams, *Keywords: A Vocabulary of Culture and Society* (New York: Oxford University Press, 1976).
2. Raymond Williams, *Keywords: A Vocabulary of Culture and Society*, 2d ed. (New York: Oxford University Press, 1983), 15.
3. Williams, *Keywords*, 23.
4. Hans Peter Luhn, "Keyword-in-Context Index for Technical Literature," *American Documentation* 11, no. 4 (1960): 288–95.
5. Daniel Rosenberg, "An Archive of Words," in Lorraine Daston, ed., *Science in the Archives: Pasts, Presents, Futures* (Chicago: University of Chicago Press, 2017), 271–310.
6. Hans Peter Luhn, "The Automatic Creation of Literature Abstracts," *IBM Journal* (April 1958): 159–65.
7. Williams, *Culture and Society*, xiv.
8. Williams, *Culture and Society*, xi.
9. Williams, *Culture and Society*, xi.
10. Williams, *Culture and Society*, xv.
11. Williams, *Culture and Society*, 3.
12. Williams, *Culture and Society*, 3.
13. Williams, *Culture and Society*, 22.
14. Williams, *Culture and Society*, 22.
15. Williams, *Culture and Society*, 35.
16. Williams, *Keywords* (1983), 14.

17. Williams, *Keywords* (1983).
18. Tony Bennett, Lawrence Grossberg, Meaghan Morris, and Raymond Williams, *New Keywords: A Revised Vocabulary of Culture and Society* (Malden, MA: Blackwell, 2005).
19. Luhn, "Literature Abstracts," 165.
20. Williams, *Culture and Society*, xi.
21. "Keyword-in-Context," 289.
22. Hans Peter Luhn, "A Business Intelligence System," *IBM Journal* (October 1958): 167.

KNOWLEDGE

CHAD WELLMON

In the "Unreasonable Effectiveness of Data," published in 2009, three Google researchers encouraged fellow scholars in natural language processing to forgo "elegant theories," "elaborate models," and complex rules, and to simply follow the data.[1] Given the increasing availability of highly structured data on the web, they suggest scholars interested in designing translation algorithms, for example, should move away from earlier concerns with hand-coded grammars, ontologies, and logic-based expert systems and take advantage of the structure already in the data. Data analysis could replace endless efforts to find linguistic rules and encode them into machines. The exhortations of the Google researchers echoed, although in less exaggerated tones, a similar injunction issued by *Wired* magazine's Chris Anderson a year earlier. Announcing the advent of what he called the "Petabyte Age," he declared that big data and applied mathematics would replace "every theory of human behavior, from linguistics to sociology. Forget taxonomy, ontology, and psychology. Who knows why people do what they do? The point is that the numbers speak for themselves."[2] Humans finally have the tools to mine not just data but knowledge, to extract it from the earth like any other inert resource.

A decade later, predictions that claimed big data will deliver knowledge without theory or causal explanations seem not only naïve but also wrong. For many, these promises turned out to be little more than the most recent return of positivism, a purportedly atheoretical empiricism for our digital age.[3] But they have also raised the prospect of an old dream, reformulated repeatedly from Plato's allegory of the cave to the life philosophy (*Lebensphilosophie*) of early twentieth-century Germany, of a knowledge closer to the truth of things, one shorn of concepts, models, and theories that get in between the world and the human mind. The desire to escape the cave of shadows, appearances, and corrupted senses and to encounter the real has long motivated not only what and how we know but also why we want to know in the first place.[4]

All the while, machine learning methods and techniques the Google researchers and Anderson touted have become features of everyday life, part of our infrastructures in everything from the recommender algorithms of Netflix to the facial-recognition algorithms of state policing and surveillance.[5] Along with this ubiquity has come more criticism and scrutiny. These more recent debates have focused, however, not on older, standard questions about AI—*what machines can do or still cannot do*—but rather cultural and social questions about justice, equity, and power.[6] Regardless of whether machines can think, the mechanical and computational processes of machine learning can obscure all-too-human biases, prejudices, and power.

In addition to criticisms on its possibly pernicious effects and uses, there are now widespread concerns about the kind of knowledge machine learning may produce. Machine learning, suggest recent critics, produces an unintelligible, possibly inscrutable type of knowledge. Confronted with processes and mechanisms that seem to defy human understanding or whose causal relations cannot be accounted for, scholars are calling for AI and machine learning researchers "to move toward greater transparency and accountability" in how they develop their training data sets and design their algorithms.[7] Concerns such as these make clear that machine learning's purported opacity, not just general ignorance about its techniques and methods, challenges long-standing epistemic ideals, especially the notion of knowledge as justified true belief: the idea that legitimate knowledge can be accounted for and explained by a human knower. This is an ideal with moral weight—real knowledge *ought* to be intelligible. The implication of these calls for greater accountability and transparency is that machine learning would be intelligible if only it were made transparent.

But what do we mean by "transparency and accountability?" And should these ideals orient our notions of what counts as trustworthy knowledge in the twenty-first century? Regardless of whether the wide-spread public interest in machine learning increases or decreases in the coming years, the increased capacities and public scrutiny of machine learning techniques provide an opportunity to reconsider the ideals and commitments underlying predominant and long-standing conceptions of knowledge in western philosophical and cultural traditions—the ideals, norms, practices, and virtues that help determine what counts as knowledge and what is mere information. Such a reconsideration need not necessarily contravene centuries of arguments that relate knowledge to individual mental states and enmesh it with human capacities. But it will show that unintelligibility and inscrutability—as epistemic anti-ideals—have a history that precedes machine learning. This history can help us better understand the ways in which knowledge—bound up not just in minds but also in media, technologies, practices, and institutions—always exceeds the capacity of any individual mind to possess it and fully account for it. Such a history will not only clarify basic epistemic ideals and norms, such as intelligibility; it will also help us imagine alternatives as we struggle to orient ourselves in our ever-evolving epistemic environments.

* * *

In the *Meno*, Socrates asks why knowledge is more valuable than "right opinion."[8] Even if right opinions happen to be true, they are not stable. They are like the statues of Daedalus, the ancient Greek craftsman who fashioned sculptures that, as legend had it, could move. Like the statues, right opinions, "are not worth much," Socrates says, "until one ties them down by (giving) an account of the reason why." Knowledge is right opinion that is fastened, grounded in a stable and clear relationship between a person who knows and some given reality or truth. Knowledge, so conceived, entails comprehension, intelligibility, and a level of certainty. In a world filled with the flux of sense impressions, images, and data, true knowledge provides a firm, reliable position. It requires reasons, justification, and, more broadly, a basis for trust.

In Socrates's account, it is the immortal soul's recollection of timeless forms that ties knowledge down, binding that soul with a reality more stable and lasting than any finite body. Although western philosophical traditions have long adopted, adapted, and rejected such a Platonic account, the basic notion that knowledge is primarily a personal and superior mental state has persisted.

From Aristotle to Aquinas, and from Locke to Kant, philosophers have tied real knowledge to individual minds, themselves generally unadorned by technologies and untouched by history. Knowledge, so understood, refers to a capacity to give reasons and to understand why. More contemporary philosophers focus on what they call the "subjective" side of knowledge, seeking to give accounts of the features, properties, and characteristics of this "highly valued state," knowledge, in which an individual person stands in relation to a given reality.[9] Despite continuous disputes and disagreements, key epistemic ideals have remained largely intact. To know, as Descartes put it in 1644, is to hold an idea or perception "very clearly and distinctly."[10] Whereas real knowledge is clear and distinct, false belief, opinion, intuition, or whatever a less-valued form of knowledge might be termed, are fuzzy, opaque, unintelligible—alien to human capacities to account for it.

Given the persistence of these epistemic ideals, what is to be made of deep neural or convolutional networks, algorithms with hidden layers whose outputs and the very steps to produce them are largely incomprehensible?[11] Even though humans have written (or at least copied and modified) the basic lines of code that constitute such machine learning algorithms and collected the training data upon which they rely, these algorithms combine ever more steps and inputs to produce outputs and behaviors that even their human designers cannot fully account for. It is becoming increasingly difficult, as Thomas Nickles puts it, "to give an account of why" they do what they do.[12]

Contemporary machine learning techniques raise the prospect of a kind of knowledge that cannot be accounted for in the way that Socrates argued was necessary to distinguish knowledge from right opinion. This seems to be the case, in particular, for the outputs of artificial neural networks (ANN), a broad set of widely used computational techniques loosely modeled on the neural structure of the human brain. Neural networks pass inputs (data sets) through a series of layers, each of which consists of processing units called neurons. Most ANNs are made up of three types of layers: input layers which receive the initial data, the hidden layers which extract or filter distinct sets of features from the input layers, and the output layers, which transfer information from the network to the outside world. As the name suggests, the hidden layers have no direct connection with the world outside the neural network. They perform their computations and transformations on the inputs, and thus produce their output from inputs from the neurons of the input layer.

It is the invisibility or hiddenness of these middle layers, where the neural network's filtering and extraction of features happens, that can make the outputs of ANNs seem opaque, inscrutable even to those who might know them best. Some critics might even deny such outputs the honorific "knowledge" and refer to them instead as *mere* information, data, or something else low on the epistemic hierarchy. If an intending knower can neither account nor take responsibility for it, then no human can claim it as her own—justified, stable, clear, distinct—belief. Real knowledge, it would seem, is always personal.

Yet, scholars and intellectuals have long relied on methods, protocols, techniques, media, and technologies to make their encounters and claims of knowledge communicable, visible, repeatable, reproducible, and navigable. Humans rely on tools and technologies not fully in their possession, not fully their own, and, oftentimes, not wholly transparent, in order to justify their opinions—in order to know. Algorithms, including the most complex of artificial neural networks, are the latest tools we use to model and know the world. The barriers to knowledge, then, may lie less with the impossibility of understanding our tools or the inscrutability of our methods and more with the complexity of the world and the finitude of human mental capacities.

From Knowing to Knowledge

Surveying the semantic shifts that "knowledge" (*Wissenschaft*) had undergone over the course of the eighteenth century, a long entry in Johann Adelung's

Dictionary of the German Language, a German multi-volume dictionary first published between 1774–1786 and then in a second edition between 1793–1801, describes a fundamental change in the conception of knowledge. At the beginning of the century, knowledge was used to describe a subjective "condition in which one knows something."[13] By 1800, however, knowledge had come to refer not only to a subjective state but to something objective, something existing beyond any one person— "general truths that were grounded in each other." The first, more "antiquated" definition of knowledge as "particular insight" or mental capacity had given way to another: knowledge as a relationship among ideas themselves and, more broadly, an increasingly distinct realm in which these ideas had taken form—in objects, systems, media, practices, and institutions. Over the course of the nineteenth century, this second notion of knowledge came to predominate, at least in German-speaking lands. Knowledge designated an objective domain that exceeded any one person's capacity to fully possess it. Knowledge was deeply—but not only—human.

In the Adelung entry, in which *Wissenschaft* was presented as the vernacular equivalent of *episteme* and *scientia*, the first definition accorded with a long philosophical tradition of defining knowledge as a personal state of true or justified belief. Consider some of the exemplary images of authoritative knowledge in the European tradition: Descartes's knowing *cogito* who thinks without books and erudition, equipped with only a method and clear and necessary ideas; Locke's individual knower confronting the flux of sense data with nothing but his own mental faculties; or Kant's critical subject who thinks with nothing but naturally endowed categories of understanding and the capacity to synthesize and schematize sensory input.

Each of these images, and the philosophical traditions that sustained and revised them, upheld epistemic self-reliance as the primary epistemic virtue.[14] The ideal of self-reliance and the image of the individual, often heroic, knower who usually accompanied it became acute as philosophers and intellectuals confronted a world they increasingly regarded as bereft of meaningful forms and a divinely guaranteed, rational order. The confidence and hope in a divinely and rationally organized world having waned, the flux and chaos of mere perception and sensory data had to be sifted and organized by human minds.

These shifts in "knowledge" were not simply semantic or philosophical. They point as well to a range of related efforts over the long eighteenth century, born of broader anxieties and anticipations, to reckon with a shared sense of material excess—the proliferation of print as well as observational and, eventually, experimental data. As knowledge came to constitute its own objective reality, scholars and scientists struggled to encounter, engage with, and make sense of an external world saturated with potential knowledge. While some celebrated the growth of this domain as a sure path to intellectual and social progress, others worried that it would soon outstrip human capacities to control and contain it. They worried about an inevitable gap between two types of knowledge: subjective and objective.

Skeptics described the newly emerging domain of supra-individual knowledge as a distinct world populated by printed things—which, in the second half of the eighteenth century, Johann Gottfried Herder called the "bibliographic Babel" and Novalis the "book world" (*Bücherwelt*)—and warned that it would soon overwhelm individual *cogitos* and minds. In 1750, Rousseau worried that knowledge had begun to outstrip human capacities and comprehension—a lament that would characterize anxieties about technological change to this day, even as the material forms and possible scales of more contemporary digital technologies have introduced new and different possibilities and concerns.[15] Similarly, Rousseau's best student, Immanuel Kant, warned in 1784 that "the book" had come "to think for us."[16] Humans had abdicated their obligation to think for themselves and, as Socrates had predicated in the *Phaedrus*, technical artifacts had come to think for them. The pervasiveness and force of these types of critiques in the final decades of the eighteenth century not only challenged the legitimacy of any extra-individual form of knowledge, they also upheld a distinct, if only implicit, anthropology: the ideal of humans without tools.

This late eighteenth-century anthropology incorporated earlier epistemic ideals rooted in *faculty psychology*, according to which different types of knowledge were ultimately grounded in the unity of the mental faculties. Adapting Bacon's map of learning in *The Advancement of Learning* (1605) and Ephraim Chambers's *Cyclopedia* (2 vols., published in 1728, with 2 supplement vols. in 1753), Diderot and D'Alembert's *Système Figuré*, published in their *Encyclopédie, ou dictionnaire raisonné des sciences, des arts et des métiers* (1751), mapped the three branches of knowledge to the three human mental faculties (memory, reason, and imagination). Even as knowledge branched out, it was rooted in mental faculties and a shared rational human capacity that allowed all humans to participate in the full flowering of knowledge.

Other scholars and intellectuals, in contrast, embraced the emergent objective domain of knowledge as a secularized space for self-realization, cultural meaning, and human belonging, calling it art, literature, religion—distinct domains of objective and subjective forms of knowledge. Decades before scholars such as Emile Durkheim and Max Weber described western modernity in terms of the differentiation of social spheres, A. W. Schlegel described literature as a distinct and aesthetically superior form of writing; Friedrich Schleiermacher described theology as a particular domain of knowledge about religious experience; and Friedrich August Wolf described philology as a science. Each of these was considered a distinct domain of knowledge with its own traditions, practices, and norms that allowed for human development or *Bildung*. By 1844, Karl Marx could hold up *Wissenschaft* as a space for freedom: "We must emancipate ourselves," he wrote, "before we can emancipate others." And the path to this freedom lay not in the old oppositions of religion— Christian and Jew—but rather in "critical, scholarly, human relationships [*Verhältnisse*]." Scholarship (*Wissenschaft*) was the "unity" through which the contradictions and illusions of metaphysics, morality, religions, and all other ideologies would be reconciled.[17]

Whether they embraced or feared these objective domains of knowledge, all scholars and intellectuals needed techniques and technologies for navigating, organizing, and searching them. If, as the article in Adelung's *Dictionary* contended, knowledge existed in an objective reality not reducible to individual minds, capacities, or propositions, then its authority and legitimacy could be wholly grounded in individual rational capacities. Furthermore, its transmission exceeded person-to-person exchanges. It had to assume some more public forms, forms that could be assessed and evaluated by a community of knowers. Objective reality was not only that with which an individual knower sought to relate; it was a reality with epistemic potential. As subjective knowledge became objective knowledge, the persona of the distinctly *modern* scholar began to include a capacity to devise and make good use of media through practices and techniques of searching.

Scholars, of course, had long sought to come to terms with the plenitude of information by managing it. Seeking to secure knowledge in the saeculum, early modern scholars developed elaborate note-taking strategies, maintained commonplace books, and formulated reference tools. In her study of how sixteenth-century scholars such as Conrad Gessner and Theodor Zwinger dealt with a prior era of information overload, Ann Blair contrasts information, those "discrete and small-sized items that have been removed from their original contexts," with knowledge, which implies "an independent knower."[18]

It was just this implication of an individual, presumably autonomous knower that nineteenth-century German scholars began to challenge. They transformed common anxieties about overload, surfeit, and proliferation—the ever-increasing material and media of knowledge from periodicals and books to astronomical observations and experimental results—into practical and communal projects for navigating, filtering, and searching the material of knowledge.[19] Scholars' practical need to orient themselves in the ever-expanding domains of knowledge, however, required not just search technologies and techniques but search practices, ideals, and virtues that could form the types of people who could use these tools and better engage with objective knowledge. However complex these domains became, knowledge and knower were never fully severed.[20]

The connections between knowledge and knower were hard won. Scholars developed and cultivated a crucial epistemic ideal: that the objectification of knowledge was also the process of making it common, shared, and universally communicable. Knowledge was not simply a private good or possession; it was a common and public good as well as an activity. Its creation and transmission required not just individual capacities, insights, and virtues; it also required social practices and virtues that bound individual knowers as scholars working together to sustain collective projects of knowledge.[21] The creation of new epistemic ideals also entailed anti-ideals. For knowledge to be legitimate, it had to be publicly searchable, and therefore could not be private. Knowledge that was not related to other knowledge was not knowledge at all; it was fanaticism, dogma, myth, prejudice—all the *epistemic idols* of modern knowledge.

Yet even as the ideals of the communicability, publicness, and sociality of knowledge became norms, the specter of its incommunicability and opacity remained. The emergence of *knowledge* as a distinct, self-regulating sphere made knowledge more public and accessible, but only for those with access to search technologies and educated in the practices, ideals, and virtues that sustained their right use. It entailed a divide between those who could access these objectified forms of knowledge and those who could not. The habits, cultures, and practices of scholarly and scientific search became key elements of a highly specialized, modern knowledge whose locus was the research university and related institutions that organized and sustained a distinct group of people, practices, and materials.

Yet few, if any, of the scholars and intellectuals who interacted within this objective domain of knowledge would have been able to give step-by-step, rule-based accounts of what they did. The practices, habits, techniques, and cultures that helped constitute knowledge were, in this sense, rarely fully transparent, intelligible, or universally accessible. The epistemic and social value that search tools, techniques, and practices acquired over the course of the late eighteenth and throughout the nineteenth century highlights the limits of publicness, transparency, and intelligibility as epistemic ideals. An unsearchable set of documents, a book not included in a bibliography, or an article with no citations referring to it amount to knowledge that effectively does not exist. What is not part of the whole of knowledge is not really knowledge at all. Whatever remains outside the whole has not been transformed, legitimated, and incorporated into the epistemic ecosystem. Whoever determines or defines the parameters of search—categories, keywords, techniques, and domains—determines what becomes visible as knowledge. Whoever shapes the conditions of access, manages the terms of search, and facilitates the movement of objects in such an environment, helps determine what can emerge as knowledge.

One of the scholars who best articulated and embodied these shifts in the concept and practice of modern, specialized knowledge was the German physiologist Hermann von Helmholtz (1821–1894), who not only made pioneering discoveries in human physiology and perception but also worked tirelessly to institutionalize knowledge as a collective and shared human enterprise. In 1862, Helmholtz addressed his faculty colleagues at the University of Heidelberg as their newly elected rector and told them that all German scholars faced the same challenge: a profusion of empirical facts. The proliferation of epistemic objects—material things that could be collected, organized, and then marshaled as evidence—had increased as the technologies and techniques for empirical observation had improved.[22] Classical philologists and comparative linguists as well as anatomists and zoologists were so "immersed" in facts that they could not "see anything beyond" the confines of their specialized disciplines. Whether in the form of epigraphic fragments from ancient objects, scattered notes in an archive, or newly collected plant specimens, the sheer stuff of scholarship had begun to make scholars "dizzy" (120).

After Hegel and amidst the rapid expansion of empirical practices and methods, "who," Helmholtz (122) asked his colleagues, would "be able to see the whole," to apprehend the unity of knowledge and maintain it as his personal mental possession? None of them individually, he argued matter-of-factly. There was simply too much to know.[23] In describing how a surfeit of "facts" becomes scholarship, Helmholtz also describes how objective reality (the fact of the world) is distilled into epistemic objects (data and information), which is then transformed into something called knowledge. He lays out a hierarchy according to which individual facts, data, and information are of lesser value than knowledge. For Helmholtz, knowledge (or *Wissenschaft*) is an honorific; it bestows not only a higher value on its referent but also entails norms and ideals about how people ought to regard it or dispose themselves to it.

One of these norms, for Helmholtz as for almost all nineteenth-century German, university-based scholars, was that no one person could account for the totality of knowledge. Helmholtz advised his Heidelberg colleagues to think of knowledge not as something to be held in an individual consciousness but rather as a collective endeavor to be participated in. It was a project sustained by a community of scholars over time. The unity of knowledge was as much an ethical and social project as it was an epistemological one. The task of scholars, philologists and physiologists alike was to develop the means, the media for rendering knowledge communicable across time and space, and to participate in the communities that sustained these media by embedding them in practices and orienting them to common ideals.[24]

In Helmholtz's account, modern knowledge existed in disciplinary domains, or *Fächer*, which balanced well-ordered objective material and well-formed subjective human capacities. Every discipline required both easily accessible and searchable material (lexica, indices, periodicals, encyclopedias) as well as distinctly human capacities (*Geistesfähigkeiten*) that had to be developed and strengthened through repeated exercise. Legitimate knowledge combined both aspects. The "external" or material organization ensured that even if knowledge could not be readily accounted for or recalled, it "could be found" by anyone at any moment.

Yet, wrote Helmholtz, knowledge could not remain "printed black on white."[25] It had to be taken up, encountered, remade, and transformed by scholars, both individually and collectively. Helmholtz described the knowledge embodied in material forms, from lexica to data sets, as resting in a "field" waiting to be cultivated. His metaphors for knowledge—earth, fields, planting, cultivating, tilling—describe an epistemic ecosystem in which knowledge emerges as the yield of an environment of human, nonhuman, and technological interactions. The task of scholars was to relate the material forms of knowledge—facts, evidence, and observations as transcribed and recorded—to each other and, crucially, to themselves. The material, external order of knowledge, he said, had to be "intellectually conquered."[26] Helmholtz had sketched many of the epistemic ideals that would come to define a distinctly *modern* knowledge: as an endless pursuit; as research; as always changing and constantly being remade; knowledge as never fully intelligible or accountable to any one person.

Google and the Limits of Knowing

How can these historical and theoretical accounts help us better understand what counts as authoritative knowledge today? Although the research universities that Helmholtz upheld as the key institutions of nineteenth-century knowledge continue to play a crucial role in our current epistemic and media environment, they increasingly do so alongside, or even at odds with, digital platforms and corporations, such as Google. Even as the trust and confidence of people across the globe in media, politicians, and universities steadily erodes as populist protests have grown, Americans, at least, continue to trust their search results.[27] And yet, Google's search algorithms remain fundamentally inscrutable, even if their training logics and search results are not.[28]

If eighteenth- and early nineteenth-century readers faced a surfeit of print, computer engineers and early users of the World Wide Web Project in the early and mid-1990s faced an exponential increase in the number of webpages. Two years after the World Wide Web Project began in 1991, there were only 130 websites. By the time Yahoo was founded in 1994, there were 2,739 websites. Four years later in 1998 when Google was founded, there were around 2,410,067 websites, and just two years later in 2000 over 17,000,000 websites. Today, in 2018, there are over 1.85 billion websites.[29]

The rapid growth of the WWW presented big challenges to the methods of early search engine companies—such as Lycos, Infoseek, AltaVista, and Yahoo—that were using automated crawlers to follow links, copy the pages, store them in an index, and then use human labor to create lists of keywords and associated websites. In their original paper outlining the "anatomy of a large scale hyper-textual Web search engine," Page and Brin proposed a different way of approaching the problem of search. They began from the insight that the web "was loosely based on the premise of citation and annotation— after all what is a link but a citation and what was the text describing that link but annotation."[30] They sought to create a model of the citational structure of the web as constituted by links among pages, and eventually developed a proprietary algorithm that modeled the links, not only the outgoing ones but also their backward paths, that constituted the web: PageRank.

The crucial distinction between Google PageRank and these first-generation web search engines was that Brin and Page had argued that the quality of a page was a function of its position within the network of webpages. What made a piece of information valuable was not the class or category to which it might belong, but rather the relationships it had to other pieces of information.

There is an important continuity between the print techniques and technologies developed over the eighteenth and nineteenth centuries and Google's early attempts "to organize the world's information." Both projects were premised on the idea that knowledge exceeded any personal mental state; it was presumed to exist independent of any one individual, embodied in printed objects or digital structures. For its first decade, Google's leaders and engineers imagined the world wide web and digital forms of knowledge in terms of print. Like their print predecessors who sought to organize the "world of books," Brin and Page sought to "brin[g] order to the web."[31]

And yet, Google PageRank can search only that which has already been linked to the web; its results are entirely imminent to the web's structure. And so, it values only that which has already been valued, that is, what has been linked to by other web pages. Because PageRank models the web, there will always be gaps in Google-knowledge. An unindexed website cannot be searched and, thus, given Google's near monopoly on search tools for the web, essentially does not exist.

Furthermore, the parameters of PageRank—every tweak, every adjustment, every added parameter to its basic algorithm—determine, in conjunction with any given search term, what websites are returned and their rank, and which ones are not. Just as those who defined and managed the parameters of nineteenth-century search technologies, those who manage Google's search engine help determine what counts as knowledge. These interventions are based on human decisions and actions that are rarely made public and are definitely not subject to public deliberation. They are the decisions of a corporation driven by capital interests.

In its first decade, Google showed little interest in content webpages. According to Google, epistemic authority or legitimacy was simply a function of the citation (link) graph of the web—the authority of a website corresponded to its popularity. Over the past decade, however, Google engineers and executives have gradually begun to discuss fundamental changes not only to its search algorithms but also to Google's evolving epistemic ideals. Google seems intent on becoming not just the organizer of "information" but the arbiter of knowledge. As one of its engineers blogged in 2012, Google was transforming itself from an "information engine" to a "knowledge engine." Frustrated by the "document-centric" character of PageRank, Google has recently sought to develop search technology that "liberates" data from documents and uses that data to create knowledge. One of its first public projects to attempt the creation of knowledge was Knol, a now defunct effort to establish a Google Wikipedia, an online encyclopedia of individually authored articles and essays.[32] Whereas PageRank legitimates a webpage by evaluating its position in the link network of the web, Knol legitimated a page by relating it to a particular person. Knol was based, that is, on a more traditional form of epistemic authority: people as worthy of trust and, thus, reliable sources upon which to justify beliefs. Such a belief is based on the reliability of a known author or authority, whose evidence and arguments can be tested and evaluated.

Although Google ultimately abandoned Knol, deleting it in 2012, the company continues to pursue the creation of knowledge over the *mere* organization of information. In a research paper published in 2015, a team of Google engineers presented a new search method that relies not on "exogenous signals" (links) but on "endogenous" ones (facts). In extracting "facts" and then evaluating websites based on the "correctness" of these facts, Google's engineers are attempting to determine the value or authority of a website based on factors or characteristics not imminent to the link graph structure of the web but on things given—facts—external to that structure. Such a process yields a trustworthiness score or, in Google talk, a *knowledge-based-trust* (KBT), that defines trustworthiness as the probability that a web source contains the correct "value for a fact."[33] This probability is largely determined by comparing an extracted "fact" to potentially similar ones collected in separate (Google owned) databases. Like Socrates's imperative to control the statues of Daedalus, Google is trying to tie down its knowledge by stabilizing its facts. But instead of tying knowledge to an immortal soul, a community of researchers, or a textual tradition, Google's engineers are tying it down to its ever-expanding collection of databases. Google's interest in *trustworthiness* exemplifies its effort not just to organize but to redefine what counts as knowledge. Instead of simply modeling the web's inherent link structure, so redolent of eighteenth- and nineteenth-century indexical print technologies, Google hopes that it might one day, as Brin put it, "understand," that it might in some sense "know."

Google's desire to transcend the document-centric web is a desire to liberate knowledge from the stubborn particularity of pages of texts and transcend the history of knowledge as the interaction of media, people, institutions, and practices, and not simply a subjective state or inert object. In a perhaps ironic historical twist in the history of knowledge, Google engineers are seeking a way of knowing that is purportedly less susceptible to the manipulations and desires of others, a way of knowing that is more stable and reliable. But what norms, practices, and values would orient this ostensible liberation of knowledge from texts? Who, as Helmholtz asked, sets the parameters and ends of search in a post-link epistemic environment?

* * *

Knowledge, writes the philosopher Linda Zagzebski, is "cognitive contact with reality."[34] Although philosophers have long focused on accounting for how such contact is possible through individual acts of intellection, any account of knowledge must also consider how such contact also requires complex relations of individual and communal or shared actions, capacities, and habits as well as their objects, technologies, and techniques. Conceiving of knowledge in these more environmental terms can help us better understand how knowledge becomes communicable, sharable, and, in some way, a common possession, not simply a personal state or belief. Doing so can also alert us to the ways in which knowledge is regulated, guarded, and controlled. Ultimately, it can help us understand knowledge as an emergent element of an epistemic ecosystem, in which the material objects of knowledge and the activities and people associated with them are coordinated.[35] Knowledge, so conceived, is not a property or evaluation of any one element—the status of a personal belief or the content of a text—but rather a good born of complex relations not always immediately intelligible and sometimes even inscrutable.

The prospect that machine learning might introduce a knowledge wholly inscrutable and alien to humans is an opportunity to reconsider our assumptions about reason, rationality, and knowledge.[36] Perhaps it is not only the inner layers of neural nets that are unintelligible, but also the norms governing how we learn, know, and orient ourselves in the world.

We need to understand better how knowledge, especially in our digital age, exceeds any individual person's capacity to justify a particular belief. The idealized individual knower, the figure of the autonomous epistemic subject—justified in her belief and capable of accounting for it—limits our understanding of the conditions of legitimate, authoritative knowledge. So too does the tendency among some media theorists to dismiss human capacities and distinctly human concerns and cares as vestiges of a romantic (or humanist or religious) ideology. Humans, both individually and as collectives, act and think in the world using their technologies, but they are not reducible to those technologies. The authority and legitimacy of knowledge is bound up not only with its material media but also with the character, capacities, and virtues of knowers who make their way in the world by means of these media.

Notes

1. Alon Halevy, Peter Norvig, and Fernando Pereira, "The Unreasonable Effectiveness of Data," *IEEE Intelligent Systems* (2009): 8–12.
2. Chris Anderson, "The End of Theory: The Data Deluge Makes the Scientific Method Obsolete," *Wired*, June 23, 2008.
3. Matthew L. Jones, "How We Became Instrumentalists (Again): Data Positivism Since World War II," *Historical Studies in the Natural Sciences* 48, no. 5 (November 2018): 673–84.
4. L. M. Sacasas, "The Allegory of the Cave for the Digital Age," The Frailest Thing, December 1, 2018, https://thefrailestthing.com/2018/12/01/the-allegory-of-the-cave-for-the-digital-age/.
5. For a largely enthusiastic account of the ubiquity of machine learning techniques, see Klaus Schwab, *The Fourth Industrial Revolution: What It Means and How to Respond*, https://www.weforum.org/about/the-fourth-industrial-revolution-by-klaus-schwab.
6. Hubert Dreyfus, *What Computers Still Can't Do* (Cambridge, MA: MIT Press, 1972). For the more recent critiques, see, for example, Ruha Benjamin, *Race After Technology: Abolitionist Tools for the New Jim Code* (Cambridge: Polity, 2019); Safiya Umoja Noble, *Algorithms of Oppression: How Search Engines Reinforce Racism* (New York: New York University Press, 2018).
7. Timnit Gebru, Jamie Morgenstern, Briana Vecchione, Jennifer Wortman Vaughan, et al., "Datasheets for Datasets," Preprint (March 23, 2018). See also Luciano Floridi, Josh Cowls, Monica Beltrametti, Raja Chatila, et al., "AI4People—an Ethical Framework for a Good AI Society: Opportunities, Principles, and Recommendations," *Minds and Machines*, November 26, 2018.
8. Plato, *Five Dialogues*, trans. G. M. A. Grube (Cambridge: Hackett, 1981), 85.
9. Linda Zagzebski, "What Is Knowledge?" in *The Blackwell Guide to Epistemology*, ed. John Greco and Ernest Sosa (Oxford: Blackwell, 1999), 92–116.
10. Descartes, *Meditations on First Philosophy*, in *The Philosophical Writings of Descartes*, vol. 2, trans. John Cottingham (Cambridge: Cambridge University Press, 2008), 1–62.
11. John Brockman, ed., *What to Think About Machines That Think* (New York: Harper Perennial, 2015).
12. Thomas Nickles, "Alien Reasoning: Is a Major Change in Scientific Research Underway?" *Topoi* (2018).
13. Johann Christoph Adelung, *Grammatisch-kritisches Wörterbuch der hochdeutschen Mundart* (Vienna: Bauer, 1811), 4:1582–83. For an extended discussion, see Chad Wellmon, *Organizing Enlightenment: Information Overload and the Invention of the Modern Research University* (Baltimore: Johns Hopkins University Press, 2015), 37–38.

14. See Linda Trinkaus Zagzebski, *Epistemic Authority: A Theory of Trust, Authority, and Autonomy in Belief* (New York: Oxford University Press, 2012).
15. Jean-Jacques Rousseau, *Discourse on the Sciences and the Arts, First Discourse*, in *The Social Contract and Discourses*, trans. G. D. H. Cole (London: Everyman, 1993).
16. Immanuel Kant, "Beantwortung der Frage: Was ist Aufklärung?" in *Gesammelte Schriften*, ed. the Königliche-preußischen Akademie der Wissenschaften, 29 vols. to date (Berlin: de Gruyter, 1902), 8:35.
17. Karl Marx and Friedrich Engels, Werke, "Zur Judenfrage" (Berlin: Karl Dietz Verlag, 1976), Band 1, 347–77, 349.
18. Ann Blair, *Too Much to Know: Managing Scholarly Information Before the Modern Age* (New Haven, CT: Yale University Press, 2010), 2.
19. Gygory Markus, "Changing Images of Science," *Thesis Eleven* 33, no. 1 (August 1992): 1–56.
20. Lorraine Daston and Peter Galison, *Objectivity* (New York: Zone, 2007), 375.
21. See Alex Csiszar, *The Scientific Journal: Authorship and the Politics of Knowledge in the Nineteenth Century* (Chicago: University of Chicago Press, 2018).
22. Hermann von Helmholtz, "Über das Verhältniss der Naturwissenschaften zur Gesammtheit der Wissenschaft," in *Vorträge und Reden*, 3d ed. (Brunswick: Friedrich Vieweg, 1884), 120, 122. Further citations included in the text.
23. For an important account of an earlier moment of felt excess, see Blair, *Too Much to Know*.
24. Lorraine Daston and Peter Galison, *Objectivity* (New York: Verso, 2010), 255.
25. Helmholtz, "Über das Verhältniss," 124.
26. Helmholtz, "Über das Verhältniss," 124.
27. Adam Epstein, "People Trust Google For Their News More Than Actual News," *Quartz*, January 18, 2016. https://qz.com/596956/people-trust-google-for-their-news-more-than-the-actual-news/.
28. See, for example, Noble, *Algorithms of Oppression*.
29. "Total Number of Websites," *Internet Live Stats*, http://www.internetlivestats.com/total-number-of-websites/#trend.
30. John Batelle, *The Search: How Google and Its Rivals Rewrote the Rules of Business and Transformed Our Culture* (New York: Portfolio, 2005), 72.
31. Sergey Brin and Lawrence Page, "The Anatomy of a Large-Scale Hypertextual Web Search Engine," *Computer Networks and ISDN Systems* 30 (1998): 107–77.
32. Udi Manber, "Encouraging People to Contribute," *Google Official Blog*, December 13, 2007, https://googleblog.blogspot.com/2007/12/encouraging-people-to-contribute.html.
33. Xin Luna Dong, Evgeniy Gabrilovich, Kevin Murphy, Van Dang, et al., "Knowledge-Based Trust: Estimating the Trustworthiness of Web Sources," *Proceedings of the VLDB Endowment* (2015).
34. Zagzebski, "What Is Knowledge," 92–116, 109.
35. Alex Csiszar, "Seriality and the Search for Order: Scientific Print and Its Problems During the Late Nineteenth Century," *History of Science* 48, nos. 3/4 (2010): 399–434.
36. For an accessible account of this concern and the formulation of "alien knowledge," see David Weinberger, "Our Machines Have Knowledge We'll Never Understand," *Wired*, April 17, 2018, https://www.wired.com/story/our-machines-now-have-knowledge-well-never-understand/.

NOISE

MATTHEW F. JORDAN

As long as people have been living in communities, they have been complaining about noise. Defined across the centuries as "unwanted sound," noise and its management have been a way to define our relationship to one another. Such ongoing conversations are fascinating, since "aural terms," writes Nick Couldry, have "advantages as a source of metaphors for thinking about the social world."[1] When we talk about consonance, harmonious sound, sound that is in harmony with our shared purpose or that supports our common ethos, we are talking about how people communicate and share space with one another effectively; talking about dissonance, on the other hand, allows us to describe and manage social anxiety about how noise and miscommunication drive us apart. Both express a great deal about the historically conditioned modes of listening that have emerged in our lifeworld.

Silence, understood as a noise-free "soundspace"—to borrow R. Murray Shafer's term—is only an idea, a relative state of acoustic consonance that falls within the socially constituted norms of acceptable or wanted sound.[2] Sound is a by-product of energy, and there is always energy in the world; so, even in an anechoic chamber, there is always sound. As Heidegger noted, "raw sound" or "pure noise"—sound without meaning—is an abstraction, since sound is always interpreted, our perception evidence that Dasein, or being-in-the-world, dwells alongside our sensations.[3] When we hear sound, our interpretation of it emerges from the flow of the recognizable and identifiable. That process, of listening, processing, and sorting sounds into categories is a complex form of consciousness that speaks to how our perception of the world is always the product of human action. A socially constructed sense of perception that Merleau-Ponty called "sensationalist prejudice"[4] is always driving the codes and the nuanced words—like clamor, racket or din—we use to describe the sounds that we come to interpret as noises invading our social world. Even our perception of "quietness," which we oppose to noise, is a socially constructed and historically contingent phenomenon.[5]

It follows that listening for, identifying, and categorizing noise has been a way for cultures to talk about communication and the social contract shaping our shared intersubjective soundspace. When we call something "noise," we constitute a normative notion of acceptable sound by placing it outside of our socially recognized norms. From our ongoing conversation about noise, a growing utilitarian discourse has issued about what we might do to mitigate or mediate our relationship to it, so as to bring our shared intersubjective space into consonance with our normative notion of acceptable sound. At first the answer was political: the first noise ordinances emerged amongst the ancient Greeks, when the council of Sybaris decreed that potters, tinsmiths, and craftsmen who banged on things for a living had to live outside the city walls. Knowing that relative "quietness" was important for the repose of citizens, Julius Caesar banned wagons in Roman streets when people were trying to sleep.[6] Noise, as Karin Bijsterveld has argued, has long been associated with social disruption,[7] yet the fluidity of the collective sense of what counts as noise speaks to the fine line between wanted and unwanted sound. Indeed, as cities and societies got bigger, the ongoing process of listening to and categorizing sound, of calling out the noise, calling for something to be done about it, became more complicated.

With the Industrial Revolution, the machines that brought social fantasies of progress, of faster production and quicker conquest of time and space, also brought with them an explosion of sounds that could not merely be talked away as a necessary by-product of modernity. Yet, as western culture applied its increasingly dominant form of instrumental reason to invent labor-saving machines that sped the plow of productivity and profit, the question of noise quickly shifted in social resonance. The political answers to problems were ceded to the engineers. R. Murray Schafer, as a pioneer of sound studies, argued that defining noise has always been about making sense of the relationship between permissible noise and the possession of technological power.[8] Industrial modernity brought with it the correlative association linking technological power, progress, and profit, and an increasingly hegemonic ideology that made noise—and most social problems for that matter—not an issue for the social body to deliberate and legislate, but rather a problem to be solved increasingly by the engineer through "better technology." Whereas critical reason applied to investigating the significance of sound or dominant modes of listening might deflect the ideology, turning over all problems to the engineer for solution only amplified the dominance of technological rationality as a cultural ideology.

James Carey has argued that the mythos of technological modernity was amplified by a quasi-religious cultural discourse, which promised a better future by way of engineering and technological progress.[9] By the end of the nineteenth century, whether it be from better architectural design on buildings to keep the noise out, or from using cotton- and sand-filled boxes over elevated railways to keep the noise in, technological fixes were increasingly seen as ways to manage the social problem of noise.

Nowhere was this "futurist ethos," as Carey called this increasingly hegemonic faith in a better engineered future, more powerful than in the realm of electricity and electrical technology. By the beginning of the twentieth century, a powerful ideological fantasy grounded in the "electrical sublime," a notion promoted endlessly by intellectuals, politicians, and advertisers, had emerged as a kind of secular theology.[10] The priests of this secular theology, the engineers, promised a future transformed by electricity and electrical power in which community and communication would be rebalanced. The world, as Samuel Morse prophesized as early as 1838, would be transformed into a harmonious global village, wired together by "nerves which are to diffuse, with the speed of thought, a knowledge of all that is occurring throughout the land, making, in fact, one neighborhood of the whole country."[11] Everywhere electrical technology was hailed as the means toward desired social change, the key to a future re-creation of human community.[12]

Though Robert Darton persuasively argues that "every age is an information age,"[13] what we have come to think of as our contemporary Information Age is supercharged with this fantasy of an "electronic sublime," an ethos directly wired to our teleological faith in technological progress enabled by the information-systems engineer and the coder. As more efficient and rationalized applications of electricity came to dominate our hopes for the future, so too did our thinking about sound and communication become wedded and wired with the electronic signal. Nowhere is this influence more audible than in discourse on information and noise.

Much of this discourse on how engineers would deal with unwanted sound in communication technology emerges from the early days of the telegraph and telephone, where engineers were listening for sounds of disturbance in these growing telecommunications systems, which, as John Durham Peters has noted, were early prototypes of the computer circuit.[14] Indeed, all kinds of early engineers were listening carefully to mechanical systems for sounds of inefficiency. Noise was a sign of wasted energy, an indication that something was wrong with the design. Karin Bijsterveld has noted that German automobile engineers, for example, taught both consumers and repairmen a complex vocabulary that corresponded to the different noises that one might hear in an automobile,[15] sounds that properly identified could aid in the diagnosis and repair of an inefficient machine. Over time, the automobile industry, through its engineers and its publicity bureaus, created a feedback loop that taught people a mode of listening that had emerged amongst telecommunications engineers. In journals like *Telephony*, engineers described problems that arose in a world increasingly connected by telecommunications systems, and the noises that corresponded to them. For example, one could hear " 'frying', cracking, and roaring noises" in the summer when communicating via the U.S. Forest Service telephone lines because high temperatures in summer created more entropy in the circuits.[16] Advertisements for the Monarch telephone touted "no noise or induction" and boasted that its engineers had solved the noise problem in the transmission of the signal. Electrical engineers described how noises tended to increase with the ever-increasing system-wide length of the circuit. One columnist in *Telephony* wrote, "We have a line which is very noisy at night. It begins at about noon and continues to get worse until about 10. Early in the morning the line is very quiet. As the day gets hotter it gets worse.... The noise does not sound like it is a ground, but is one clear pop almost continuously."[17] "Objectionable noises" in communications technology powered by the electronic signal could have many causes, but the solution had a singular aim: they could be eliminated through better design. For the engineer, listening for noise was an essential part of a process aimed at an ideal technologized future.

In the twentieth century, as "information" became one of the master tropes used to define and conceptualize the communications traffic between people, groups, and systems, noise has remained a durable metaphor, even as the modes of listening have shifted. The function of discourse on noise in information theory tells us much about the kinds of listening that have emerged and become dominant in our Information Age. Though what computer scientists and coders listen for and how they listen have changed, we still hear echoes of the same promise of a quieter world made possible by technology and the engineer. Noise cancelation products, smart homes, quiet cars, sound productivity or "ambient sound" apps and sleep aids are just some of the many applications of this original promise abundantly represented in the consumer world today.

Whereas early writing on electronic communication was charged with aural listening tropes that echoed age-old social debates about unwanted noise getting in the way of social consonance, "listening" has become more conceptual as the diagnostic field has moved from sound to mathematical data. Even so, the metaphorics of noise are still central to the engineering problem. Then, as now, the engineer aimed his thinking at the technological sublime, a fantasy-infused neutral medium where a message could be sent over vast distances without disturbance or entropy. A perfectly engineered system would, by definition, be a system without noise.

By the time the consequential texts of information theory were written by Claude Shannon, Warren Weaver, and their colleagues at the Bell Systems Laboratory, the function of noise as a trope for understanding efficiently engineered systems had become fixed. Indeed, in the modern communications theory inspired by the cybernetic ethos of Shannon, Weaver, Norbert Wiener, John von Neumann, and Alan Turing, the metaphorics of noise echoes throughout. Paradoxically, however, for the engineers, noise became increasingly associated with the visual. Always present was the wire as a visual and conceptual heuristic. Whatever the graphic might be, the "transmitter" moved toward the central term, a "channel," and ended up at a "receiver." Noise has always been understood and located in relation to the central term. In Shannon's influential article, "A Mathematical Theory of Communication," it was visualized as an external interference or obstacle in the otherwise linear transmission of message, an unwanted side effect to be excised or scrubbed away.[18]

In the years since, the linguistic frames of information theory have been pulled into a variety of interpretive hermeneutic traditions. As they have, the wire-based visual scheme has remained the dominant metaphor for communication, even when thinking about noise. According to this diagram, during transmission, the signal encounters "noise" from a third source or from the environment in general. The noise getting in the way of the reception of the signal must be diagnosed and eliminated. Crucially, in Shannon, the experience of signal noise was not a listening situation linked to social conversation about how to negotiate our shared intersubjective space; rather, it was a problem for the engineer to solve.

For the systems engineer, noise is a disruption in the statistical distribution of energy that confuses the act of intention and reception. Intrusive noise threatens reception by making it impossible to accurately determine the intent of the signal and to accurately re-present it. According to Jonathan Sterne, a similar fetish for a "noiseless" system has also dominated the engineering of sound

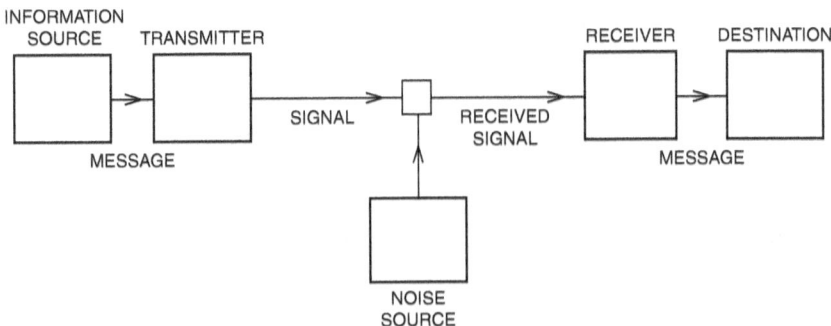

11.1 C. E. Shannon's schematic diagram of a general communication system.

reproduction technology, where perfect noiseless reproduction is the teleological desire of all technological innovation.[19] Importantly, it is the engineer who decides what counts as good sound in coding and designing components.[20] Yet, in both fields, the perfect communication system was always hypothetical, a heuristic concept; noise will always be present in any physical system, foiling perfect efficiency.

The Bell Systems lab mathematicians who set the parameters for information theory were less interested in sound-for-sound's sake. Rather, their writing, and those who followed them in this line of inquiry, indicated that sound was conceived as data points for the systems' sake. Shannon and Weaver, for example, argued that problems in the transmission of the signal, of the sending and receiving of information, create uncertainty, and "uncertainty which arises because of errors or because of the influence of noise is undesirable uncertainty."[21] They strove for "certainty" within the system; information theory, as such, has continued to be concerned with eliminating ambiguity in the interplay between the intention of the signal and its reception, eliminating the noise—read "uncertainty"— getting in the way of perfect efficiency. Importantly, "information," within Shannon and Weaver's model, is not the same as the content that would be perfectly received by the receiver. Indeed, in the mathematical model, information was directly proportional to the effect of entropy in the system. As Umberto Eco points out, Weaver makes it clear that "the word information . . . is used in a special sense that must not be confused with its ordinary usage. In particular, information must not be confused with meaning."[22] The communication system—and it follows noise—is always considered from a statistical perspective, and the performance of that system is never described in a phenomenological sense. Sound, energy, and noise are always understood as statistical data. Even Norbert Wiener, who knew that information could "say something," especially if it was different from what was expected in the "[c]ommunity's previous common stock of information," seemed unconcerned about the differences between information and meaning. Eco argues that this lack of concern is because Wiener, like Shannon and Weaver, was again exploring the *theoretical* power of a cybernetic electronic brain rather than exploring how human beings interpret meaning as emerging from a system, which will always, as there is always entropy in the physical world, include noise.

Shannon was quite clear that meaning was unimportant to such mathematical and statistical modeling of a noiseless channel:

> Frequently the messages have *meaning*; that is, they refer to or are correlated according to some system with certain physical or conceptual entities. These semantic aspects of communication are irrelevant to the engineering problem. The significant aspect is that the actual message is one selected from a set of

possible messages. The system must be designed to operate for each possible selection, not just the one which will actually be chosen since this is unknown at the time of design.[23]

The engineering question for information theory was always primarily about establishing an ever-more advantageous signal-to-noise ratio and for compensating for whatever signal disturbance existed within the system by creating code that added redundancy to counter-act the noise disturbance.

The emphasis on system efficiency and the de-emphasis on the ways in which meaning is interpreted by individuals receiving information from the system has not stopped social scientists from echoing the sender-wire-receiver metaphor. Roman Jakobson, for example, who knew Weaver through their mutual affiliation with the Rockefeller Foundation's Natural Sciences Division, began applying "integrated parallelism" to linguistics after reading a paper Weaver sent him. The way the Bell Systems scientists were analyzing sounds as discrete objects in the service of synthetizing speech intrigued him at a time when he was thinking about the meaning of phoneme sounds.[24] Similarly, Piaget applied information theory's metaphoric frames to his developmental theories of the system of perception. Claude Lévi-Strauss—Shannon's neighbor during the war—drew from information theory at a time when French structuralists were translating human meaning into mathematical formulae. As he developed a theory to conceptualize how "primitive cultures" circulated meaning, he began to talk about how the "entire process of human knowledge thus assumes the character of a closed system" that worked as a system of codes, messages, and relays.[25] Indeed, even while the scientific ethos came to dominate the study of humans and culture in the academy, information theory began exerting a powerful exogenous influence in thinking about communication phenomena across the humanities. Its tropes have even found their way into unlikely fields, such as literary studies, where thinkers like W. R. Paulson have taken to describing literature as a system. "Literature is a noisy transmission channel," which makes it richer in information because "noise can create complexity, can augment the total information of a system."[26]

Yet, as Robert Craig noted, much of this application has been grounded in a common error, a misreading of information theory as a theory of communication due to its powerful connection to the scientific and technological zeitgeist of the post-war era, a misreading symptomatic of the dominance of technocratic ideology in our lifeworld. "Shannon's mathematical theory of information (Shannon & Weaver, 1948), which communication scholars touted as evidence of their field's potential scientific status even though they had nothing whatever to do with creating it, often poorly understood it, and seldom found any real use for it in their research."[27] The persuasiveness of the rhetoric in the technocratic age led many scholars to submit their field to this

Procrustean bed. Nowhere is this application of information theory more problematic in the humanities than in the conception of noise and its impact on listening.

What is the mode of listening that information theory promotes in its focus on eliminating noise? The convenient assumption is that a message conveys unit information, and that this is what the listener should be trying to interpret. That is not how Shannon and Weaver conceived of it, however. Rather, in their mathematical modeling, they insisted that the concept of information applies not to the meaning of an individual message (a chunk of information sent and received) but rather to the situation as a whole. Avoiding the ambiguous power-infused nature of noise as a socially constructed phenomenon, where one communicator's message might well be another's noise, they limited themselves to perfecting the efficiency of the mediation machine at hand. Perhaps this is why Roman Jakobson, despite having borrowed from information theory to conceptualize the information contained in a linguistic unit of sound, never really made use of the concept of noise.

Rather than listening for *meaning* that is concealed by or contained in noise, computer scientists and mathematicians are "listening" for problems in the system, glitches or errors, that can be silenced or compensated for with better code.[28] Information theory's phenomenology of noise—and its mode of listening—is not motivated by concerns about our shared aural space, or our shared intersubjective world of sound; rather, it cultivates a kind of listening that is less social, less physical, and less material. It is statistical and conceptual. Importantly, in a lifeworld increasingly mediated by technology, faithful consumers are subjected to conditions of mediation increasingly dominated by this regime of engineer-listening, where sound is translated into data. As a result, our soundspace is increasingly determined by the engineers and coders who design the products we buy.

What might it imply if the engineers of today's digital platforms ignore social content as they listen for the glitches in the system to fix? After all, as Shannon wrote, "Semantic aspects of communication are irrelevant to the engineering problem."[29] Information—within the statistical models—relates to the *quantity* of what is sent, not the *quality* or sense of what is received, so it makes sense that the engineer is listening and accounting for statistical anomalies that get in the way of the maximum efficiency of the system. Though certainly these anomalies might also have sound, noise is increasingly used metaphorically rather than phenomenologically. Shannon and many of his Bell Lab colleagues attempted to define the amount of information from a semi-axiomatic point of view, studying the flow of information in the existing system and comparing it to an ideal "noiseless channel" or medium. Say one was engineering a "social network" like Facebook, whose system efficiency and profitability depended on being able to transmit messages from advertisers to the consumer.

From the engineer's, or coder's perspective, dissenting views or disturbance within the system would be defined as "noise." Working toward the ideal would mean filtering out the inefficiencies as noise, which is to say eliminating the very intersubjective differences which are intrinsic to pluralistic society.

In information theory, the efficiency of the whole, the system, is greater than the sum of its parts, so its mode of listening is always related to the efficiency of the system rather than to the meaning of a message. Systemic interference, or noise, is a sign of disturbance or error in the channel. "Noise-free" becomes a telos in theorem building, a mathematical ideal driving system design. The guiding spirit of information theory is hence Tayloristic: by listening for the presence or absence of noise and eliminating it, it is possible to approach the limits of efficiency.

Yet if entropy is commensurate with the drag of noise on the energy of the signal, then the amount of information contained in the signal is directly proportional to the amount of noise and entropy that the receiver encounters. In short, an information-rich communication situation is at odds with the engineering telos of maximum efficiency. This is where the heuristic orientation of information theory puts it at odds with most of the humanities disciplines that have applied its language. This misapplication was cultivated, in part, by Norbert Wiener. With his scientific teleology always firmly fixed in what *might be possible* if the perfect system was engineered, he declared, "we have decided to call the entire field of control and communication theory, whether in the machine or in the animal, by the name of cybernetics." From an ethical standpoint, listening to what a speaker is trying to say and listening for noise in a system represent very different modes of listening. The obligation of the engineer is not, as John Rawls might say, grounded in a moral "duty of civility," which implies a "willingness to listen to others."[30] In fact, the situational morality of engineer-listening involves avoiding this ethical obligation altogether by focusing narrowly on the modeling of the system.

In information theory, the two words "information" and "uncertainty," and one could say "noise," often serve the same function in mathematical modeling. *Meaning*, on the other hand, has an inverse correlation to information in the context of system design. As Weaver wrote, "One has the vague feeling that information and meaning may prove to be something like a pair of canonically conjugate variables in quantum theory, they being subject to some joint restriction that condemns a person to the sacrifice of the one as he insists on having much of the other."[31] Shannon implies that it is possible to communicate information at an ideal rate with utmost reliability in the presence of "noise," and engineers have applied statistical models that emphasize redundancy as a way to contribute to the intelligibility of the message in the presence of noise. Noise, however, remains a variable to be compensated for through better design that filters it out, or nullified by better code that builds in redundancy.

Paradoxically, engineering solutions to the problem of noise lead to an information-deprived system, because the more noise that exists within the communication situation, the more information it is said to contain. For the engineer and the coder, a noisy, information-rich system is an inefficient system, a problem to be fixed. Certainly, one sees the importance of listening for inefficiency in modeling as it applies to cyberwarfare, where hackers also scan for noise and systemic weakness. It is up to the engineer to eliminate systemic weakness to protect the integrity of the whole. For the coder trying to make a system more secure, the noise-probability matrix becomes a variable to be dealt with by way of encoding in discrete channels to account for it. In our technocratic age, which is over-determined by algorithmic coders looking to maximize the efficiency of the system, what we hear is increasingly dictated by the code.

In some ways, the coder is not unlike the everyday listener: there is an idea of an ideal "soundscape," a range of expected sound, that both entities would appeal to as a heuristic to identify noise. Yet the way they listen is worlds apart. The code designer's mode of listening, like the information-systems engineer, is machine mediated. Since the advent of decibel meters, engineers have used an ever-expanding range of finely tuned machines that "hear" sounds that people cannot, devices that translate sound into data points used to model system efficiency in relation to a "noiseless channel." Engineer-listening has a complex vocabulary of "noise" terms that circulate in the mathematical world of coders and system designers. More than descriptive of phenomenological sound, the taxonomy of engineer "noises" is related to Stochastic processes, describing numbers that fall outside the range of expectation in the models.

Some of the terms are overtly statistical. For example, "Gaussian noise" describes sound data with a normal distribution in the time domain and with an average time domain value of zero. It is a way of saying that the noise in the system is within a normal distribution, therefore not wholly unexpected. Other terms have an indexical relation to this. "Additive Gaussian noise," for instance, designates a statistical model designed to mimic the effect of random processes that might occur in nature. "Additive" here connotes noise that is beyond what is expected based on probability models.

Some noise terms used in information theory are closer to actual physical sounds. The term "burst noise," for example, describes a sound often heard in systems integrating semiconductors and ultra-thin gate oxide films. This sound, also called "popcorn noise," "impulse noise," "bi-stable noise," or "RTS noise," came to be recognized by engineers as a feature of diagnostic listening. Similarly, "thermal noise" (also known as Johnson-Nyquist noise) is a long-heard phenomenon related to the system circuitry being heated by the sun. The statistical modeling which emerges from this phenomenological listening accounts for the randomness of interference within the system, making the noise heard proportional to temperature.

Most noise terms used in engineer-listening, however, do not refer linguistically to sounds, but rather to optical phenomena; they are symptoms of the shift to machine-based listening. Information scientists writing equations and code to compensate for the disturbances within the system listen by way of technological mediation, through machines that translate energy into visible data. Noise comes to be understood through a plane of virtual mediation.[32] White noise, for example, is a product of the early analysis of television and radio reception and describes a signal that distributes uniform power and data points across all ranges of the spectrum channel. As expected, mathematical modeling also accounts for "Non-Gaussian White Noise," and "Additive White Gaussian noise."

"Flicker noise"—another sight-based virtual term—describes a type of low frequency disturbance that flickers between high-frequency and "flat-band" noise. It has an even Gaussian distribution and is time reversible. When translated into the simulated spectral densities as a function of its frequency through machine listening, this kind of noise (which has density proportional to $1/f$) is called "pink noise." Many other noises are registered for engineers as virtual optical phenomena via technologies of mediation and machine listening. These include "red noise," also sometimes called "brown noise" because of its statistical approximation of Brownian motion; "blue noise," a type of signal with minimal low-frequency components and no concentrated spikes in energy; "violet noise," a kind of differentiated white noise, that not only appears purple on the simulation machines, but is also similar to the acoustic "thermal noise" of water. The term "grey noise" describes random "white noise" subjected to a "psychoacoustic equal loudness curve," meaning that the sound phenomenon is perceived by everyday listeners to be equally loud at all frequencies, whereas humans often hear White noise as not-equally distributed because of our perceptual biases; the term "green noise" describes a signal that uses the mid-frequency components of white noise. At the extreme of noise coloration is "black noise," which is frequently used to describe the paradoxically "noisy" experience of "silence."

Just as noise for information-science engineers is increasingly perceived and comprehended through machines that translate sound into virtual colors, some noise—data about system interference—is used for designing and coding optical devices. "Shot noise," for example, modeled by a Poisson process, describes a disruptive signal originating from the discrete nature of an electrical charge. It is effectively a random occurrence, one that often appears in photon counting in optical devices. Giving a sense of what nonphenomenological engineer-listening has become, "shot noise" is a kind of data disturbance associated with the particle nature of light. This "noise" has no perceptual connection to our soundspace.

Though viewed as a problem for the system, noise is not always eliminated by the engineer. Sometimes more noise is added as part of the coding, a homeopathic remedy to the problem of systemic noise. "Dithering," for example, describes how noise is added to reduce overall noise in the bandwidth based on stochastic resonance. Usually, "blue noise" or "green noise" are added to mask noises that might make the signal too burdened with entropy or information to be receivable. Phase cancellation modeling, used in most noise cancelation technology, is based upon advances in psychoacoustics. It uses machine listening to eliminate the perception of unwanted sounds for the consumer by adding more noise, masking sounds that "cancel" the perceivable sound for the user. The problem of unwanted sound is managed and mitigated by code that adds sound to the system, creating so much information that the receiver can recognize nothing within the sound environment except what the coder wants them to hear.

System optimization is always the aim of the engineer. Noise is filtered out by design or accounted for in code. Yet a mode of listening behind the system design—one looking to eliminate noise or code for maximum redundancy to compensate for it—means, paradoxically, that systems might tend toward an increasingly information-deprived environment. If coding is about maximizing efficiency in our Taylorized information systems, then the coding of the web is increasingly a function of the monopoly application of information theory by the oligopolies that own them. The efficiencies are aimed toward the desired outcome of those who own the systems: maximizing profit. And as society becomes increasingly wired into these systems of mediation conditioned by the engineer, the future is ominous. Will the Information Age engineer show the same consequence-blind amoral rationality as the Cold War nuclear engineer?

In the digital era, as demonstrated by recent revelations about Cambridge Analytica's mercenary role in dumping dithering redundancies into the platform to amplify the efficiency of political messaging that targets the vulnerable, cyber warfare will be waged through "information dominance." This design is not anomalous to information theory, but the logical extension of its Tayloristic spirit. It should give scholars in the humanities pause. Noise, ever a problem to be eliminated in the service of maximizing the efficiency of the system or to be used to deafen the consumer to the existence of unwanted sound within that system, may be a feature that the humanities should attend to with more care. As Kate Lacey has argued, rather than forever striving to eliminate "unwanted sound" as part of our mode of "listening in," we should learn to "listen out."[33] Rather than always allowing an engineered lifeworld to cancel out the sounds that we are convinced are getting in the way of the efficiency of the system and our corresponding consumer fantasies, we should attend to the unwanted noises that the other might make. Allowing for contingent, unexpected, and, perhaps, unwanted sounds to enter our lifeworld and listening for what they mean without the aid of machine-driven mediation just might be the kind of listening we need to cultivate.

Notes

1. Nick Couldry, *Listening Beyond the Echoes: Media, Ethics, and Agency in an Uncertain World* (Boulder: Paradigm, 2006), 6.
2. R. Murray Shafer, *The Soundscape: Our Sonic Environment and the Tuning of the World* (New York: Simon and Schuster, 1993).
3. Martin Heidegger, *Being and Time*, trans. John Macquarrie and Edward Robinson (Oxford: Blackwell, 1962), 164.
4. Maurice Merleau-Ponty, *The Primacy of Perception: And Other Essays on Phenomenological Psychology, the Philosophy of Art, History and Politics* (Evanston, IL: Northwestern University Press, 1964), 134.
5. See Matthew F. Jordan, "Becoming Quiet: On Mediation, Noise Cancellation, and Commodity Quietness," in *Conditions of Mediation: Phenomenological Perspectives on Media*, ed. Tim Markham and Scott Rodgers (London: Peter Lang, 2017), 237–47.
6. Mike Goldsmith, *Discord: The Story of Noise* (Oxford: Oxford University Press, 2012).
7. Karin Bijsterveld, *Mechanical Sound: Technology, Culture and the Public Problems of Noise in the Twentieth Century* (Cambridge, MA: MIT Press, 2008), 34.
8. Bijsterveld, *Mechanical Sound*, 35.
9. James Carey, *Communication as Culture: Essays on Media and Society* (New York: Routledge, 2009).
10. Carey, *Communication as Culture*, 94.
11. Carey, *Communication as Culture*, 160.
12. Carey, *Communication as Culture*, 88.
13. Robert Darnton, "An Early Information Society: News and the Media in Eighteenth-Century Paris," *American Historical Review* 105, no. 1 (February 2000): 1–35.
14. John Durham Peters, "Technology and Ideology: The Case of the Telegraph Revisited," in *Thinking with James Carey: Essays on Communications, Transportation, History*, ed. Jeremy Packer and Craig Robertson (New York: Peter Lang, 2006), 137–56.
15. Karin Bijsterveld, Eefje Cleophas, Stefan Krebs, and Gijs Mom, *Sound and Safe: A History of Listening Behind the Wheel* (Oxford: Oxford University Press, 2014), 7.
16. "Practical Subjects-Discussions," *Telephony* (August 4, 1917): 32.
17. "Queries on Theory and Practice," *Telephony* (September 15, 1917): 33.
18. C. E. Shannon, "A Mathematical Theory of Communication," *Bell System Technical Journal* 27, no. 3 (July 1948): 381.
19. Jonathan Sterne, *The Audible Past: Cultural Origins of Sound Reproduction* (Durham, NC: Duke University Press, 2003).
20. Jonathan Sterne, *MP3: The Meaning of a Format* (Durham, NC: Duke University Press, 2012).
21. Warren Weaver, "Contributions to the Mathematical Theory of Communication," in Claude Shannon and Warren Weaver, *The Mathematical Theory of Communication* (Urbana: University of Illinois Press, 1949), 109.

22. Umberto Eco, *The Open Work* (Cambridge, MA: MIT Press, 1989), 57.
23. Shannon, "A Mathematical Theory of Communication," 379.
24. Bernard Dionysius Geoghegan, "From Information Theory to French Theory: Jakobson, Lévi-Strauss, and the Cybernetic Apparatus," *Critical Inquiry* 38, no. 1 (Autumn 2011): 105.
25. Claude Lévi-Strauss, *The Savage Mind* (Chicago: University of Chicago Press, 1962), 269.
26. W. R. Paulson, *The Noise of Culture: Literary Texts in a World of Information* (Ithaca: Cornell University Press, 1988), 73.
27. Robert T. Craig, "Communication Theory as Field," *Communication Theory* 9, no. 2 (May 1999): 141.
28. Peter Krapp, *Noise Channels: Glitches and Error in Digital Culture* (Minneapolis: University of Minnesota Press, 2011).
29. Shannon, "A Mathematical Theory of Communication," 379.
30. John Rawls, *Political Liberalism* (New York: Columbia University Press, 2005), 217.
31. Shannon and Weaver, *The Mathematical Theory of Communication*, 28.
32. Greg Hainge, *Noise Matters: Toward an Ontology of Noise* (London: Bloomsbury, 2013), 22.
33. Kate Lacey, *Listening Publics: The Politics and Experience of Listening in the Media Age* (London: Polity, 2013).

SCREEN

FRANCESCO CASETTI AND BERNARD
DIONYSIUS GEOGHEGAN

The Electronic Screen

Since the invention of radar in the 1940s, the electronic screen has stood out among the primary instruments used to establish and maintain the continuous flow of information between humans and complex machine systems. Indeed, with the rise of automatic information-based machinery in the twentieth century, the electronic screen (able to figure diverse forms of data in user-friendly formats) has become a—perhaps *the*—vital instrument for ensuring real-time bidirectional and recursive communication between humans and machines. More than merely "representing" information to a user, however, the modern electronic screen maintains flows among diverse bodies and spaces. Television screens network a nation, producing national identities and sustaining community across vast distances.[1] Mobile screens on smart phones allow individual users to interact in real-time with information systems distributed in spaces, maintaining instantaneous communication with friends, databases, colleagues, and the like. Thanks to the figurative power of the screen, diverse and abstract flows gain a user-friendly quality that permits immediate human participation and feedback with digital systems. Social media platforms such as Facebook and Twitter are impressive systems for collecting and disseminating data; yet, their ability to do so depends on the visual interfaces and glowing screens that enable users to participate in real-time communications with the platform. In short, the electronic screen represents information systems, to be sure, but more importantly than that it *articulates* these systems. It produces a human-machine digital synthesis that cuts across spaces, audiences, bodies, and components.

Radar

Many of the key functions of electronic screens can be found in the history of the radar screen. With the introduction of technologies including high-speed flight, vastly more powerful artillery, and underwater ships into modern warfare, the classical frontiers of battling armies disappeared. Suddenly battles took place deep within a territory, without warning, as munitions travelled at distances and speeds that outpaced standard human perception. As early as the 1910s, engineers of war devised new families of information processing systems for predicting the locations of enemies and their munitions, for example at sea, as well as primitive visualization technologies that translated machine calculations into user-friendly displays.[2] As the speed of war accelerated and information systems—particularly those involving computers—grew increasingly complex, the need for dynamic screens that would allow humans to monitor and steer the work of these systems grew. In the 1940s, this led to the deployment of radar screens as the first widely used electronic visualization devices purpose-built for allowing human users to provide real-time feedback to information systems. Consider the celebrated SCR-584 automated radar defense system deployed in the V-1 raids on England in the 1950s. Depending on its exact configuration, an SCR-584 setup included not only an apparatus emitting and receiving radio waves but also computers, antiartillery weaponry, the soldiers in the field manning the antiartillery devices, and humans in a shed capable of sorting signal from noise in radar signals displayed on a screen.[3] The screen had less to do with displaying the internal operations of the machine than with providing an intelligible representation of space on which human operators acted as a link for regulating the flow of information across the whole system. The electronic screen opened the machine to the human user and joined the aptitudes of the human users—discretion, judgment, experience, intuition—with the mathematical operations of the machine. The result was the production of a new kind of information system as well as new kinds of hybrid spaces whose dimensions related to the human-machine assemblages (radars, tanks, planes, maps, military command structures, etc.) operating within them.

Not until the 1950s did early forms of the modern computer screen begin taking shape. The American SAGE (semi-automatic ground environment) missile defense system, deployed in the late 1950s, implemented the first use of screens with digital computers on a large-scale basis.[4] In a complex chain of radar and other defense systems distributed along the American coast, hundreds of screens displayed to human operators a real-time image of airspace provided by computers and supplemented by vast databases of preplanned flight information. Computers did much of the work of tracking and targeting the enemy, but the screens enabled teams of humans to get an overview of this work and provide vital feedback to the machine. For a brief time in the 1980s and 1990s, the work of the screen in coordinating bodies and spaces, and providing real-time feedback to systems, was overshadowed by the rise of non-networked personal computing. The Macs and PCs of this period seemed like solitary machines that simply showed an individual user the state of play in a game, or text in word processing. Yet in government and industry, computers often remained the backbone of collaborative patterns of work, with screens providing the instrument for ensuring the constant flow of information across bodies and spaces. The rise of the World Wide Web in the '90s and the subsequent proliferation of smart mobile devices, however, re-emphasized the role of the screen in articulating information systems across diverse bodies and spaces.

Which Screen's Archaeology?

In this filiation from radar to the electronic screen, where can we accommodate the traditional magic lantern or cinema screens? Do we have to conceive of two different lineages, one for the screens that support flows, the other for screens that simply display images? There is a recurring tendency to split the screen's history, as if the emergence of the electronic screen had started a totally new screen family. Our suggestion, instead, is to adopt a wider perspective: if we want to trace a reliable screen archaeology, we must go beyond the today-so-usual connectivity; moreover, we must go beyond the electronic format, and even beyond the visibility that seemingly monopolizes the human senses in the screens of today. Screens enjoy a long history in which diverse kinds of information have played different roles and elicited different forms of action.

For example, screens have not always been optical devices. Since the fifteenth century, the English word *screen*, as well as the French *écran*, the Italian *schermo*, and the German *Schirm*, has denoted objects that perform functions other than supporting a projected representation. A screen was a contrivance for warding off the heat of a fire or a draft of air; a partition of wood or stone dividing a room or building in two parts; a wall thrown out in front of a building to mask the façade; a tactical deployment of soldiers to conceal the movement of an army; or an apparatus used in the sifting of grain and coal. It was a filter, a divide, a shelter, a camouflage. These functions underscored not so much the optical qualities of a screen as its environmental character—its nature as a prop to be used within and in relation to a space. The primacy of the optical character of the screen only emerged in the first decades of the nineteenth century, when the word started to designate the surfaces supporting images generated by media like microscopes and the phantasmagoria.[5] In the latter, for example, a transparent cloth was aimed at hiding the projector located in the rear, while at the same time hosting its images: the cloth was called "screen" because of its role as a filter and camouflage; once its predominant role as a surface or support for images came to the fore, the word "screen" came to primarily denote an optical device—a meaning soon extended to other dispositives (a la Deleuze) based on a projection, like the magic lantern. At the end of the nineteenth century, cinema endorsed the primacy of the visual connotation of the word.

The current explosion of digital screens lends a new currency to the old and seemingly antiquated meanings of the word *screen*. Digital and social media expand the functions of screens beyond the optical. Surveillance cameras provide protection and defense from the outside. In retrieving information, computers sift (or filter and "screen") data according to the needs of users. Hand-held devices help to create a bubble in which users can find intimacy and refuge even in public spaces. Global Positioning Systems parse territory and identify right and wrong routes. Interfaces underline a separation between different worlds and keep a door open between them. Pixelated media-façades envelop entire buildings and hide them from view. Screens have become, once again, filters, shelters, divides, and camouflage. They remain surfaces that display images and data, and yet their opticality is deeply rooted in their spatial and environmental conditions.

How may we better grasp the connotations of these multiple screens, and the back and forth between them? And, more generally, how may we conceive of a screen archeology which bears witness at once to screens' multiple ways of working and to their possible commonality?

Becoming-Screen

A good starting point is the fact that we can't delineate a screen "as such," as if it were a freestanding and self-contained device existing independent of its context. The screens of the SCR-584 or the SAGE missile defense system are only meaningful and effective insofar as they link together the operations and actors of the information systems to which they belong. The same holds for the screen of a cinema, whose function becomes apparent only in connection with a projector, an audience, and a space intended for immersion into real and imaginary worlds. A screen becomes a screen only when inserted in a dispositive—or better put, an assemblage, to use Deleuze's term[6]—and when connected with a set of practices that produce it as a screen. Screen's nature either as a display or a shelter or a filter, as well as its orientation either toward the optical or toward the environmental can consequently be read in connection with the emergence of certain kinds of assemblages, respectively aimed at intercepting, directing, and entertaining the gaze, or at arranging space so that it becomes more functional and/or safe. The screen is a function of these assemblages—its performance or role being tied not to its substance or its physicality, but to its affordance and its availability. It is not by chance that in early cinema there are many fixtures that can function as a screen, from glass surfaces to white walls, and from translucent surfaces to canvases.[7] If they become a screen it is because they fit an overall design and support a set of operations.

What matters is not the being but rather the becoming of the screen. In this process of *becoming-screen*, there are no clear preconditions. All we have is the coalescence of a set of elements, which converge to perform certain functions, and to fulfill certain goals, putting the ensemble of elements to work in a new manner. No doubt that social needs, as well as a technology's internal development, play some part in this emergence. Yet, the playground on which an assemblage performs its action or envisions its goals, does not *primarily* respond to these external factors, but finds its characterization at the moment in which the assemblage surfaces. This is true for all dispositives—and it is also true for screen dispositives. The early twentieth century silver screen of cinema, the interactive computer screen associated with American radar defense (i.e., SAGE), and the mobile screen of the cell phone allied with complex geospatial functions are not so much "invented" to serve this or that need as they are the organic result of a certain number of pressures and affordances within which a certain screen became possible and desirable. The screen, then, is not clearly the invention of an individual or an inventor but rather something that emerges as the event of an entire network of habits, practices, instruments, lines of technical development, and so on. The screen is an index of an assemblage, and the assemblage is the necessary context in which a screen can surface and display its affordances.

The birth of an assemblage is not necessarily the final stage of a teleological course of development: it looks much more like a "big bang" from which a new universe of opportunities and relations surfaces. The metaphor of the "big bang" underlines the idea that the constitution of an assemblage implies not causality but *contingency* and *conjuncture*. On the one hand, it is something which "happens"—it is an "event." We can express the same idea by saying that an assemblage is something that "emerges" within a field of possibilities and circumstances: something that was potentially there suddenly materializes, with its fixtures, its dispositions, and its operations. The becoming-screen, as well as its orientation towards the optical or the environmental, has the quality of an *emergence*.[8] On the other hand, an emergence is always an *emergency*: it responds to urgency. In this sense, we cannot exclude the presence of active forces that exert a certain pressure on the constitution of an assemblage—or, better, that help it to happen. These forces may also lead the device in one direction or another: the screen's optical turn likely had to do with the political and economic interests that in early modernity favored visual data—and more in general the processes of "visualization," to use Bruno Latour's word.[9] The current environmental re-orientation of screens (dreams of ubiquitous computing, the proliferation of interfaces from gas pumps to the backs of airplane seats, and the insistent association of these screens with GPS-enabled techniques) likely responds to the needs of a society that, obsessed more by control than discipline, as Gilles Deleuze would say,[10] finds itself ill-at-ease with the surveillance of both macro- and micro-territories. In the same vein, we cannot exclude the presence of a project in a proper sense—the obsession of an individual, or research by a company—that pushes for the creation of an assemblage. After all, devices deal also with patents and copyrights. Yet the possible reasons that underpinned the emergence of an assemblage can be detected only after the fact. Which means that, post facto, we recognize as preconditions to the screen something that the assemblage itself helped define. These preconditions were not present as such until the birth—or the rebirth[11]—of the assemblage; it is the assemblage's emergence—or its resurgence in a new instantiation—that unfolds these preconditions and produces this or that screen as such.

This peculiar dynamic between the screen and its assemblage troubles the effort to write its history, for the identification of what causes the emergence of an assemblage is an effect of its emergence. It is what happens later that shapes our detection of what there was before. This is equally true for the precursor of an assemblage. The pre- is a consequence of what comes after: a precinematic screen or a predigital screen does not exist without the advent of cinema or digital technologies. Media philologists have to keep this principle in mind if they want to escape some of the usual pitfalls of media archaeologies: a purely chronological order of facts, a causal explication of the events, and a teleological interpretation of the innovations.[12] Put in other terms, a historical account must be grounded not on an idea of a simple past, but on an idea of an anterior future: paraphrasing Roland Barthes, "something has been" because "something will be."[13] Indeed, it is because of the triumph of optical machines that we can retrace the screen's complicity with the processes of visualization; and it is because of the recent emergence of environmental implications that we now look back at the screen's original meanings. The idea of an independent "it was" is baseless.

Finally, a big bang not only retro-acts on its potential preconditions and precursors to a screen: it also pro-acts on the context in which a dispositive would work. The constitution of an assemblage as an effect of contingent conjunctions defines or redefines the general framework that orients our perception of the world: it elicits conceptual oppositions not yet shaped, convergences between elements not yet conceived, new relevance, and new colors and shades. Consequently, a new conceptual articulation comes to the fore. It was not by chance that in the history of screens, the advent of the new optical media redefined the forms and implications of opticality in the eighteenth and nineteenth centuries, and in the same way the increasing presence of a great number of environmental media today reshapes the idea of environment anew. The emergence of an assemblage is the emergence of a cognitive map. Such a map can last for a long time, especially in periods of transition, and can apply to incipient dispositives: in the mid-nineteenth century, the magic lantern was associated with the microscope, because of their common concern with the creation of "magnified" images. A new map would be accepted in coincidence with the full social recognition of a new assemblage. The becoming-screen takes place in a complex ontogenetic process.

The Phantasmagoria vs. Panorama

An example—even though roughly cut and sharply summarized—could help. Let's think of two contemporary and competing dispositives: the panorama and the phantasmagoria. Born in the late 18th century,[14] both these dispositives responded to the same urge: they intercepted and mobilized an emerging need for exposition and exposure, as well as for privatization and discipline, in an age in which visuality was blooming.[15] At the same time, the phantasmagoria and the panorama shared the same basic configuration: they both provided a spectacle that was offered to a gathered audience in a dedicated interior space and was based on impermanent images hosted on a permanent support—respectively a transparent cloth on which slides were projected and a wall on which a temporary canvas was hung. .

Despite these similarities, the panorama and the phantasmagoria are deeply contrasted in their roots and in their orientation. The panorama resumed representational techniques activated by frescoes, landscape watercolors, and military sketches. It entailed the use of perspective, and consequently it recalled the camera obscura; it also practiced an unframed depiction of a scene (whose potential model was Baciccia's ceiling in the baroque Chiesa del Gesù in Rome), and large formats. The phantasmagoria, by contrast, drew from the magic lantern and the fascination of projected images; it enacted a composite spectacle, in which the wonders of nature complemented the charm of the magic, and where the spectators' reactions were part of the show. Hence, two different arrangements emerge from seemingly similar assemblages—and, consequently, two diverse accents were placed upon the image supports, with the screen of the phantasmagoria becoming a key element, and the wall of the panorama remaining a mere functional component.

Such a contrast in the dispositives' arrangements was redoubled by a contrast in their ideological purposes. The panorama staged an appropriation of the world and a celebration of history. It moved within a culture of empire, with its obsession for a territory that has to be conquered and protected in order to make possible the circulation of commodities and the extraction of resources. Hence, it became a representation that brought certain visions to the fore of attention while repressing others. It allowed some images (the celebration of industrial and military deeds) and obstructed others (e.g., perspectives of the colonial other), through a set of operations that included (among others) the exhibition of data, spectacularization of landscapes, and a complexity of point of view. The phantasmagoria enacted a different set of screening dynamics. Through the projection of images of ghosts, or the spectral reinterpretation of contemporary events, it put spectators into *contact* with the kingdom of the dead and ultimately with the uncanny aspects of the surrounding reality, going beyond merely *representing* them. It did not simply move within a culture of magic: the intense and provoking show, with images that were moving, growing, and shrinking, aroused audiences' emotions; spectators were facing their own fears and desires. In this sense, the constant check of the audience's reactions by the projectionist-conjurer worked as a sort of "screen test." In a way, the panorama enacted geopolitical expansion while the phantasmagoria dealt with spiritual entities, an emotional bond, and ultimately a sort of transcendental network. The former was a political machine, aimed at preserving historical memories and at exploring the physical reality; the latter was a psychoanalytical one, engaged with the spectators' "inner world."

With the panorama and the phantasmagoria, we have two different tracks toward the optical, two different legacies to which to refer, and two different types of instances to be heralded and embodied. The concurrent emergence of these assemblages provides two conceptual maps through which to read the past and the present, and consequently two divergent frameworks in which a screen operates, the one entrenched into the history of visual representation, the other open to a logic of connectivity. These maps would endure through the entirety of the nineteenth century, establishing distinctions as well as complementarity. It was the advent of film that would rearticulate these maps and seemingly bring visuality to its climax.

Cinema

Within the screen-based media, cinema is undoubtedly a canonical case study. Indeed, film perfected the transformation of the screen into an optical device. Cinema's silver screen was the emblem of a tool totally devoted to the spectatorial gaze. Not by chance, classical film theory considered the screen not only at the service of moving images, but also ready to disappear behind them—incurring in this way a true paradox, since it often assigned the status of reality to a representation made of shadow and light, and denied materiality to a prop made of real fabric. Yet, while fully acquiring an optical status, film's screen did not lose its previous environmental resonances. In film theory it is also possible to find thinkers who recall the original meanings of the word. For example, a consideration of silver screen as a *filter* that allows the fictional events to pour into the film theatre is recursive in many novels, but also in the critical notes of a writer like Joseph Roth,[16] and it is central in one of the last texts by Sergei Eisenstein, devoted to stereoscopy.[17] A definition of the silver screen as a *divide* that separates the fictional world and the world of the everyday is heralded by the Filmology movement, in particular by Albert Michotte who speaks of a "segregation of spaces."[18] The idea that the silver screen is a sort of *shelter* emerges in some film reviews of the 1920s and 1930s, which make fun of the fact that adventure movies and exotic documentaries are screened in comfortable film theatres that allow spectators to feel protected. The image of a shelter is also evoked with political implications by Siegfried Kracauer[19] in his description of the salaried masses as "homeless," and it would find its ultimate instantiation in Stanley Cavell's considerations that at the movies spectators are "absent" to the fiction, and consequently not as "exposed" to events as real witnesses are.[20] Finally, the main thesis of the so-called Apparatus theory is that the silver screen, in displaying an image close to the real, hides the only reality which matters, its mode of production: in this sense it works as *camouflage*.[21]

This body of scattered but not whispered statements helps us to capture a sometimes-forgotten process. Assemblages tend to preserve a sort of "memory" of their past. The smartphone, even though voice calls are now just one of its functions—and not necessarily the most important one—is still called *phone*. In many assemblages, these old functions are manifested by their components that migrated to the new device from a previous one. This is the case of a printer connected with my computer that allows the latter to produce a real printed text, and not only virtual writing. These old functions generally constitute a sort of remainder: in the new assemblage they represent a point of dissipation, if not of disturbance. And yet they give a sort of "thickness" to the new assemblage: they provide ways of working that for the moment must be kept in reserve, but that can also be considered as a possible or even a prospective use of the dispositive. The old functions are still there, even if on standby; the new assemblage can activate them when necessary. This retention of the past enables a medium to carry within itself other potential media, ready to emerge or re-emerge when contingent circumstances and an active conjuncture make it possible. In the cinema, when the screen recalls its old functions, as it does in the film theories that we have mentioned, the potential medium that resides in its folds can come to the surface. Indeed, these theories disclose cinema's concealed undergirding: if at the moment it is a quintessential visual art, it is also a constitutively environmental medium.

The Screen's Future

The analytical framework offered by our example enables us to reconsider the current flourishing of screens. Their environmental connotations, which we have underscored at the very beginning of this text, represent a discontinuity, but not an antagonistic break with respect to the optical. In the screens' history, the environmental and the optical orientations not only alternated, but also coexisted in the same dispositive. As cinema demonstrates, optical screens always retained the full memory of their previous environmental functions in the form of a potentiality ready to surface. This lets us return to cinema its rightful share: its multifaceted nature provides a relevant background from which new media, more inclined towards the environmental, can emerge. Many of the contemporary artworks, and in particular installations inspired by film and exploring the allocation of screens in space by artists like Christian Marclay or Douglas Gordon, perfectly understand this derivation.[22] At the same time, our counter-genealogy of the movie screen authorizes an extension of media archaeology beyond its usual borders into a broader and necessarily interdisciplinary project. If not only film, but every medium is able to hold potential media in its folds, there are no exclusive lineages: "ancestors" come from everywhere. Consequently, while it is correct to find specific archaeological threads for the contemporary media—for example, radar as a predecessor of the computer screen—it is more appropriate to take into consideration the wider processes of deterritorialization and reterritorialization that ground an assemblage.[23] Media archaeology becomes an open field. The screen never was exclusively optical, and opticality was never exclusively located in a few specific media; in the same vein, it never worked as a mere display, and instead was always entrusted with some form of connectivity and flow. This would be equally true for the current screens: in light of their emergence today, we must also look at their own potentialities, and detect their own hidden sides.

Notes

1. For two takes on the role of television screens in producing real-time communities across distances, see Raymond Williams, *Television: Technology and Cultural Form* (New York: Schocken, 1974); and Mary Ann Doane, "Information, Crisis, Catastrophe," in *New Media, Old Media: A History and Theory Reader*, ed. Wendy Hui Kyong Chun and Thomas Keenan (New York: Routledge, 2006), 251–64.
2. David A. Mindell, *Between Human and Machine: Feedback, Control, and Computing Before Cybernetics* (Baltimore: Johns Hopkins University Press, 2002), 30–33.
3. Mindell, *Between Human and Machine*, 248–59.
4. For more on SAGE, see Paul N. Edwards, *The Closed World: Computers and the Politics of Discourse in Cold War America* (Cambridge, MA: MIT Press, 1996), 75–112.

5. Among the early uses of the word "screen" with optical connotations, see Henry Baker who, in *The Microscope Made Easy* (London: Doldsley, 1744), 23, 25–26, speaks of a "screen" and a "paper screen" on which the magnified image appears. For the Phantasmagoria, see two notices referring to the patent granted to Paul de Philipsthal on January 26, 1802, respectively published in *Cobbett's Political Register* (London: Cox and Baylis, 1802), 2:1053, and in the *Monthly Magazine* 87 (June 1802): 488. The two reports read "transparent screen," while, quite curiously, the text of the patent published a few months before in *The Repertory of Arts and Manufactures*, vol. 16 (London: Nichols, 1802), 303–5, reads "transparent body."
6. On the concept of assemblage, which translates the French term *agencement*, see Gilles Deleuze, "What Is a *Dispositif*?" in *Two Regimes of Madness: Texts and Interviews, 1975–1995* (New York: Semiotext(e), 2006), 338–48.
7. *Richardson's Handbook of Projection* (New York: Chalmers, 1923): 226–33.
8. On emergence, and emergence as an event, see Michel Foucault, "Nietzsche, Genealogy, History," in *Language, Counter-Memory, Practice: Selected Essays and Interviews*, ed. D. F. Bouchard (Ithaca: Cornell University Press, 1977), 139–64.
9. Bruno Latour, "Visualization and Cognition: Thinking with Eyes and Hands," *Knowledge and Society* 6 (1986): 1–40.
10. Gilles Deleuze, "Postscript on the Societies of Control," *October* 59 (Winter, 1992), 3–7.
11. In the process of media change, we can consider the birth of a dispositive as a process that includes different steps and is open to different dispositives' instantiations. For cinema, a persuasive analysis in André Gaudreault and Philippe Marion, "A Medium Is Always Born Twice . . .," *Early Popular Visual Culture* 3, no. 1 (May 2005): 3–15.
12. The same concern is expressed by Thomas Elsaesser, *Film History as Media Archaeology—Tracking Digital Cinema* (Amsterdam: Amsterdam University Press, 2016).
13. Roland Barthes, *Camera Lucida: Reflections on Photography*, trans. Richard Howard (New York: Hill and Wang, 1981): 38–39.
14. Robert Barker's Panorama boomed in London in 1792, after a first attempt in Edinburgh, where his patent was filed in 1787; Paul Philidor's Phantasmagoria opened in Paris also in 1792, even though it was for only a few months (Etienne-Gaspard Robert, known as Robertson, would provide a more stable show at the Pavillon de l'Echiquier in 1798, and in the cloister of the Couvent des Capucines the following year). On Panorama's history, see Stephan Oettermann, *The Panorama: History of a Mass Medium*, trans. Deborah Lucas Schneider (New York: Zone, 1997). On Phantasmagoria's history, see Laurent Mannoni, *The Great Art of Light and Shadow: Archaeology of Cinema* (Exeter: University of Exeter Press, 2000); and Mervyn Heard, *Phantasmagoria: The Secret Life of the Magic Lantern* (Hastings, UK: Projection Box, 2006).
15. On the visual culture toward the end of the eighteenth century and the beginning of the nineteenth century, see Jonathan Crary, "Géricault, the Panorama, and Sites of Reality in the Early Nineteenth Century," *Grey Room*, no. 9 (Autumn 2002): 5–25.
16. Joseph Roth, "Ein Kino im Hafen," in *Drei Sensationen und zwei Katastrophen: Feuilletons zur Welt des Kinos*, ed. Helmut Peschina and Rainer-Joachim Siegel (Göttingen: Wallstein, 2014); or *Frankfurter Zeitung*, November 4, 1925. See also Joseph Roth, *Antichrist* (Amsterdam: Albert de Lange, 1934).
17. Sergei Eisenstein, "About Stereoscopic Cinema," *Penguin Film Review* 8 (1949): 35–45.
18. A[lbert] Michotte, "Le Caractère de 'réalité' des projections cinématographiques," *Revue Internationale de Filmologie* 3–4 (October 1948): 249–61.

19. Siegfried Kracauer, *Die Angestellten: Aus dem neusten Deutschland* (Frankfurt: Societats Verlag, 1930), serial publication in *Frankfurter Zeitung*, 1929.
20. Stanley Cavell, *The World Viewed: Enlarged Edition* (Cambridge, MA: Harvard University Press, 1979), 24.
21. Jean-Louis Baudry, "Ideological Effects of the Basic Cinematographic Apparatus," in *Narrative, Apparatus, Ideology*, ed. Philip Rosen (New York: Columbia University Press, 1986), 286–98, and see "Cinéma: *effets idéologiques* produits par l'appareil de base," *Cinéthique* 7–8 (1970): 1–8.
22. For a wide exploration of screen installations, see Giuliana Bruno, *Surface: Matters of Aesthetics, Materiality, and Media* (Chicago: University of Chicago Press, 2014).
23. On the process of de- and reterritorialization, see Gilles Deleuze and Felix Guattari, *Anti-Oedipus: Capitalism and Schizophrenia* (New York: Viking, 1977).

SEARCH

DAVID L. MARSHALL

In this chapter, I hope to indicate that contemporary search technologies are linked to older intellectual traditions, rhetoric chief among them. Working back through search engines and search areas to search arts, I connect contemporary algorithmic topic modeling to the ancient Greco-Roman art of topics. Drawing on the work of the cultural historian Robin Bernstein, I end with a very brief summative reading of an often-white-supremacist topos known as "Topsy," a character from Harriet Beecher Stowe's *Uncle Tom's Cabin*. As a keyword in Google Images, "Topsy" continues to call up a remarkably tight set of results, but the topos also exemplifies a series of very precise and important cultural processes. In order to understand what these processes are, and how they are linked to Topsy, we need to work through several discourses.

Search Engines

The basic situation of an engine like Google Search is quite remarkable. Constantly crawling the web, downloading a version of it, identifying the parts to be updated most frequently, generating searchable inverted indexes from the downloaded information, mapping that world of data onto search queries from users, choosing retrieval models with Boolean or probabilistic modes of determining relevance, optimizing results on the basis of user behavior, constructing and updating models of both individual users and topics that organize relations among searchable terms—all of this infrastructure is to be built so that any given user will wait no more than, say, a second for results.[1]

To some, internet-based search is a form of democracy. Every user becomes an enfranchised citizen. Using is voting, because clicking is endorsing. Famously, one of the original competitive advantages for Google Search was its incorporation of linking into PageRank, as if pointing to another webpage were a form of voting for it. Sergey Brin and Larry Page, the founders of Google, projected a kind of statisticalized democracy when they spoke in 1998 of this link metric in terms of a "random surfer." The metaphor of "surfing" may now be dated, but the logic of the stipulation holds: "the probability that the random surfer visits a page is its PageRank."[2] In the long term, the page linked to by many other pages is a more likely landing site if one pursues a relentlessly random click-through practice.

We can complicate the association of search with democracy in various ways. In the previous paragraph, it was assumed that all parts of the web are connected at least to some degree and that the web is not so "Balkanized" that the starting point of one's random click-through trial would skew the results. Mutual citation or closed circuits of citation—the "link exchange network" or the "link farm"—present fundamental challenges to the desire to see a citation as a vote.[3] In such schemes, one is not so much casting one's vote as bartering it or manufacturing it in order to rig an election. As deployed in these discourses, "democracy" is input optimization. The desire is to make all interaction countable. We must understand, though, that input-optimization here entails a clarification of the stakes of the click only for the vote-counters. There is no corollary presumption that voters themselves should be told clearly when they are voting or for what. After all, when one clicks on an image, one is voting not for "it" but instead for the various ways in which it has been rendered machine-readable.

Beyond the technical "hows" of the search engine and the contested status of clicking as voting, search raises a raft of properly metaphysical issues about basic presuppositions. The knowable is at stake: desire that takes Google as its object is the reinvention of an older "desire for a universal index or library."[4] Presentness is newly palpable: Google's agglomeration mechanisms affect our sense of the contemporary by providing metrics on "the trending"—via "zeitgeist" (now "trends"). Desire becomes countable: "the trending" itself is now widely dispersed both as a category and as an experience, but it emerges out of what in 2005 John Battelle memorably called "the Database of Intentions."[5] Search establishes a database of intentions because, when I search, I am often looking to do something in the near future. Further in this direction, we have "providence" as "foresight" and nothing other than "the Church of Google." The notion is that Google is our best approximation of God: omniscient, omnipresent, potentially immortal, infinite, all-remembering, omnibenevolent, and so on.[6] These issues are so basic that they defy categorization.

Beyond these metaphysical issues, there is a critical politics of the algorithm that challenges the democratic gloss of the click as a vote. In Adrian Chen's paraphrase of Joy Buolamwini's point, "just as the male gaze sees the world on its own terms, as a place made for men's pleasure, the coded gaze sees everything according to the data sets on which its creators trained it."[7] Trevor Paglen reports that in 2016 a deep learning network trained on the ImageNet dataset routinely misread Manet's *Olympia* as a burrito. It would read the Manet as a "burrito" modeled on the Mission-style San Francisco burrito. Why? Because the Bay Area is a place where algorithms are born.[8] Voting requires counting, which requires classifying, and it is impossible to agree with Barbara Cassin when she says that "the algorithm as such is not a rhetoric; it is only a means of classifying."[9] Classificatory terms have rhetorical effects when they structure fields of sensitivity to input.

In 2015, for example, Google's "photo application . . . automatically tagged African Americans as 'apes' and 'animals.'"[10] Classification is intrinsically political, but search engine models do not err simply because their base samples are misleading. Classification is also political in the sense that it continually involves making decisions about whether, in a particular case, it is the counting mechanism or the input that is, for example, racist. "Yes, the structure of our engine has contributed to that result," one can say, or "No, if you don't like the result, don't shoot the messenger."[11] To be sure, the essence of an algorithm will be its automatic application of rule procedures, and algorithms do work on algorithms optimizing them in an essentially rule-bound manner. Nevertheless, as Annette Vee attests, "algorithms are constantly being tweaked by the companies in charge of them, sometimes amid loud protests from users."[12] Garry Kasparov cried foul when he suspected programmers of intervening mid-match when he was playing the IBM chess computer Deep Blue. In the "game" of search, however, the technicians are continually at work under the hood.

The politics of search algorithms is inseparable from their political economy. As Safiya Noble relays, when a search for "black girls" suggests a pornographic site as a first result, we should not see this as the marker of some democratic internet majority that has been looking for sexual content when conducting this search. Why not? Because that result has been monetized in ways both obvious and subtle by Adwords, and by a variety of search engine optimization practices.[13] There is an economy in which words like "mesothelioma" are expensive.[14] In response to Google, Cassin says that "Europe needs a search engine that does not depend on a search engine from elsewhere." She misses the deeper point that is articulated forcefully by Noble: "what we need are public search engine alternatives . . . to ensure that the public has access to the highest quality information possible."[15] The argument is that public funding of search engines would be a necessary but not sufficient condition for anything approaching a "democracy of clicks." We do not need to protect European cultural forms from Google-led American cultural imperialism. We need to protect search from monetization in an era during which, as Trevor Paglen says, "smaller and smaller moments of human life are being transformed into capital."[16] Monetizing the click is a miracle of capitalist miniaturization.

There is a political economy of algorithmic classification, but there is also a politics of unsupervised topic modeling, in which the world is purportedly sorted into kinds that are invisible to, as it were, the naked eye. Supervised topic modeling is the process of mimicking classifications that are intuitive to human beings (or at least conventional in a given culture). An algorithm can aim to automate this kind of differentiation. Unsupervised topic modeling is the process of using the distant reading capabilities of algorithms to generate topics that did not previously exist. As David Mimno points out, "manually curated subject headings," the subject headings curated by the Library of Congress, for example, "have been in development for centuries."[17] Such work is "expensive, fraught with political and philosophical conflicts, and prone to obsolescence," he goes on to say, so why not automate the production of topics?[18] Automating the generation of topics constitutes an algorithmic transformation of *sensus communis*. The Latin phrase specifies not only a knowledge of what others know but also a sensitivity to how others may react to a particular prompt. Computationally generated topics organize the common points of reference to which a community refers. As Facebook demonstrates in a thousand ways, shared orientations may be a blessing or a curse.

Search itself is intimately concerned with topic modeling. Here, we have what has come to be called the "cluster hypothesis"—namely, the hypothesis that "closely associated documents tend to be relevant to the same requests," where "closely associated" is understood in terms of topics qua keyword "distributions over a vocabulary."[19] One can generate topics by identifying the word least likely to be used in the vicinity of a given anchor word, by making that least likely word a second anchor word, and by replicating this procedure to identify further anchors.[20] And one can specify that "a good summary term should be both distinctive specifically to one topic and probable in that topic."[21] One can work top-down with a divisive clustering algorithm starting with all instances in one topic or bottom-up with an agglomerative clustering algorithm assuming initially that each instance is its own topic.[22] One can adopt a k-means cluster mode of analysis that stipulates how many topics one should end up with at the end of the sorting process.[23] Once topics have been constituted algorithmically in these ways, the question can be, "What has the algorithm 'seen,' in the course of its agglomerations, and should we attend to seeing that too?"

Search Areas

The contemporary experience of search is paradoxical: we search for ordinary things, but the hidden and costly apparatus of search is extraordinary. The banalization of search covers over a closely associated phenomenon—namely, exploration. Many of the processes developed to improve search engines are also used in a variety of fields to explore spaces of possibility. Music and dance are two such fields. Developing user profiles on the basis of data obtained during querying and exploring results is one way that corporations have commoditized search. Without losing sight of this political economy, we may also add that user profiles are descriptions of personal style. What will this kind of person do next?

Tailoring search results to the querier as well as the query does run the risk of generating what Eli Pariser famously termed "filter bubbles" (where algorithmic predictions of one's tastes diminish the "info-diversity" of one's environment), but these approximations of style can rejuvenate not only one's own creative practice but also one's ability to listen and respond to the creative performances of others. Eitan Wilf is investigating precisely this kind of sensitivity when he conducts ethnographies of jazz musicians interacting with a marimba-playing robot named Shimon developed by a team at Georgia Tech. Like some other computationally generated jazz, Shimon has used Markov chains modeled from the repertoires of past jazz greats. Markov chains are a statistical method of constructing and weighting possibility spaces around particular sequences. In the corpus of performances called "Charlie Parker," for instance, what array of continuations attaches to the note sequence "A, B?" As Wilf explains it, Shimon is good at generating the conditions of possibility for greater creativity in listening because the robot produces music by combining different styles—say, one third Thelonious Monk, one third John Coltrane, and one third a musician interacting with Shimon in real time. Wilf understands this hybridization in direct analogy to an observation made by Pariser in relation to filter bubbles: "Google or Facebook could place a slider bar running from 'only stuff I like' to 'stuff other people like that I'll probably hate' at the top of search results and the News Feed, allowing users to set their own balance between tight personalization and a more diverse [or contrarian] informational flow."[24] In the context of jazz improvisation, Wilf understands this cross-pollination of styles in terms of a "training ground" dedicated to the cultivation of "basic dimensions of human agency."[25] These training grounds are "contextually meaningful" in the sense that they make it possible to specify a search domain in the vicinity of what one takes to be particularly interesting performances.[26]

Eitan Wilf focuses on how we can construct dialogue spaces of listening and being listened to, but is this move transferable to other domains? In dance, this might be a kinaesthetic dialogue with an algorithmic approximation of oneself. Here, "search" takes the form of exploring a possibility space of motions. The dancer, choreographer, and computer programmer Sarah Fdili Alaoui has been using motion-capture technology to generate real-time interactions between dancers and algorithmically generated stylizations of their motion. Partnered with projections on a screen, one dances with an algorithmically modulated remix of oneself. The result is a dialogical space, dubbed "Double Skin, Double Mind" (DS/DM). By mimicking my movements, DS/DM enters into dialogue with me and replicates my dancerly habits. Because it uses a variety of transformation rules for such input, however, DS/DM can also model or suggest ways of developing habitual positions with continuations that I have not yet explored.[27]

We see the connection between search and the construction of personalized possibility spaces very clearly in the famous "notecases" (*Zettelkästen*) of the German systems theorist Niklas Luhmann. In the notecases, having a matrix of previous thoughts literally at one's fingertips is part of a communicative process in which writing and thinking become symbiotic. The analogy with Fdili Alaoui's DS/DM is provisionally confirmed: just as DS/DM explores the "kinesphere" (defined by Rudolf Laban as "the individual area that the body is moving within"), so Luhmann emphasized the importance of constructing a notecard system that would always be within the "reach" (*Reichweite*) of the seated thinker.[28] These notecases were very simple: notecards each with a line or so (sometimes quoted, often composed), stored in old-school card catalog drawers, organized loosely by very general topic with a place fixed by number for each notecard, augmentable at any point by means of numerical interpolation, indexed by a separate subject catalogue, and networked by means of cross-referencing. Cross-referencing is linking. It materializes sequences of "next" or "previous" or "concomitant" thoughts, and the progressive articulation of these cross-references constructs something akin to the possibility spaces just discussed in relation to music and dance. In Luhmann's case, the playing partner is one's past self. Importantly, "the notecases need a number of years to achieve a critical mass." To excavate a rich space of possibilities, the notecases have to incorporate alternatives and become, as it were, a garden of forking paths. They reach critical mass when one has laid down potential tracks for one's thoughts in a quantity that is large enough to generate both a sense of alternatives and a sense that one cannot remember everything that ensues if one goes down any given path.[29] Cross-references are inserted intentionally at a piecemeal level, but over time the amalgam of cross-references issuing from or pointing to a particular notecard constitutes a tissue of thoughts that had no single external guide and is more appropriately thought of as an autopoetically emergent topos.

When Luhmann's notecases were included in an exhibition at the Kunsthalle Bielefeld in 2015, the overarching thematic was "serendipity," and we can understand this association of search with chance in terms of browsing. To browse the notecases was to turn oneself over to chance proximities between notecards in the midst of a curated space. Librarians often find themselves thinking about this connection between curation and serendipity. As the American physicist, Philip M. Morse, put it in 1970, "browsing may be defined as a search, hopefully serendipitous."[30] Chance may be harnessed by meandering in places where the odds of a happy find are good. According to Morse, "the librarian should arrange ... collections so as to be obviously differentiable," so that each user has a better than average chance of selecting a happy hunting ground.[31] With her coauthors, Kate Joranson—a librarian at the University of Pittsburgh—has argued that "'discovery' is best understood as a complex interplay between both searching and browsing," even as these two latter terms "have become conflated in the library literature."[32] One searches with key terms in a variety of fields; one browses in spaces that have been curated ahead of time by others. The "shelves" one browses—whether digital or physical—may be designed for general users, or they may be curated with particular users in mind. The point is that, once again, we may understand the library as a possibility space, where the curation of collocation arranges proximities.

Philip Morse's foundational paper on browsing as a mode of search advocated for the curation of subject areas because he thought this would increase the chances of productive browsing, but ironically this article was itself the product of a transposition from one subject area to another. Morse explained that "search theory was developed in World War II in connection with antisubmarine warfare."[33] As he presents it, naval tactics of finding were then transposed into libraries. This transposition raises the question of whether subject divisions may be understood not simply as preparations for browsing but also as means to the end of analogy-driven search and discovery *between* domains. One builds the silo in order to opportunistically overcome it later. Of course, these domains are not only the subject headings maintained by the Library of Congress but also the departments that slice and dice academic inquiry into what seem like more manageable fields in modern research universities.

We are once again dealing with search when we ask ourselves whether there are computational aids that might assist in discovering analogies. This question informs work by Christian Schunn and others on a discovery architecture called OpenIDEO. OpenIDEO is an online platform for the sharing and selection of solutions to queries such as "How can we manage e-waste & discarded electronics to safeguard human health & protect our environment?"[34] The platform includes a field in which proposers indicate where their idea came from. Deploying the kinds of topic modeling discussed earlier, Schunn and his fellow researchers use this field to develop a metric for the distance traversed by an idea from source domain to target domain. Against those who emphasize—and *desire* to emphasize—the ingeniousness of the far-fetched comparison, Schunn et al. conclude that there is such a thing as "too far afield" when it comes to analogies. They hypothesize that "a computational design tool that could find analogies in the 'sweet spot' [between too close and too far] ... could be exceedingly helpful to facilitating the practical use of the design-by-analogy method."[35] Search provides options; search by analogy can too.

Search Arts

I have made two points: we should attend to the search areas that contemporary search engines bring into being via automated classification and clustering; and the exploration of these search areas are forms of creativity extending across a large number of domains, from music and dance to intellectual invention itself. I now want to add a third claim: there are earlier search arts that help us understand the cultural processes at work here. I am thinking of rhetorical *artes topica*. These arts have registered important intuitions about what takes place in search areas and about how the search area is itself progressively elaborated by transformation rules working on earlier discoveries within the area. That sounds quite abstract. Let me explain. There are seven key steps here.

First, search engines cluster topics in order to tailor results to queries, and we can see this process in action in the computational perspicacity recently developed on the corpus of images that the art historian and art theorist Aby Warburg (1866–1929) collected in his unfinished final project, the *Bilderatlas Mnemosyne*. In this "atlas," Warburg arranged images, mostly from European high art traditions, into particular zones of affective intensity that he termed "pathos formulas." Pathos formulas are representations of bodies seized by passion that circulate and become recognizable codes in particular visual cultures. Many but not all of the figures in the image atlas exhibit pathos formulas. Leonardo Impett, a digital humanities scholar, has asked whether we can operationalize Warburg's pathos formulas by specifying machine-readable descriptions that function as search terms. That is, can we reenact a Warburgian gaze computationally? To quantify the pathos formulas, Impett and his collaborators manually transcribed stick-figure skeletons from the image atlas. These skeletons marked angles between head and spine, shoulder and upper arm, upper arm and lower arm, spine and upper leg, upper leg and lower leg. These measurements became the data from which clusters could be elicited. Using a k-means clustering algorithm set at sixteen, Impett has had success differentiating pathos formulas from nonpathos formulas. About four-fifths of the pathos formulas are located within the first of the sixteen computationally generated clusters, and the remaining fifth is adjacent. As yet, he has not succeeded in reenacting computationally the Warburgian differentiation of pathos formulas into kinds.[36] Perhaps Warburg's subclassifications cannot be replicated because they specify nothing real. Or perhaps Warburg's individual image tables were dedicated not to the agglomeration of similars, but rather to the setting out of extremes within a particular emotional constellation.

Second, Impett's investigation of Warburg's pathos formula does not yet understand the image atlas as a collection of search areas in which creative work can be done. Elsewhere, I have explored the search area of Table 52 in some detail. This table identifies a topos called "the ethical inversion of victor affect." In effect, the search area of Table 52 is a results page for the query, "What are the various ways in which one can put a public face on either winning or losing?" One can explore the distances between poses. One can examine the difference between the form of loss that is mute and the form that is vocalized, for instance, when the opening of a mouth implies the addition of vocal utterance to gesture. To transform the results page into a search area, we can treat individual images as combinable into, for example, potential Markov chains that begin but do not end animated sequences.[37]

Third, we should understand search areas as zones of creative work in relation to what Giambattista Vico called "sensory topics" (*topica sensibile*). A sensory topos gathers tokens of a type and proposes their compatibility. Alongside "the ethical inversion of victor affect," the name "Achilles" is a good example of a sensory topos. Vico was saying that topoi were zones of shared sensitivity to the registration of new detail. For Vico, Homer was not an individual poet but rather the proper name of an orally transmitted storage structure for small acts of innovation executed by a dispersed collective of unnamed rhapsodic performers. Achilles may have originated in a moment when an act of courage became conspicuous and was registered in cultural memory. Nevertheless, for Vico, this node only really became Achilles when someone added the detail that this character was motivated to public acts of courage by merely private grievances. The confabulation of Achilles was simply the emergent product of piecemeal sutures attaching new and sometimes transformative details to the *Iliad* cycle of Achilles material.

Fourth, search arts can make sense of creative practices in search areas such as Achilles. Crucial here are the transformation rules facilitating the discovery of variations within the possibility space of a search area. Vico discussed Achilles in the context of his "poetic logic," which made arguments about the tropic engines of thought. Tropic substitutions that were metaphoric, synecdochic, metonymic, and ironic in form drove thought. These tropes were transformation rules operating within sensory topoi such as Achilles. Do you wish to discover further stories within the Achilles topos? Then look for addenda in the zones marked similarity, part-whole, cause-effect, and contradiction. Create a substory in which Achilles's acts of courage are the opposite of what they seem, not public and noble but private and ignoble—irony. Weave this contradiction into the Achilles topos by describing these ignoble acts as effects of causes such as humiliation or retribution—metonymy.[38]

Fifth, we can connect early modern practices of commonplacing such as Vico's with ancient practices of articulating topoi not as particular arguments but as areas in which certain forms of argumentation can be found. Commonplacing was a predominantly early modern practice of excerpting quotable lines from original contexts, storing them under variously organized subject headings, and keeping them ready for deployment in a variety of cento-poem-like genres. In his *De Copia* (first published in 1512), Erasmus cast commonplacing as an alternative to an older art of topics. This older art described *forms* of argumentation. Erasmus was channeling that older art when he reported that "arguments are in general derived from definition, from description, from etymology, which is a kind or species of definition, from those things that pertain to the nature of definition: class, species, peculiarity, differences, partition, division ...; from the introduction of similes and *dissimilia*; from contraries, contradictions, consequences; from relatives, causes, events; from comparison, which is threefold, the greater, the lesser, the equal."[39] Erasmus attributed this *ars topica* to Aristotle and Boethius, Cicero and Quintilian—a simplification. He added, simply but epochally, "most powerful for proof, and therefore for copia, is the force of *exempla*, which the Greeks called *paradeigmata*."[40] We see here a certain narrowing of the frame for topical search and accumulation arts.

Sixth, as the tropic transformation rules in Vico's sensory topics discovered new plot arcs for Achilles, so attention to forms of argument can uncover new arguments in the search area of an early modern commonplace file. With no knowledge of modern search engines, Aristotle understood the importance of a name as a search vector. "We must define the kinds of categories in which ... are found" the modes of predication that are definition (*oros*), property (*idion*), genus (*genos*), and accident (*symbebekos*), he said in the *Topics*. Those categories can be listed as "essence, quantity, quality, relation, place, time, position, state, activity, passivity."[41] These categories are places in which to find arguments, but they are also ways of changing subject-predicate relations by distinguishing a phenomenon in various ways. Topical categories are modes of exploring relations between subject and predicate. One may take an appearance as a definition, as the manifestation of a distinguishing but not defining mark, as one of many similar appearances, and as the exhibition of aspects of a phenomenon that are entirely immaterial to its essence.

Seventh, there is a de-essentializing politics at work when we distinguish a subject from its predicates, but this is part of a broader process of discerning new names. From this, we learn that naming is deeply related to the project of perspicacious de-essentializing. The appearance that is its own definition seems glorious, and there have been thinkers—Heidegger is one—for whom such appearances are moments in which beauty coincides with truth. A captivating appearance seems to name without remainder. But this is a trap. Warburg himself was suspicious of the appearance that purported to function as its own definition. His image tables were so many machines for exercising a capacity to resist associations between, for instance, the appearance of Mussolini and, for instance, the definition of leadership. The appropriate response to "name-fixation" of this kind is not less naming but more. Warburg's image tables were birthplaces of names, because they constituted search areas in which to discern not only the provisional definitions of affective intensities but also the provisionality of their properties, analogues, and accidents. Agreeing with this account entails support for iterative processes of more dynamic naming. Perhaps Achilles was the ur-character of the *Iliad*. In the end, though, he was only one amid a diversity of heroisms.

Coda

The sequence of claims pursued here connecting search engines to search areas to search arts appears to be highly abstract. As the argument progresses, perhaps it also seems to move further away from the kinds of cultural and political work we might prefer to be doing today. But these lines of argument are actually quite pertinent to contemporary concerns. In closing, I very briefly take up an example discussed by Robin Bernstein. In her cultural historical work on the racializations of childhood in the United States during the nineteenth century, Bernstein attends to Topsy, a character from *Uncle Tom's Cabin*. Harriet Beecher Stowe was a foundational figure in the invention of "Topsy" as a search space, but Bernstein widens the lens. Stowe established a place upon which the cultural maelstrom of the antebellum and postbellum United States deposited traces. A large number of Americans became co-creators of Topsy in the course of adding their lines to the topos. These "lines" were not only literary or theatrical initiatives undertaken in the slipstream of the literary artifact called *Uncle Tom's Cabin*. All manner of incursions into the material culture of Topsy, including things like children's dolls, also constituted lines. To this day, "Topsy" remains a remarkably effective search term. Specified by "Uncle Tom's Cabin," a Google Image search for "Topsy" routinely locates a wealth of cultural historical materials. The results page for "Topsy" is itself a search area in which to discern both local transformation rules and particular continuations of the Topsy topos. Even within a sensory topos like Topsy that is very often put to work in support of white supremacy, there can be room for irony as a transformation rule. We see this in the instance of the topsy-turvy doll. Without pretending that attempts to perform such inversions will always be either successful or prudent, I end with the words of Robin Bernstein: "if an enslaved woman sews an obscene doll" that is "a sign of systematic rapes" (because the white half and the black half are like siblings, each emerging from "beneath the skirt"), and if that enslaved woman gives that doll "to a glorified, white slaveholding child, who cuddles and kisses and adores it and takes it to bed while slaveholding adults look on in obtuse approval, *that's funny*" in a bitter, shocking, and political way.[42] Folded back upon itself, the topos skewers.

Notes

1. W. Bruce Croft, Donald Metzler, and Trevor Strohman, *Search Engines: Information Retrieval in Practice* (Boston: Pearson, 2010).
2. Sergey Brin and Lawrence Page, "The Anatomy of a Large-Scale Hypertextual Web Search Engine," *Computer Networks and ISDN Systems* 30 (1998): 110.
3. Croft, Metzler, and Strohman, *Search Engines*, 365–66.
4. Ken Hillis, Michael Petit, and Kylie Jarrett, *Google and the Culture of Search* (New York: Routledge, 2013), 9. See also Dennis Duncan's chapter on "index" in this volume.
5. John Battelle, *The Search: How Google and Its Rivals Rewrote the Rules of Business and Transformed Our Culture* (Boston: Nicholas Brealey, 2005), 6.
6. "Proof Google Is God . . . ," Church of Google, accessed June 6, 2018, http://www.thechurchofgoogle.org/proof-google-is-god/.
7. Adrian Chen, "The Google Arts and Culture App and the Rise of the 'Coded Gaze,'" *New Yorker*, January 26, 2018 (accessed June 6, 2018), https://www.newyorker.com/tech/elements/the-google-arts-and-culture-app-and-the-rise-of-the-coded-gaze-doppelganger.
8. Trevor Paglen, "Invisible Images (Your Pictures Are Looking at You)," *New Inquiry*, December 8, 2016 (accessed January 10, 2018), https://thenewinquiry.com/invisible-images-your-pictures-are-looking-at-you/.
9. Barbara Cassin, "Google Control: Entretien avec Barbara Cassin," *Cités* 39 (2009): 101. See also the entry on "algorithm" by Jeremy David Johnson in this volume.
10. Safiya Umoja Noble, *Algorithms of Oppression: How Search Engines Reinforce Racism* (New York: New York University Press, 2018), 13.
11. Noble, *Algorithms of Oppression*, 134.
12. Annette Vee, *Coding Literacy: How Computer Programming Is Changing Writing* (Cambridge, MA: MIT Press, 2017), 37.
13. Noble, *Algorithms of Oppression*, 11; see also 67.
14. Barbara Cassin, *Google Me: One-Click Democracy*, trans. Michael Syrotinski (New York: Fordham University Press, 2018), 68.
15. Cassin, *Google Me*, 6 (see also 109); Noble, *Algorithms of Oppression*, 123–24.
16. Paglen, "Invisible Images," 10.
17. David Mimno, "Topic Regression" (PhD diss., University of Massachusetts Amherst, 2012), 6.
18. Mimno, "Topic Regression," 6.
19. C. J. van Rijsbergen, *Information Retrieval* (London: Butterworths, 1979), cited in Croft, Metzler, and Strohman, *Search Engines*, 389; Sanjeev Arora, Rong Ge, Yoni Halpern, and David Mimno, et al., "A Practical Algorithm for Topic Modeling with Provable Guarantees," *Proceedings of the Thirtieth International Conference on Machine Learning* (ICML, 2013).
20. Moontae Lee and David Mimno, "Low-Dimensional Embeddings for Interpretable Anchor-Based Topic Inference," Conference on Empirical Methods in Natural Language Processing, accessed June 8, 2018, http://emnlp2014.org/papers/pdf/EMNLP2014138.pdf, 1319–20.

21. Lee and Mimno, "Low-Dimensional Embeddings," 1320.
22. Croft, Metzler, and Strohman, *Search Engines*, 375.
23. Croft, Metzler, and Strohman, *Search Engines*, 383.
24. Eli Pariser, *The Filter Bubble: What the Internet Is Hiding from You* (New York: Penguin, 2011).
25. Eitan Wilf, "Contingency and the Semiotic Mediation of Distributed Agency," in *Distributed Agency*, ed. N. J. Enfield and Paul Kockelman (Oxford: Oxford University Press, 2017), 199.
26. Wilf, "Contingency," 204.
27. Sarah Fdili Alaoui, Frédéric Bevilacqua, and Christian Jacquemin, "Interactive Visuals as Metaphors for Dance Movement Qualities," *ACM Transactions on Interactive Intelligent Systems* 5, no. 3 (2015): 6, article 13.
28. Sarah Fdili Alaoui, Frédéric Bevilacqua, Bertha Bermudez Pascual, and Christian Jacquemin, "Dance Interaction with Physical Model Visuals Based on Movement Qualities," *International Journal of Arts and Technology* 6, no. 4 (2013): 364; Friedrich Meschede, "Vom Glück des Findens," in *Serendipity: Vom Glück des Findens*, ed. Friedrich Meschede with assistance from Meta Marina Beeck (Bielefeld: Kunsthalle Bielefeld, 2015), 67.
29. Niklas Luhmann, "Kommunikation mit Zettelkästen," in *Universität als Milieu: Kleine Schriften*, ed. André Kieserling (Bielefeld: Haux, 1992), 57.
30. Philip M. Morse, *On Browsing: The Use of Search Theory in the Search for Information* (Cambridge, MA: MIT Press, 1970), 1.
31. Morse, *On Browsing*, 14.
32. Kate M. Joranson, Steve Van Tuyl, and Nina Clements, "E-Browsing: Serendipity and Questions of Access and Discovery" (accessed June 6, 2018), http://dx.doi.org/10.5703/1288284315272.
33. Morse, *On Browsing*, 1.
34. Joel Chan and Christian D. Schunn, "The Importance of Iteration in Creative Conceptual Combination," *Cognition* 145 (2015): 113.
35. Katherine Fu, Joel Chan, Jonathan Cagan, Kenneth Kotovsky, et al., "The Meaning of 'Near' and 'Far': The Impact of Structuring Design Databases and the Effect of Distance of Analogy on Design Output," *Journal of Mechanical Design* 135 (2013): 9.
36. See Leonardo Impett, "From Mnemosyne to Terpsichore—the Bilderatlas After the Image," Digital Humanities Conference 2017 (accessed June 8, 2018), https://dh2017.adho.org/abstracts/525/525.pdf.
37. David L. Marshall, "Warburgian Maxims for Visual Rhetoric," *Rhetoric Society Quarterly* 48 (2018): 352–79.
38. I am thinking of tropes in relation to transformation rules as discussed by Alfred Gell, *Art and Agency: An Anthropological Theory* (Oxford: Clarendon, 1998), especially 216–17.
39. Desiderius Erasmus, *On Copia of Words and Ideas*, trans. Donald B. King and H. David Rix (Milwaukee, WI: Marquette University Press, 1963), 67.
40. Erasmus, *On Copia*, 67.
41. Aristotle, *Topics*, 103b20–24.
42. Robin Bernstein, *Racial Innocence: Performing American Childhood from Slavery to Civil Rights* (New York: New York University Press, 2011), 89.

SELF-TRACKING

DEBORAH LUPTON

Self-tracking is a form of personal knowledge creation. The term "personal informatics" is sometimes used to describe this process, particularly by researchers in computer science. A recent community of self-tracking enthusiasts refer to "the quantified self" to describe their activities. "Lifelogging" is a variant of self-tracking that received attention for a while before the quantified self largely replaced it. I define self-tracking as a voluntary, reflexive mode of practice that is adopted by people as a way of learning more about themselves by noticing and recording aspects of their lives, and then using the information that is gathered to reflect on and make sense of their lives. Self-tracking is often undertaken as a way of optimizing or improving life in some way. It can also simply involve using personal information to engage in a process of self-discovery, self-awareness, and supplementing memory. Some self-trackers keep their personal data to themselves as a private practice; others choose to share their information. Indeed, many social media sites and specific self-tracking platforms actively encourage people to share personal details with each other and comment on other users' content as ways of strengthening social ties and providing support.

Almost any aspect of life can be tracked, from bodily functions and activities to work performance, finances, energy consumption, sexual encounters, and moods. Self-tracking may be simply a mental strategy, a mode of self-awareness in which individuals take care to notice specific features of their lives and make mental notes and comparisons. Alternatively, a raft of technologies may be used to collect and store this information, from the time-honored paper-and-pen method (as in journal or diary writing), to the recent digital tools of mobile cameras, computer spreadsheets, online platforms, mobile apps, wearable devices, and even insertable or ingestible devices that go inside the human body. If digital technologies are used for self-tracking, other actors and agencies are often able to access and use self-trackers' data.

It is on these novel forms of self-tracking, and the digitized forms of information generated from them, that I focus in this essay. At first glance, self-tracking may be considered a banal, solipsistic, and even narcissistic pastime, and the information it creates mundane. However, particularly in the light of new ecologies of connected digital devices and software, and the emergence of the digital data economy, closer examination reveals self-tracking and personal data to be profound phenomena in many ways. What is new about personal digital data from self-tracking, compared to other forms of information about the self, is their highly detailed, intimate, continually generated, often metricized and automated nature; the opportunities that are now available to readily share this information with many others; threats to the privacy and security of these data posed by their digitization; and the implications for selfhood, embodiment, and the ways in which people conceptualize and engage with information about themselves.

While people have engaged in tracking and recording aspects of their bodies and lives using journals, written numbers or mental awareness since antiquity, new digital technologies provide opportunities to accomplish these activities in unprecedented ways. Many of the devices and software designed for self-tracking are partly or fully autonomized, and generate data throughout the day (and in some cases, during sleep). Digital cameras in mobile or wearable devices facilitate image-taking that records elements of a person's life. Social media platforms can also produce personal information: how many friends or followers a person has, how other users respond to the content a person uploads, and so on. Productivity apps and platforms monitor how people spend their time. Some self-tracking technologies use digital sensors, which can monitor a wide range of bodily functions and activities that were previously not readily detected or recorded by the human senses. These include steps taken, heart rate, stress levels, energy expended, food and liquids consumed, and sleep patterns. Smartphones with tracking apps are carried on or strapped to the body. Wearable devices such as smartwatches and "smart" wristbands, ankle bands, headbands, gloves, pendants, rings, clothing, and footwear with digital sensors are designed to be worn on the body. "Smart" bottles and forks monitor water and food consumption. Insertable devices such as blood glucose monitors and "smart" tablets that are swallowed record bodily functions from within the body and send signals to digital devices worn on the body. Some self-tracking devices are embedded into physical environments, such as "smart" pillows, mattresses, floors, chairs or rooms with sensors that can record bodily movement, and digital home energy use and security systems that can monitor inhabitants' electricity use and movements in and out of their houses.

Many interesting theoretical issues are raised by the emergence of digitized self-tracking technologies and the personal information they generate. Advocates and developers of self-tracking apps and devices frequently draw on a discourse of motivation, behavior change, and self-improvement when attempting to promote these technologies. Thus, for example, the Fitbit company, which manufactures popular wearable devices for fitness tracking, promotes its wares on its website with claims such as: "Fitbit motivates you to reach your health and fitness goals by tracking your activity, exercise, sleep, weight and more." Prospective customers are invited to seek further information on the website by reading stories from "real people" to "see how Fitbit is changing lives." Many such representations of the affordances of digital self-tracking technologies, including not only commercial actors seeking to promote their wares but also researchers in fields such as persuasive computing, champion their potential to "nudge" users into behavior change.[1] These representations tend to position such devices as possessing almost magical powers of inserting themselves into people's mundane routines, influence human action, and consequently improve human lives. Indeed, in the tech industry the term "enchanted objects" is often used to describe products that resonate with human desires and needs and create emotional connections.[2]

Some social researchers and ethicists have suggested that digital technologies designed and marketed for self-tracking may detract from human agency, by transferring autonomous action and deliberation from the user to the automated device.[3] Drawing on feminist new materialism provides an alternative perspective.[4] Rather than viewing humans and technologies as separate entities, the feminist new materialism approach positions them as coming together as assemblages to generate agential capacities.[5] A distributed and relational understanding of affordances positions them as more-than-human potentials generated when people use their technologies. Affordance is a term that is often used in media studies to describe the opportunities for action that digital technologies invite, allow, demand, close-off, or refuse to human users.[6] An affordance may or may not be enacted in the ways anticipated by the makers of the technology. Humans take up technologies and incorporate them into everyday habits by responding to and engaging with these affordances.

A feminist new materialism perspective emphasizes that human bodies possess their own affordances: for example, sensory and memory capabilities. Technological affordances may also close off agential capacities. Humans may improvise with, resist, or reinvent the technological affordances in a multitude of ways. This approach involves recognizing that the affordances of technologies invite human responses in certain defined, and often very obvious ways, but that these affordances are not realized unless in action with the human user.

Humans and technologies work together as part of a continual becoming of artefacts and embodiment. These assemblages are never finished or complete, but are always emergent.[7]

A similar approach can be applied to understanding the digital data assemblages generated when humans come together with self-tracking technologies. Humans and nonhumans work together to make new things ("information") that can be used and reused, configured and reconfigured. The information that is produced from digitized self-tracking is both about and for humans. It is a more-than-human entity, however, as it is generated with and through assemblages of humans and nonhumans. These assemblages are lively, constantly emerging, joining, and coming apart. They involve distributed and relational agencies, capacities and affective forces.[8] Humans use their embodied senses and memory to configure and interpret this information, working with digital sensors in a digital-human sensory enactment. This perspective goes well beyond the notions of "information literacy" or "data literacy" that are often espoused in information and informatics studies. It acknowledges the role of the fleshly body beyond cognitive processing, and positions sense-making as coconstitutive between humans and technologies.

From Cyborg Bodies to Human-Digital-Data Assemblages

The concept of the cyborg became a popular way of imagining the cybernetic possibilities of the human-digital technology relationship in the late twentieth century, both in popular culture (such as the *Terminator* and *Robocop* series of films, and television series such as *Six Million Dollar Man* and *Star Trek*) as well as in social and cultural theory. The cyborg has particularly inspired cultural theorists who have written about the implications of computerized technologies for human embodiment and subjectivity. For Donna Haraway and others writing on cyborg bodies, the technologies that humans used were conceptualized as prosthetic enhancements of fleshly embodiment. Haraway's major contribution was to also use the figure of the cyborg metaphorically as part of her socialist feminist politics. She focused on the blurring of boundaries represented by the cyborg body, contending that humans are always hybrid and more-than-human, always becoming-with-others, their bodies extending from their fleshly envelope into the world and back again.[9]

Over the past few decades, Haraway has revised and refined her cyborg theory. She now prefers to conceptualize human-nonhuman relationships using the metaphor of compost.[10] Haraway envisages humans as intertwined with companion species of other living and nonhuman entities in a rich, dense matter in which the boundaries between objects cannot be distinguished, so that "we make with, and we become with each other."[11] In what is "more than a joke" and "a refusal to be quite so serious about categories, and to let categories sit a bit lightly with the complexities of the world,"[12] Haraway now proclaims herself as a "compost-ist" rather than a posthumanist.[13] She argues that this rich matter of human-nonhuman entanglements can include nonliving things (like digital technologies and digital data): "I don't think compost excludes cyborgian politics. It doesn't exclude cyborg entities at all."[14] As Haraway points out, compost heaps often involve nonorganic materials, such as plastics and metals. Her "tentacular thinking" draws attention to the connections between things in this dense entanglement of objects, while her compost metaphor highlights the relationship between life, decay, and death.[15]

Developed before Haraway's compost philosophy, Jane Bennett's concept of "thing-power" similarly draws attention to the vitality and vibrancy of assemblages of humans and nonhumans, both organic and nonorganic.[16] Bennett defines thing-power as "the curious ability of inanimate things to animate, to act, to product effects dramatic and subtle."[17] Both Bennett and Haraway can be described as part of a vitalist materialism scholarship, in which these kinds of affects, capacities, and forces emerging in, through, and with human-technological assemblages are foregrounded.

In my work on the onto-epistemology of digital data, I draw on a related idea that conceptualizes data as lively, referring not only to their unceasing generation and recombination, but also to their relationship to human lives.[18] In more recent times, with the emergence of mobile and wearable technologies that can be constantly connected to digitized wireless networks, the boundaries between human bodies and digital technologies have become increasingly difficult to distinguish. Another significant change is that digitized humans now generate flows of digital data. When people are routinely moving through their everyday lives connected to and monitored by the internet, carrying or wearing mobile digital devices on their bodies or tracked by digital sensors embedded in smart environments and spaces, continually generating digital traces, they become human-digital-data assemblages. Human bodies are located in webs of intersecting smart objects—often referred to as "the internet of things," or now even "the internet of everything"—in which they are one node among many data-emitting and -exchanging nodes, human and nonhuman. Far more than prosthetics, smart objects are entangled with human bodies—and each other. Cyborgs are now no longer a species apart, threatening, alien, and superhuman. They are everywhere and everyone: they are Us, not the Other.

Personal digital data assemblages have their own social lives as they circulate in the digital data economy and are accessed and exploited by many potential actors and agencies. They are also lively in the sense that they are about elements of human life and they possess biovalue as increasingly commodified objects in the digital data economy. These assemblages are always mutable, dynamic, responsive to new inputs and interpretations. Building on this metaphor of lively data, I have further suggested that we can think of digital data assemblages as companion species, and of humans as living and co-evolving with their data, each responding to the other in a synergistic encounter. Like compost, these assemblages are permanently in states of movement, composition, and decomposition.

Visuality, Metrics, and Personal Informatics

The design and development of digital self-tracking technologies takes place within the computer and information sciences. The field of personal informatics develops a model of the human-computer relationship in which key foci are the technical features of the representation, processing, storage, and communication of information. Within this paradigm, information is conceptualized as matter that can be incorporated within computerized systems (denoted by the term "informatics"). Contemporary concepts and practices of informatics tend to be disembodied, aspiring to the objective of stripping down its sensory and affective force. Information should ideally be "clean," "objective," and "neutral," cognitive rather than intuitive or visceral.

Digital monitoring practices tend to position the body as a data repository, with specific digital sensors and other monitoring devices used to target various parts or functions of the body to uncover and extract the information contained within so that it may be rendered useful. Tropes of dissection and flaying of the body, as well as those referring to x-ray visions, depict data collecting practices and technologies as bringing previously invisible bodily information into plain sight.[19] Digitized self-tracking technologies similarly participate in regimes of truth, drawing on their imputed scientific neutrality to do so. Many proponents of these technologies, and their users, champion their ability to uncover previously hidden and mysterious aspects of and patterns in self-trackers' behaviors and bodies. They suggest that the human senses and modes of recording and remembering information are ideally augmented by the affordances of these technologies. These data are commonly represented as allowing fine details of humans to be identified, and analyzed, and brought together in new ways to generate further insights.

This approach is evident in the Quantified Self community. The dedicated website of this group has as its motto "self-knowledge through numbers" and announces its mission "to support new discoveries about ourselves and our communities that are grounded in accurate observation and enlivened by a spirit of friendship."[20] Contributors to the personal informatics literature in human-computer interaction studies also tend to represent digital tools and data as superior to human capacities, as in this claim by leading personal informatics researchers: "Personal informatics systems provide an advantage over simply trying to remember information about the self, because pure self-reflection is often flawed. This is because people have limited memory, cannot directly observe some behaviors (e.g., sleep apnea), and may not have the time to constantly and consistently observe some behaviors (e.g., manually counting steps throughout the day)."[21] Many digitized modes of self-tracking single out specific aspects that can be monitored and recorded by the user. An app to monitor physical activity, for example, structures what the definition of "activity" is, how it should be measured and how the information is algorithmically analyzed and the format in which it is delivered back to the user. (A common, and completely arbitrary metric used in digital step-counters is that of the "10,000 steps a day" target.) The digital sensors that are used in wearable devices detect very specific and limited signals from the body: blood flow, pulse rate, some types of movement, spatial location. These affordances pay a major role in structuring and shaping humans' engagements with the technologies, including the type of information that can be generated and how this information is represented to users.

The informatics perspective dominates existing research on how people make sense of their personal data and incorporate them into their lives. Humans are positioned as the "emitters" and "receivers" of their personal information, which is mediated through digital technologies and presented back to them for their "processing." They are conceptualized as part of the computing system, their brains operating in a stepwise series of commands. Other sensory ways of knowing and understanding ourselves are closed off when the visual is privileged. Very few materializations of digital self-tracked data present this information in tangible form, for example. We can see our data, but we cannot usually touch, smell, taste, or hear them.[22]

Through the processes of digital self-tracking, therefore, embodied elements involving fleshly responses and signals become reduced to visual materializations of information. These personal data are usually materialized in the form of numbers and graphs, encouraging users to think about their information in quantifiable and quantified formats. These affordances ignore, or close off, other modes of knowing, recording and understanding the elements of selfhood and embodiment. Other aspects of the body are left unacknowledged by these processes because they are not brought into the field of visibility created by the technologies. Bodily digitization, therefore, is both generative and reductive.

Self-tracking, Selfhood, and Surveillance

Although the cyborg figure has lost much of its cultural power through its gradual incorporation into the bodies of ordinary citizens, personal digital data assemblages have begun to attract a similar admixture of utopian visions and unsettling affects. In my book *The Quantified Self: A Sociology of Self-Tracking*, I discussed self-tracking as a sociocultural set of practices underpinned by dominant assumptions about selfhood, embodiment, and social relations.[23] I drew attention to a particular focus in popular discourses and practices that represent digitized self-tracking as a mode for eliciting self-knowledge via digital datasets which is then used to optimize the self or record aspects of practitioners' everyday lives as a form of documentation. As I noted, there are strong associations in discourses on self-tracking with neoliberal values of self-responsibility for life opportunities and outcomes, as well as the importance of viewing selfhood as an entrepreneurial project.

The findings from a series of empirical studies that colleagues and I have conducted involving people who engage in self-tracking revealed that many of them ascribe to these discourses and ideals in order to explain their practices and rationales.[24] The participants articulated a range of reasons for why they engage in self-tracking: to manage chronic illness or finances, become physically fitter, lose weight, sleep better, achieve a more nutritious diet, become more productive, use their time more wisely, and achieve a better level of wellbeing. They talked about achieving knowledge, awareness, and problem-solving; taking control; and feeling better. As many self-trackers noted, "it feels good" to maintain self-tracking practices, both in the sense that they feel more in control of their life, but also because their bodies feel stronger, fitter, or healthier, or because they feel that they have achieved greater awareness about themselves.[25] While many participants were not interested in sharing or comparing their personal data with others, some found this affordance particularly motivating.[26]

Information in the form of digital data is often represented as immaterial, intangible, invisible, and otherwise not available to the senses. And yet, digital data are generated with and through tangible devices and are transmitted and stored using material technologies. They are matter that can also have material effects.[27] When this information is about human bodies, it can be folded back into the body: responded to with affective force and inspiring continued habitual embodied action, or supporting a change in everyday practices of embodiment. Berson uses the term "instrumented" to describe the phenomenology of the process by which digital sensors are attached to human bodies to measure aspects of function and movement.[28] He contends that kinaesthetic acculturation is required of bodies undergoing these processes, as they adjust to engaging with these sensors and the data that are generated. New bodily habits and registers of meaning and communication are required when bodily movement is mediated with digital sensors and data. The human senses play a key role in these configurations, as do digital data when bodies are monitored by sensors.[29] Self-tracking can help people become more sensitized to the sensory dimensions of their bodies by encouraging them to notice how they feel. They can act in pedagogical ways, instructing people on how to interpret the meaning of their bodily sensations and perceptions.[30]

The continuous production of information about oneself, particularly via digital tracking devices, can potentially lead to anxiety, fear, and frustration because of their sheer volume, which may itself inspire feelings of lack of control over data. So too, loss of control may be experienced in relation to the use of personal self-tracked data by other actors or agencies. Unlike forms of personal information in previous eras, digitized data have value beyond the person who generates them. Personal data can be used for self-monitoring and self-surveillance purposes, but their availability to other actors and agencies means that they can be used in surveillance of individuals by others.

In the digital data economy, personal data have taken on commercial and governmental value for a range of actors, in what has been termed "surveillance capitalism."[31] A growing literature in critical data studies has drawn attention to the ways in which personal data can be exploited by third parties.[32] When information about the self is gathered and stored by using mental awareness or paper records, it is not readily accessible by other actors or agencies. New modes of personal data generation and storage, in contrast, tend to involve transmission to cloud-based digital archives. At any stage in the collection, transmission and storage processes, this information may be open to access by other people, either legally or illicitly by hackers and cybercriminals. The liveliness of digital data and their constant movement and recombination in the data economy render it difficult for people to understand exactly where their personal data go and who has access to them. The "black boxes" of algorithmic processing and profiling data systems also serve to make third-party uses of personal data opaque and difficult to challenge.[33]

Cultural critics often call for new stories to be imagined and told when conceptualizing the futures of science and technology: Haraway calls this "speculative fabulation."[34] One source of new and alternative fabulations are artists, creative writers, and designers who have engaged in projects that seek to challenge taken-for-granted assumptions about personal digital data. These works draw attention not only to the liveliness of digital data assemblages, but also their potential for reinvention, exploitation, and deterioration.

In one art project, the members of the panGenerator studio developed an interactive installation, "hash2hash—Everything Saved Will Be Lost" for the National Ethnographic Museum in Warsaw.[35] The installation invited visitors to take a selfie and load it onto the large installation screen. They watch as the digital image of themselves gradually deteriorates, the screen emitting real flakes of ash that fall to make a pile around a tombstone inscribed with the hashtag symbol. The idea of the exhibition was to encourage visitors to reflect on their mortality and the limited lifespan of their personal data. Other artists and designers have experimented with ways of recording, storing, and materializing personal data that move beyond standard metrics and graphics to invite alternative and multisensory engagements. Tega Brain's "Smell Dating" invites people to select potential romantic partners by responding to a piece of fabric infused with their body odors.[36] Luke Munn's "Domestic Data" uses the contents of a home vacuum cleaner filter bag as data that can reveal patterns of activity of the home's inhabitants, including pets.[37]

Several artists and arts collectives have produced works that emphasize the politics of data and algorithmic governance. In an artwork intended to critique the exploitation of human bodies for profit, the Institute of Human Obsolescence team asks participants to wear clothing embedded with sensors to harvest the heat from their bodies.[38] The heat generates electricity, which is then transformed into cryptocurrency. In a similar project, British artist Max Dovey's Respiratory Mining uses human respiration to mine cryptocurrencies. Dovey employs this concept as a provocation to consider the ways in which a human bodily attribute—breath—can generate digital data, which in turn can become a universal currency, algorithmically processed to generate commercial value on digital systems such as the blockchain. In her provocation, Jennifer Lyn Morone has critiqued the commodification of personal data by turning herself into an "incorporated person" (entitled "Jennifer Lyn Morone, Inc.").[39] She claims on her website that by collecting as much information about oneself as possible, a person can increase their commercial value: "Jennifer Lyn Morone, Inc has advanced into the inevitable next stage of Capitalism by becoming an incorporated person. This model allows you to turn your health, genetics, personality, capabilities, experience, potential, virtues and vices into profit. You are the founder, CEO, shareholder and product using your own resources."

These art and design enquiries and provocations are important in challenging often unacknowledged assumptions concerning what digital self-tracking technologies can and should do. They highlight the sensory and affective forces and engagements generated by digital data assemblages. As we live with and alongside our digital data assemblages and co-evolve with them, they can contribute to our agential capacities but also cruelly make visible our vulnerabilities; such interventions highlight important questions about where we might see the future of self-tracking and personal data.

Notes

1. Deborah Lupton, *The Quantified Self: A Sociology of Self-Tracking* (Cambridge: Polity, 2016).
2. See, for example, the influential book by David Rose, *Enchanted Objects: Design, Human Desire, and the Internet of Things* (New York: Scribner, 2014).
3. Natasha Dow Schüll, "Data for Life: Wearable Technology and the Design of Self Care," *BioSocieties* 11, no. 3 (2016): 317–33; John Owens and Alan Cribb, "'My Fitbit Thinks I

Can Do Better!': Do Health Promoting Wearable Technologies Support Personal Autonomy?" *Philosophy and Technology* 32 (2019): 23–38.
4. For example, Jane Bennett, *The Enchantment of Modern Life: Attachments, Crossings, and Ethics* (Princeton: Princeton University Press, 2001); Jane Bennett, *Vibrant Matter: A Political Ecology of Things* (Durham, NC: Duke University Press, 2009); Donna Haraway, *Staying with the Trouble: Making Kin in the Chthulucene* (Durham, NC: Duke University Press, 2016); Karen Barad, "Posthumanist Performativity: Toward an Understanding of How Matter Comes to Matter," *Signs* 28, no. 3 (2003): 801–31; Rosi Braidotti, *The Posthuman* (Cambridge: Polity, 2013).
5. Deborah Lupton, "How Do Data Come to Matter? Living and Becoming with Personal Data," *Big Data and Society* 5, no. 2 (2018) (accessed July 6, 2018), doi:10.1177/2053951718786314.
6. Jenny L. Davis and James B. Chouinard, "Theorizing Affordances: From Request to Refuse," *Bulletin of Science, Technology and Society* 36, no. 4 (2016): 241–48.
7. Lupton, "How Do Data Come to Matter?"
8. Lupton, "How Do Data Come to Matter?"
9. Donna Haraway, *Simians, Cyborgs, and Women: The Reinvention of Nature* (London: Free Association, 1991).
10. Donna Haraway, "Anthropocene, Capitalocene, Plantationocene, Chthulucene: Making Kin," *Environmental Humanities* 6, no. 1 (2015): 159–65; Sarah Franklin and Donna Haraway, "Staying with the Manifesto: An Interview with Donna Haraway," *Theory, Culture, and Society* 34, no. 4 (2017): 49–63; Haraway, *Staying with the Trouble*.
11. Franklin and Haraway, "Staying with the Manifesto," 50.
12. Franklin and Haraway, "Staying with the Manifesto," 50.
13. Haraway, "Anthropocene, Capitalocene, Plantationocene, Chthulucene," 161.
14. Franklin and Haraway, "Staying with the Manifesto," 54.
15. Haraway, *Staying with the Trouble*; Franklin and Haraway, "Staying with the Manifesto."
16. Bennett, *Vibrant Matter*; Jane Bennett, "The Force of Things: Steps Toward an Ecology of Matter," *Political Theory* 32, no. 3 (2004): 347–72.
17. Bennett, "The Force of Things," 351.
18. Lupton, *The Quantified Self*; Deborah Lupton, "Lively Data, Social Fitness and Biovalue: The Intersections of Health Self-Tracking and Social Media," in *The Sage Handbook of Social Media*, ed. Jean Burgess, Alice Marwick, and Thomas Poell, 562–78 (London: Sage, 2018); Deborah Lupton, "Personal Data Practices in the Age of Lively Data," in *Digital Sociologies*, ed. Jessie Daniels, Karen Gregory, and Tressie McMillan Cottom, 339–54 (Bristol: Policy, 2017); Deborah Lupton, "Feeling Your Data: Touch and Making Sense of Personal Digital Data," *New Media and Society* 19, no. 10 (2017): 1599–614.
19. Yuliya Grinberg, "The Emperor's New Data Clothes: Implications of 'Nudity' as a Racialized and Gendered Metaphor in Discourse on Personal Digital Data," in *Digital Sociologies*, ed. Jessie Daniels, Karen Gregory, and Tressie McMillan Cottom (Bristol: Policy, 2017), 421–33; Louise Amoore and Alexandra Hall, "Taking People Apart: Digitized Dissection and the Body at the Border," *Environment and Planning D: Society and Space* 27, no. 3 (2009):444–64; Lupton, *The Quantified Self*.
20. "About the Quantified Self," *Quantified Self* (accessed February 2, 2018), http://quantifiedself.com/about/.
21. Ian Li, Anind K. Dey, and Jodi Forlizzi, "A Stage-Based Model of Personal Informatics Systems," Proceedings of the SIGCHI Conference on Human Factors in Computing Systems, Atlanta (2010), 557–66.
22. Lupton, "Feeling Your Data."

23. Lupton, *The Quantified Self*.
24. These studies included interviews and focus groups conducted with the following separate groups in Australia: 1. women who were pregnant or had a child aged three and under; 2. commuting cyclists; 3. people who identified as self-trackers; and 4. women who were asked about their use of digital health technologies.
25. Deborah Lupton and Gavin J. D. Smith, "'A Much Better Person': The Agential Capacities of Self-Tracking Practices," in *Metric Culture: Ontologies of Self-Tracking Practices*, ed. Btihaj Ajana (London: Emerald, 2018), 57–73; Deborah Lupton, Sarah Pink, Christine Heyes LaBond, and Shanti Sumartojo, "Personal Data Contexts, Data Sense and Self-Tracking Cycling," *International Journal of Communication* 12 (2018); Deborah Lupton, "'I Just Want It to Be Done, Done, Done!' Food Tracking Apps, Affects, and Agential Capacities," *Multimodal Technologies and Interaction* 2, no. 2 (2018), accessed May 23, 2018, doi:10.3390/mti2020029; Lupton, "Personal Data Practices in the Age of Lively Data"; Deborah Lupton and Sarah Maslen, "The More-Than-Human Sensorium: Sensory Engagements with Digital Self-Tracking Technologies," *The Senses and Society* 13, no. 2 (2018): 190–202.
26. Lupton et al., "Personal Data Contexts, Data Sense, and Self-Tracking Cycling."
27. Lupton, "Feeling Your Data."
28. Josh Berson, *Computable Bodies: Instrumented Life and the Human Somatic Niche* (London: Bloomsbury, 2015).
29. Lupton, "Feeling Your Data."
30. Lupton, "Feeling Your Data"; Lupton and Maslen, "The More-Than-Human Sensorium."
31. Shoshana Zuboff, "Big Other: Surveillance Capitalism and the Prospects of an Information Civilization," *Journal of Information Technology* 30, no. 1 (2015): 75–89.
32. Zuboff, "Big Other"; Christian Fuchs, *Social Media: A Critical Introduction*, 2d ed. (London: Sage, 2017); José van Dijck, *The Culture of Connectivity: A Critical History of Social Media* (Oxford: Oxford University Press, 2013).
33. Frank Pasquale, *The Black Box Society: The Secret Algorithms That Control Money and Information* (Cambridge, MA: Harvard University Press, 2015).
34. Franklin and Haraway, "Staying with the Manifesto."
35. PanGenerator studio, "hash2hash—Everything Saved Will Be Lost" (accessed February 23, 2018), https://vimeo.com/254393034.
36. Tega Brain, "Smell Dating," 2018 (accessed February 16, 2018), http://smell.dating/.
37. Luke Munn, "Domestic Data" (2017), accessed February 26, 2018, http://www.lukemunn.com/2017/domestic-data/.
38. "Institute of Human Obsolescence" (accessed February 25, 2018), http://speculative.capital.
39. "Jennifer Lyn Morone, Inc." (accessed October 21, 2018), http://jenniferlynmorone.com/.

TELE (Τῆλε)

WOLF KITTLER

The morpheme *tele-* originated in a rich paradigm of words in Greek antiquity. In early modernity, it was revived as a prefix for a new scientific instrument, the telescope, and it is now ubiquitous in the fields of communication, robotics, and artificial intelligence. The Greek adverb *tēle*, "at a distance," and the compounds derived from it, are key terms in the epics of Homer, the odes of Pindar, and the tragedies of Aeschylus, Sophocles, and Euripides. Both the Achaeans' and the Trojans' allies fight "far from their friends and their native land."[1] The action of the *Odyssey* can get started because "Poseidon had gone among the far-off Ethiopians."[2] And Odysseus is said again and again to have perished in a faraway place by both his enemies and friends.[3] The word captures the tension between those characters convinced that Odysseus has met his death far from home and the friends and small group of intimates who know better. Part of this second group are the listeners of the song, or the readers of the story. This tension is further heightened by Homer's frequent references to the fate of King Agamemnon, who, immediately after having returned from the Trojan war, was killed by his wife Clytemnestra because of what Pindar calls "the sacrificial slaying" of their daughter "Iphigeneia at Euripus far from her homeland."[4] A comforting reply to Pindar's gloomy formulation of Iphigeneia's fate are the words which the heroine herself addresses to the chorus of Greek women in Euripides's tragedy *Iphigenia Among the Taurians*:

> Far from your fatherland and mine
> I have been taken where, it is thought,
> I lie in luckless slaughter.[5]

Yet, the words derived from the root *tēle* do not only stand for the Mediterranean spaces which Greek sailors had already colonized in Homer's time; they also define the difference between near and far in a more corporeal sense, and, by implication, between knowing and not knowing, between gaining or lacking information. Hit by a big wave, Odysseus falls "far from his raft."[6] The most drastic formulation, however, is this: "Achilles, striking [Deucalion] with the sword on his neck, hurled afar his head and with it his helmet."[7]

Compounded with verbal roots, the prefix *tēle-* serves to denote the ways in which humans relate to the space they inhabit. These include the perception of distant objects through eye and ear, as well as the overcoming of spatial differences not only through gestures and the voice, but also with weapons and technical media. Among the most frequent epithets applied to the heroes of Homer's epics is the word *tēlekleitos*, "far-" or "widely famed," but only an Achilles deserves the "far-shining tomb" that Agamemnon erects in his honor.[8]

A compound comprising the root *tēle-*, not documented in Homer, but used in the Homeric Hymns to Helios and Selene,[9] is the word *tēlaugēs*, from *augeō*, "I shine," and *augē*, "light of the sun." It is one of Pindar's terms for the splendor of the heroes and the athletes.[10] In the first century of the current area, however, the word must have lost its relation to the notion of distance and only refers to a sharp vision. In this sense, it appears in the story of the healing of the blind man in the gospel according to Mark: "After that he put his hands again upon his eyes, and made him look up: and he was restored, and saw every man clearly" (8.25). And in Julian's *Hymn to the Mother of Gods*, the formula *tēlaugeis aitias* simply means "clear and manifest reasons."[11]

The chorus of clouds in Aristophanes's *Clouds* plays on a whole family of words connoting distant vision:

> Clouds everlasting,
> let us arise, revealing our dewy bright form,
> from deep roaring father Ocean
> onto high mountain peaks
> with tresses of trees, whence
> to behold heights of distant vantage [in ancient Greek, *tēlephaneis skopias aphorōmetha*],
> and holy earth whose crops we water,
> and divine rivers' rushing,
> and the sea crashing with deep thunder.
> For heaven's tireless eye is ablaze

with gleaming rays.
So let us shake off the rainy haze
from our deathless shape and survey
the land, with telescopic eye.[12]

Not only shining into the distance, and, thus, visible from a distant vantage point, *tēlephanēs*, but also looking or even gazing into the distance are the mountain tops, *skopia*, a word derived from *skopiazō*, "I see." And from there, the clouds look down with a "far-seeing eye," *tēleskopos omma*, onto the earth, which ether's tireless eye illuminates with bright sunlight, *augē*. Reveling in optical metaphors and images, this song is a poetic parody of the Socratic notion of "the idea." Taking his cue from that term's etymological relation to *idein*, aorist of *oraō*, "I see," Aristophanes mocks the concept's fuzzy nature, and its tendency to dissipate, at a closer look, like clouds in the sun.

The clouds' word *tēleskopos*, a hapax legomenon in Antiquity, had a renaissance when it was transferred to the instrument that opened up the space of the universe in modernity. As Edward Rosen has shown, Galileo was neither the one who invented it nor the first one to conduct astronomical observations,[13] nor did he coin the word telescope:

> On the basis of the available documents . . . we may reasonably conclude that *the term telescope was originally devised by Demasiani and publicly unveiled by Ceci*[14] *at the banquet in Galileo's honor on April 14, 1611*. . . . Unless we have seriously blundered, it was the Greek John Demasiani of Cephalonia, a poet and theologian rather than a scientist, who fostered, if he did not initiate, the curious categorical imperative which ordains that modern scientific instruments shall bear ancient Greek names.[15]

In his book *Istoria e dimonstrazioni intorno alle macchie solari e loro accidenti*,[16] Galileo introduced the new word to the scientific community, whereupon Johannes Kepler, the most important astronomer of his time, confirmed it in a letter dated July 18, 1613.[17]

It is conceivable that Demasiani took his inspiration from Aristophanes's *Clouds* and/or from Hesiod's version of the Prometheus myth.[18] And the imperative he initiated applies not only to scientific instruments, but also to their offspring: media technologies. Telegraphy, the first one to be named in this vein, has a long history, starting with the description of the way in which news of the Greek victory over Troy was transmitted via beacon signals in Aeschylus's tragedy *Agamemnon*. Within this context, Aeschylus coins the hapax legomenon *tēlepompos*,[19] an adjective derived from the verb *pempō*, "I send forth or away," "dismiss," "send home," "discharge," "shoot," "conduct," "escort," which can be used for people,[20] things such as the wind,[21] as well as for letters.[22] The term telepomp never became part of the large family of words carrying the prefix *tēle*-, but it could well serve as the general term for all telecommunication media today.

Philologists have long pondered over whether it is possible to perceive light signals over such large distances as that between Mount Athos and one of the mountains on the island of Euboea. As far as I can see, the question has been settled: under favorable atmospheric conditions, this is, indeed, possible. Yet, this leaves another question open which only a few have posed: does this prove that it was possible to transmit messages at such a speed across the beacon line that Aeschylus describes with such accurate geographic detail? And if this system was so efficient, why, then, is it that none of the great military leaders, no Alexander, no Hannibal, no Caesar, ever thought of using it? Why is it that the first functioning telegraph was invented only during the French Revolution?

The last, and I think decisive, reason for doubts about the efficiency of Aeschylus's beacon line, however, is the simple fact that this system only transmits one message: news of the Greek victory. What if they had lost? In short, Aeschylus' system carries zero information per Shannon's formula:

$$H = -1 \log_2 1 = 0$$

Picking up the problem where Aeschylus had left it, Polybius (c. 200 BCE) proposes two methods of coding. 1: Take two synchronized water clocks, insert two rods into them, onto which a few messages are inscribed at equal intervals.[23] If beacon signals are used to start and stop these two clocks synchronously, the messages can be safely transmitted. Yet, because their number is limited, Polybius proposes a second, more sophisticated code. 2: If you plot the Greek alphabet in a 5*5 matrix, you can signal the position of each letter by means of two times five torches.[24] This invention comes close to Morse's telegraph code, and one wonders why Polybius's ideas did not bear fruit for more than a millennium after his time. Thus, Louis de Jaucourt, in his entry for the term *signal* in the *Encyclopédie*, 1765, could only tell the age-old stories of the beacon fires from Homer to Aeschylus and Polybius one more time.[25] Abbé Claude Chappe, the inventor of the first truly functioning telegraph, may have studied this text. We know, in any case, that the first experiments he conducted were done with "harmonized,"[26] or synchronized clocks, which were not water clocks anymore, but the mechanical marvels of the eighteenth century. Chappe, who is known to have published at least five papers on electricity, first thought of employing that medium for the start and stop signals of these clocks, but, finally, gave up on it because the insulation of the wires turned out to be a problem too difficult to solve with the means at his disposal.[27] Therefore, he fell back on a system of optical signals, which he developed with the help of the famous horologist Abraham-Louis Breguet.[28] Composed of one large beam, the regulator, and two smaller ones, the indicators, at its ends, the device looks like the blowup of a human figure gesticulating with its arms. Yet, unlike the limbs of a human body, these beams rotate in full circles like the hands of a clock, which differs from an ordinary clock only in so far as the revolutions, rather than being concentric, are eccentric in three points. The code consists of 4 * 7 * 7 = 196 symbols, further subdivided into two sections, one half for the messages proper, the rest for control signals.

What distinguishes Chappe's telegraph from all previous telecommunication systems is the fact that the symbols, rather than being simply fed one after the other into the channel, are clocked, as it were, according to the formula: "En deux temps et trois mouvements."[29] According to this rule, each signal is transmitted in three distinct steps. The first one has two functions: (a) like a telephone ring tone, it alerts the operator down the line to expect an incoming message; (b) depending on the inclination of the regulator to either the right or the left side, this signal already indicates from which one of the two sets the incoming message will be chosen. In the second step, the signal itself is given in a preliminary form with the regulator still inclined 45° in relation to the horizon. The third and final step "finishes" the signal by rotating the regulator back into the horizontal position while keeping the constellation of the indicators unchanged. This transmission protocol guarantees that the system is synchronized not just from any one station to the next, but beyond the line of sight to the second next station, and, thus, to all the stations in the line.

If Polybius overcame the weakness of Aeschylus's beacon line by solving the problem of coding, then Chappe took the final step by combining Polybius's two systems into a single one. His telegraph consists of an elaborate code for an unlimited number of possible messages and a protocol for the synchronization of their transmission. Because of this, the Chappe telegraph is the first functioning telecommunication system in human history, a truly modern medium.[30] The story of its naming is told in Count André François Miot de Melito's memoirs:

> Mr. Chappe, the inventor of the telegraph, or the one who is at least considered to be its inventor, paid me a visit at the war department. The famous painter David had brought him along. Chappe explained the use of his machine to me, for which he had coined the name *tachygraph* (fast writer). I suggested that he substitute that imperfect name with that of *telegraph* (distance writer). He adopted this change. The name telegraph has remained, and it has, as they say, made a fortune.[31]

Dated as late as 1858, Miot de Melito's account is not absolutely reliable, but we know that the neologism was already used in Joseph Lakanal's *Rapport sur le télégraphe*, which was published by the French *Imprimerie nationale* in

September/October 1794.[32] From that moment on, the long series of compound nouns formed with the prefix *tēle-* was preprogrammed. Already in 1796, Gottfried Huth coined a new such term in one of the supplements to his translation of Johann Heinrich Lambert's treatise on the physical properties of what he calls "Portevoix,"[33] a bullhorn to amplify the human voice:

> It is commonly known how successfully ... the French, during their conquest of the Austrian Netherlands, used the telegraph or the art to transmit messages ... within few minutes to far away locations by means of characters that can be sent over great distances. The invention of the instrument they used on that occasion is a great tribute to Mr. Chappe because, while of a simple construction, it can represent a great number of characters whose various combinations and manifold interpretations can serve as cyphers of a very secret language.... If there is anything to criticize about this invention, it is the costliness of its use, because of the need for good telescopes, as well as the deficiency it shares with all telegraphs using optical signals that one has to abandon their use when the atmosphere is dim, and that even in clear nights one cannot use them without costly additional equipment.
>
> If the speech tube is used, the telescope and the telegraphic machine for the representation of the characters are no longer necessary; now, instead of visible objects, articulated audible ones are being used for the same purpose. This essential difference may well warrant and necessitate a different name for the telegraphic medium that operates by means of the speech tube. And which name would be more appropriate here than the one equally borrowed from Greek: telephone, or distance speaker.[34]

The acoustician Ernst Florens Friedrich Chladni describes this new medium in one sentence: "Mr. Huth recommends speech tubes for the transmission of information over great distances by means of intermediate stations; such a *telephone* could be useful, above all, if, due to fog, etc., one cannot use the telegraph."[35] Thus, neither the first telegraph nor the first telephone were powered by electricity, though shortly after they were invented, the development of their electric replacements was well underway. As early as 1753, an anonymous writer C. M. had devised "An expeditious method of conveying intelligence" based on the following argument: "It is well known to all conversant in electrical experiments, that the electric power may be propagated along a small wire, without being sensibly abated by the length of its progress. Let then a set of wires, equal in number to the letters of the alphabet, be extended horizontally between two given places, parallel to one another, and each of them an inch distant form the next of it."[36] Messages sent over this contraption would be powered by a Leyden jar, a brand new device, and made visible at the receiving end by the electrostatic force exerted by small metal balls on scraps of paper representing the letters of the alphabet:[37] "All things constructed as above, and the minute previously fixed, I begin the conversation with my distant friend in this manner.... [A]nd my correspondent, almost in the same instant, observes these several characters rise in order to the electrified balls at his end of the wires."[38] Chappe wrote five papers on such topics as the polarity of electricity,[39] the measurement of electricity,[40] the phenomenon of electrolysis,[41] which had been discovered one year earlier,[42] on the voltaic pile, and on the effects of electricity on the growth of living organisms.[43] It is all the more ironic that it was his optical telegraph, which, only four years after Chappe's suicide, on January 25, 1805, inspired the first prototype of a truly functioning electric telegraph, a machine which was powered by a voltaic pile, and which represented pairs of alphabetic letters whose order was determined by the difference between the quantity of oxygen and hydrogen bubbles arising from the anode and the cathode in a tank of water. The history of this invention was told by an anonymous writer at its fiftieth anniversary:

> It appears that an event in connection with the war brought on by Austria against France fifty years ago, in 1809, caused the galvanic telegraph to be invented and made.
>
> The Austrian army had on the 9th of April that year begun to cross the river Inn, and to enter Bavaria. King Maximilian had hardly been informed of this, when he, on the 11th, with his family, in all haste, retired from Munich to the western frontier of his kingdom, to the town of Dillingen....
>
> By means of the line of Chappe's optico-mechanical telegraphs, established all the way from the French frontier to Paris, the Emperor Napoleon I got there the information of the Austrian army having entered Bavaria much sooner than it had been thought possible by the Austrians, namely on the 12th, and he, without delay, departed from Paris for Bavaria on the way to his army. He came so totally unexpected to Dillingen, that he found King Maximilian in bed...
>
> Baron Montgelas [the head of the Foreign and Home Departments] had been witness of the surprise caused by the French Emperor's unexpected arrival at Dillingen. Under his extensive administration was also the Munich Academy of Sciences. Dr. Samuel Thomas Soemmerring, the well-known anatomist and physiologist, who had been since 1805 a member of that Academy, was from time to time invited to come to dine with the minister Mongelas at Bogenhausen, near Munich, where he lived. This was the case on the 5th of July, 1809, when the minister expressed to him the wish to get from the Academy of Sciences proposals for telegraphs, having, it is to be supposed, in view no other but improved optical telegraphs.
>
> Soemmerring, who had, like Humboldt, very early paid attention to galvanism, in hopes of being able to make its study useful to clear up some of the

most mysterious portions of physiology,[44] and who also had now closely followed and noted the brilliant chemical discoveries made by Davy with the galvanic battery in the laboratory of the Royal Institution in London, at once resolved to try whether the evolution of gases from the decomposition of water by the action of the galvanic current might not be applied to telegraphic purposes.

From the time of the above mentioned dinner at the minister's, he gave himself no rest in his endeavours to construct a galvano-chemical telegraph.[45]

Soemmerring's telegraph marks the beginning of a new epoch, the epoch of electric and electromagnetic media, the beginning of our time. From then on, the number of words composed using the prefix *tēle-* increases substantially and rapidly. "Television," introduced by Constantin Perskyi in 1900, is but one of them.[46] It became so popular that, at the end of the nineteenth century, it made its way into the discourse of parapsychology. In 1882, the members of the Literary Committee of the Society for Psychical Research coined the terms *tele-aesthesia* and *telepathy*, subspecies of "thought-transference,"[47] and meant "to cover all cases of impression received at a distance without the normal operation of the recognised sense organs."[48] They alluded to the concept of *actio in distans*, which was and still is a much-discussed problem in physics. The perception of that which happens to an absent person is called teleaesthesia. And telepathy is the transference of pain over great distances from one person to another. With the decline of the first of these two words, this subtle difference has disappeared and, with it, the relation of the term telepathy to physical pain.

A strange encounter between telepathy and another telecommunication medium happens within Alan Turing's *Imitation Game*, which is played, as he writes, "with three people, a man (A), a woman (B), and an interrogator (C) who may be of either sex. The interrogator stays in a room apart from the other two. The object of the game for the interrogator is to determine which of the other two is the man and which is the woman."[49] To ensure that the decision is being reached independently of the physical appearance of the two contestants, Turing stipulates: "the answers should be written, or better still, typewritten. The ideal arrangement is to have a teleprinter communicating between the two rooms."[50] Suggesting that one of the two humans be exchanged with a digital computer, Turing wonders how well such a machine might do in this game. And he poses the question: What would happen, if "ESP," such as "telepathy, clairvoyance, precognition and psychokinesis," were to overwrite the teleprinter? Answer: "With E.S.P. anything may happen."[51] Telepathy, in this sense, is the ultimate medium. It is the phantasm that eliminates the necessity of telecommunication media once and for all. Charles Fort, in his book *Lo!* (1931) took the idea of action at a distance to its limit: "Mostly in this book I shall specialize upon indications that there exists a transportory force that I shall call

Teleportation.... There may even be teleportative voyages from planet to planet."[52] In 1993, a paper on "Teleporting an unknown quantum state via classical and Einstein-Podolsky-Rosen channels"[53] introduced Fort's neologism into particle physics, an event which was strange enough to elicit the following comment from a colleague: "To have the word 'teleporting' in the title of a physics paper was quite unusual at the time, since teleportation was considered to be part of science fiction and a somewhat shaky topic. But apparently, there was no better name for the interesting theoretical discovery these people made, and it was a very fitting name indeed."[54] The prefix *tēle-* did not only play a prominent role in the history of telecommunication, but also in that of weaponry and warfare. Odysseus, the archer, named his son *Tēlemachos*, "the one who fights at a distance." And Pindar, in his third Pythian ode, speaks of "a far-flung stone."[55] Most noteworthy, however, is an agreement between the cities of Euboea "that forbids the use of long-distance missiles."[56]

Today, such missiles are not only far-reaching, but remote controlled, or, with a word coined by Burnet Hershey shortly before the end of World War II, telearchic.[57] Another neologism for modern weapon systems such as guided submarines, robots, or drones, is telechirics, a compound word composed of *tēle-* and *cheir*, "hand," which John W. Clarke introduced in an article on "Remote Control in Hostile Environments."[58] With this term, we are far away from the beautiful hapax legomenon *tēlephilon* in Theocritus's third idyll:

> I was wondering if you loved me,
> and the smack didn't make the distant-love stick:
> it shriveled away uselessly on my smooth forearm.[59]

The passage refers to a form of divination. You were lucky in love if a petal of the plant distant-love, when put on one's arm, remained stuck. Jaufre Rudel, in his poem "Lanquan li jorn ...," probably not knowing what he did, translated the word into Provençal: *Amor de lonh*.[60] But I guess the classical philologist and Theocritus connoisseur Friedrich Nietzsche knew what he was saying when he wrote, "The charm and most powerful effect of women is, to speak in the language of philosophers, an effect at a distance, an actio in distans: yet, this involves first and above all—distance."[61] A less romantic, but perhaps more practical replay of these ideas is currently being promoted by a newly founded company which advertises its services as follows: "The SymPulse is at the forefront of an effort called 'tele-empathy': using technology to improve insight into the patient experience. Movement disorders like Parkinson's are one aspect of this work, but there are others."[62] Obviously not so sure whether the message from Agamemnon's victory could possibly be transmitted over the long beacon line he invented for this purpose, Aeschylus had the good news duplicated not only by a real herald a few scenes later, but—and again not much later—by

King Agamemnon himself.⁶³ Thus, the transmission of messages and the transport of objects or freight remained, in principle, one and the same until the end of the eighteenth century: they both had to be entrusted to real human or animal legs, as in the case of the horse-drawn stagecoaches of the Turn and Taxis family from medieval to modern Europe, or of the Pony Express in the American West. The concept of information as an immaterial entity in its own right could only be conceived of after Aeschylus's dream of a fast telecommunication system was, finally, fulfilled, first, by the optical, and, shortly thereafter, by the electric telegraph, which, as Heinrich von Kleist said so pointedly in 1809, was able to transmit messages "on wings of the thunderbolt,"⁶⁴ a metaphor which combines the age old experience that only physical bodies can carry messages and the new insight that it can be transferred by light or electricity, that information is, in other words, interchangeable with energy.

Norbert Wiener's book *Cybernetics or Control and Communication in the Animal and the Machine*,⁶⁵ 1948, goes the final step, so far at least: inspired by Samuel Butler's formative claim that living bodies, including those of humans, and machines are principally the same,⁶⁶ Wiener ties information back to the world of physical objects. Control and communication constitute the feedback loops that govern the movements not only of organisms, but of robots as well. Based on his work on automated antiaircraft artillery systems in World War II, Wiener's book on *Cybernetics* heralds a time in which information can not only be conveyed at large distances with minimal temporal delays, but can activate machines at large distances as well.

Notes

1. Homer, *Iliad*, vol. 1 and vol. 2, trans. A. T. Murray (Cambridge, MA: Harvard University Press, 1924), 11.817 and 16.539. For texts in Greek, I cite line numbers.
2. Homer, *Odyssey*, vol. 1, trans. A. T. Murray (Cambridge, MA: Harvard University Press, 1919), 1.22.
3. Homer, *Odyssey*, 2.165; 2.182–84; 2.332–33; 17.251–53; 17.312; 23.67–68.
4. Pindar, *Olympian Odes and Pythian Odes*, trans. William H. Race (Cambridge, MA: Harvard University Press, 1997), 11.22–23.
5. Euripides, *Iphigenia Among the Taurians*, trans. David Kovacs (Cambridge, MA: Harvard University Press, 1999), 175–78.
6. Homer, *Odyssey*, 5.315.
7. Homer, *Iliad*, 20.481–82.
8. Homer, *Odyssey*, 24.80–84.
9. *Homeric Hymns. Homeric Apocrypha. Lives of Homer.*, ed. and trans. Martin L. West (Cambridge, MA: Harvard University Press, 2003), 31.10–14 and 32.8.
10. Pindar, *Nemean Odes*, ed. and trans. William H. Race (Cambridge, MA: Harvard University Press, 1997), 3.64.

11. Julian, *Volume I: Orations 1–5*, trans. Wilmer C. Wright (Cambridge, MA: Harvard University Press, 1913), 5.174d.
12. Aristophanes, *The Clouds*, ed. and trans. Jeffrey Henderson (Cambridge, MA: Harvard University Press, 1998), 277–90.
13. Edward Rosen, *The Naming of the Telescope* (New York: Henry Schuman, 1947); and Edward Rosen, "Galileo and the Telescope," *The Scientific Monthly* 72, no. 3 (March 1951): 180–82.
14. Prince Frederico Cesi founded the *Academia dei Lincei*.
15. Rosen, *The Naming of the Telescope*, 67–68.
16. Galileo Galilei, *Istoria e demostrazioni intorno alle macchie solari e loro accidenti* (Giacomo Mascardi: Rome, 1613).
17. Rosen, *The Naming of the Telescope*, 39–40.
18. Hesiod, *Theogony*, in *Theogony. Works and Days. Testimonia.*, trans. Glenn W. Most (Cambridge, MA: Harvard University Press, 2007), 566, 569.
19. Aeschylus, *Agamemnon*, in *Oresteia. Agamemnon. Libation Bearers. Eumenides.*, ed. and trans. Alan H. Sommerstein (Cambridge, MA: Harvard University Press, 2009), 300.
20. Homer, *Odyssey*, 13.48; 10.18.
21. Homer, *Odyssey*, 5.167.
22. Thucydides, *History of the Peloponnesian War*, vol. 1, books 1–2, trans. C. F. Smith (Cambridge, MA: Harvard University Press, 1919), I.129.2.
23. Polybius, *The Histories*, vol. 4, books 9–15, transl. W. R. Paton, revised F. W. Walbank (Cambridge, MA: Harvard University Press, 2011), X.44.6.
24. Polybius, *The Histories*, X.45–47.
25. *Encyclopédie, ou Dictionnaire des Sciences, des Arts, et des Métiers*, vol. XV: *Sen-Tch* (Neufchatel: Samuel Faulche, 1765), s.v. *Signal*, 183–87. Unless marked otherwise, all translations mine.
26. *Rapport sur le télégraphe / Fait / Au nom du comité de l'instruction publique, réuni à la commission nommée par le décret du 27 avril dernier (vieux style), / Par Lakanal* (Paris: Imprimerie nationale, Vendémiaire, l'an III [September/October 1794]), 1–11, quote p. 4
27. *Rapport sur le télégraphe*, p. 4.
28. Édouard Gerspach, *Histoire administrative de la télégraphie aérienne en France* (Paris: E. Lacroix, 1861), 9. Cf. *La Décade Philosophique, Littéraire et Politique: par une société de gens de lettres* (Paris: Bureau de la Décade Philosophique: l'an 6 [1797]), 365.
29. "In two times, and three movements or phases."
30. Cf. Jean Marie Dilhac, "The Telegraph of Claude Chappe—an Optical Telecommunication Network for the XVIIIth Century," http://ethw.org/w/images/1/17/Dilhac.pdf (accessed March 22, 2018).
31. *Mémoires du Comte Miot de Melito*, vol. 1 (Paris: Michel Lévy Frères, 1858), 38, n. 1.
32. Lakanal, *Rapport*, 1–11.
33. Johann Heinrich Lambert, "Sur quelques instruments acoustiques," in *Histoire de l'académie royale des sciences et belles lettres de Berlin* (Berlin: Haude and Spener, 1763), 87–124, quote p. 87: https://archive.org/stream/berlin-histoire-1763-pub1770#page/no/mode/2up (accessed March 25, 2018).
34. Gottfried Huth, *J. H. Lamberts Abhandlung über einige akustische Instrumente. Aus dem Französischen übersetzt nebst Zusätzen über das sogenannte Horn Alexanders des Grossen, über Erfahrungen mit einem elliptischen Sprachrohre und über die Anwendung*

der Sprachröhre zur Telegraphie (Berlin: Königliche Realschul-Buchhandlung, 1796), 94–129, quotes pp. 94, 96, 97, 109.

35. Ernst Florens Friedrich Chladni, *Traité d'acoustique* (Paris: Courcier, 1809), 289–90.
36. C. M., "To the Author of the Scots Magazine," *Scot's Magazine* XV (February 17, 1753): 73–74, quote p. 73.
37. The Leyden jar was invented by Ewald von Kleist in 1745, and by Pieter van Musschenbroek in 1745–1746. Cf. Alanna Mitchell, *The Spinning Magnet: The Electromagnetic Force that Created the Modern World and Destroyed It* (New York: Random House, 2018).
38. C. M., "To the Author of the Scots Magazine," 73.
39. Claude Chappe, "Lettre de M. l'abbé Chappe à M. de la Métherie, Sur un Appareil propre à distinguer les deux espèces d'Électrisation," *Observations et Mémoires sur la Physique, sur l'Histoire Naturelle et sur les Arts et Métiers* 34 (January 1789): 62–63, and Plate II.
40. Claude Chappe, "Lettre de M. l'abbé Chappe a M. de la Métherie Sur un Électromètre," May 1789, 370–71, and figs. 1–3.
41. Claude Chappe, "Lettre de M. Sylvestre et M. l'abbé Chappe, à M. de Fourcroy," in *Annales de Chimie; ou Recueil de Mémoires Concernant la Chimie et les Arts qui en dépendent*, vol. 6 (1790): 121–26.
42. Adriaan Paets van Troostwyk and Jan Rudolph Deiman, "Lettre de MM. Paets van Troostwyk et Deiman, à M. de la Métherie, Sur une manière de décomposer l'Eau en Air inflammable & en Air vital," *Observations sur la Physique, sur l'Histoire naturelle et les Arts* 35, part II, (1789): 369–78.
43. Claude Chappe, "Physique," *Bulletin de la Société Philomatique, à ses correspondants*, no. 21 (March 1793): 2–4; Claude Chappe, "Nouvelles experiences Qui tendent à prouver que l'Electricité ne favorise pas sensiblement l'acroissement des parties animals," *Observations et Mémoires sur la Physique, sur l'Histoire Naturelle et sur les Arts et Métiers* 40 (January 1792): 62–64.
44. One of these books is S[amuel]. Th[omas]. Sömmerring, *Über das Organ der Seele*, Friedrich Nicolovius: Königsberg 1796, which contains a letter by none other than Immanuel Kant who argues that there cannot be such a thing as an "organ of the soul" because the soul can neither be located in space nor dated in time.
45. "The Origin of the Electric Telegraph," *Journal of the Society of Arts* (Mai 13, 1859): 453.
46. M. Constantin Perskyi, "Télévision au moyen d'électricité," in *Exposition universelle internationale de 1900. Rapports et procès-verbaux*, ed. M. E. Hospitalier (Paris: Gauthier-Villars, 1901), 54–56.
47. "Report of the Literary Committee," in *Proceedings of the Society for Psychical Research* 1: 1882–1883 (Ludgate Hill: Trübner, 1883): 118.
48. "Report of the Literary Committee," 147.
49. Alan M. Turing, "Computing Machinery and Intelligence," *Mind* 59, no. 236 (1950): 433–60, quote p. 433.
50. Turing, "Computing Machinery and Intelligence," 434.
51. Turing, "Computing Machinery and Intelligence," 454.
52. Charles Fort, *Lo!*, 553 and 574: http://www.sacred-texts.com/fort/lo/index.htm. Accessed March 29, 2018.
53. Charles H. Bennet, Giles Brassard, Claude Crépeau, Richard Jozsa, Asher Peres, and William K. Wootters, "Teleporting an Unknown Quantum State via Dual Classical and Einstein-Podolski-Rosen channels," *Physical Review Letters* 70, no. 13 (March 1993): 1895–99.

54. Anton Zeilinger, *Dance of the Photons* (New York: Farrar, Straus and Giroux, 2010), 46.
55. Pindar, *Pythian* 3, in *Olympian Odes. Pythian Odes., Pindar*, vol. I, trans. William H. Race (Cambridge, MA: Harvard University Press, 1997), 47–49. Cf. Strabo, *Geography*, vol. III: Books 3–5, trans. Horace Leonard Jones (Cambridge, MA: Harvard University Press, 1923), IV.3.
56. Strabo, *Geography*, vol. 5, books 10–12, X.12.
57. Burnet Hershey, *Skyways of Tomorrow* (New York: Foreign Policy Association, 1944), 13–16.
58. John W. Clarke, "Remote Control in Hostile Environments," *New Scientist* 22, no. 389 (April 30, 1964): 300–303, quote p. 300.
59. Theocritus, *Idylls*, in *Theocritus. Moschus. Bion.*, ed. and trans. Neil Hopkinson (Cambridge, MA: Harvard University Press, 2015), 3.28–30; translation altered.
60. *Lark in the Morning. The Verses of the Troubadours. A Bilingual Edition*, ed. Robert Kehew, trans. Ezra Pound, W. D. Snodgrass and Robert Kehew (Chicago: University of Chicago Press, 2005), 62–65.
61. Friedrich Nietzsche, *Die fröhliche Wissenschaft*, Nr. 60, http://gutenberg.spiegel.de/buch/die-frohliche-wissenschaft-3245/5. Accessed August 11, 2017.
62. Sandeep Jauhar, "Empathy Gadgets," *The New York Times: Sunday Review*, July 30, 2017, p. 10. Cf. " 'Tele-Empathy' Device Allows Caregivers to Really Feel Parkinson's Symptoms," *CTV News*, April 24, 2017. http://www.ctvnews.ca/health/tele-empathy-device-allows-caregivers-to-really-feel-parkinson-s-symptoms-1.3381948. Cf. also Klick Lab's SymPulse™: https://www.klick.com/sympulse. Both accessed August 13, 2017.
63. Aeschylus, *Agamemnon*, loc. cit., entrance of the herald, line 503; entrance of Agamemnon line 680.
64. Heinrich von Kleist, "Nützliche Erfindungen. Entwurf einer Bombenpost," in *Sämtliche Werke und Briefe*, ed. Helmut Sembdner (Munich: Carl Hanser, 1964), 2:385–88, quote p. 385: "auf Flügeln des Blitzes."
65. Norbert Wiener, *Cybernetics or Control and Communication in the Animal and the Machine* (New York: Wiley, 1948).
66. Samuel Butler, "The Book of the Machines," chapters 21–23, in *Erewhon: or, Over the Range* (London: Trübner, 1872), 190–223.

CONTRIBUTORS

Michele Kennerly is associate professor of communication arts and sciences and of classics and ancient Mediterranean studies at the Pennsylvania State University. She is the author of *Editorial Bodies: Perfection and Rejection in Ancient Rhetoric and Poetics* (University of South Carolina Press, 2018), coeditor of the volume *Ancient Rhetorics and Digital Networks* (2018), and coeditor of the incipient book series Rhetoric + Digitality, both from the University of Alabama Press. One of her current projects explores invocations of ancient Athens in discourse about automation and digitization. She serves as president of the American Society for the History of Rhetoric (2019–2021).

Samuel Frederick is associate professor of German at the Pennsylvania State University. He is the author of *Narratives Unsettled: Digression in Robert Walser, Thomas Bernhard, and Adalbert Stifter* (Northwestern University Press, 2012) and the coeditor of *Robert Walser: A Companion* (Northwestern University Press, 2018). With the poet Graham Foust, he has translated three volumes of Ernst Meister's late poetry (Wave Books, 2012, 2014, 2015). His newest book, *The Redemption of Things: Collecting and Dispersal in German Realism and Modernism*, will be published by Cornell University Press.

Jonathan E. Abel is associate professor of Japanese studies and comparative literature, and director of the Global and International Studies Program at the Pennsylvania State University. His book *Redacted: The Archives of Censorship in Transwar Japan* (University of California Press, 2012) won the Weatherhead East Asia Institute First Book Prize. His current book project explores the role of Japanese new media in transforming the world in unexpected ways.

Contributors

***

Francesco Casetti is the Thomas E. Donnelley Professor of Humanities and Film and Media Studies at Yale University. Among various books and essays, he is the author of *Eye of the Century: Film, Experience, Modernity* (2005), and *The Lumière Galaxy: Seven Key Words for the Cinema to Come* (2015), both from Columbia University Press. His current research focuses on early film theory, especially the cinephobic stances of the first half of the twentieth century, and on a reconsideration of the screen in its spatial connotations and as a component of our current "mediascapes."

Dennis Duncan is a lecturer in English at University College London. His publications include *Book Parts* (2019), coedited with Adam Smyth, and *The Oulipo and Modern Thought* (2019), while *Babel: Adventures in Translation* appeared in 2018 to accompany an exhibition of the same name at the Bodleian Libarary, Oxford. Another monograph, *Index, A History of the*, is due out with Penguin in 2021.

Bernard Dionysius Geoghegan is a writer, media theorist, and historian of science. His research explores how digital technology—as an ensemble of instruments, practices, inscriptions, and concepts—shapes science, culture, and the environment. He teaches courses on the history and theory of digital media at King's College London.

N. Katherine Hayles is a Distinguished Research Professor of English at the University of California, Los Angeles, and the James B. Duke Professor Emerita of Literature at Duke University. Her 11 print books include *Unthought: The Power of the Cognitive Nonconscious* (University of Chicago Press, 2017) and *How We Think: Digital Media and Contemporary Technogenesis* (University of Chicago Press, 2015), in addition to over 100 peer-reviewed articles. Her books have won several prizes, and she has been recognized by many fellowships and awards, including two honorary degrees. She is a member of the American Academy of Arts and Sciences. She is currently at work on *Cyber-Bio-Symbiosis: A General Ecology of Cognitive Assemblages*, under contract to Columbia University Press.

Laura Helton is assistant professor of English and history at the University of Delaware, where she teaches print and material culture, African American literature, and public humanities. An archivist and historian by training, her research focuses on the history of collecting in American life. Her current book project, "Collecting and Collectivity: Black Archival Publics, 1910–1950," traces the making of African American archives and libraries to show how historical recuperation shaped forms of racial imagination in the early twentieth century.

Elizabeth Horodowich is professor of history at New Mexico State University. Her research focuses on the history of Venice, the history of Italy, and global history in the period between 1400–1600, and she is the author of four books and many scholarly articles on these subjects. She is the recipient of awards and fellowships from a variety of foundations, including Harvard University, the National Endowment for the Humanities, and the American Historical Association.

Jeremy David Johnson is visiting assistant professor in communication at the University of the Pacific. His research investigates how networked platforms and algorithms shape public deliberation, and how citizens and designers can shape more just digital systems. His works have appeared in the journals *Computers and Composition* and *Argumentation and Advocacy* and in the edited volumes *Ancient Rhetorics and Digital Networks* and *Theorizing Digital Rhetoric*.

Matthew F. Jordan is associate professor of media studies at Penn State University. His research explores how popular media forms and technologies are used to constitute and reify aspects of personal identity and cultural ideology. He is currently working on two books that examine the technological management and mediation of sound in global modernity. The first tells the story of the rise and fall of the Klaxon automobile horn; the second traces the genealogy of "quietness" technologies, critiquing the increasingly ubiquitous phenomenon of "commodity quietness" in contemporary culture as a normative response to the problem of noise.

Wolf Kittler is professor of German and comparative literature at the University of California, Santa Barbara. His writings include monographs on Heinrich von Kleist and Franz Kafka, as well as essays on literature, art, music, philosophy, the history of science, the history of warfare, and media theory. He is currently working on a book titled *On Wings of Light: A Cultural History of Telecommunication from Antiquity to the Present*.

Deborah Lupton is SHARP Professor in the faculty of Arts and Social Sciences, UNSW Sydney, working in the Centre for Social Research in Health and the Social Policy Research Centre and leading the Vitalities Lab. Professor Lupton is a chief investigator and leader of the UNSW Node of the Australian Research Council Centre of Excellence in Automated Decision-Making and Society (2020–2026). She is a fellow of the Academy of the Social Sciences in Australia and holds an honorary degree awarded by the University of Copenhagen.

David L. Marshall is associate professor of communication at the University of Pittsburgh. He is primarily an intellectual historian of the period starting 1650. His first book was *Vico and the Transformation of Rhetoric in Early Modern Europe* (Cambridge University Press, 2010). His second book was *The Weimar Origins of Rhetorical Inquiry* (University of Chicago Press, 2020). His most recent work revolves around Aby Warburg, the art historian and art theorist. That project has proposed to him a connection between the rhetorical art of topics and contemporary topic modeling that he is continuing to explore.

Damien Smith Pfister is associate professor of communication at the University of Maryland. He studies the intersections of the digital and the rhetorical, with a special emphasis on the cultural and deliberative consequences of media technology. He is the author of *Networked Media, Networked Rhetorics:*

Attention and Deliberation in the Early Blogosphere (Pennsylvania State University, 2014), coeditor of *Ancient Rhetorics and Digital Networks* (2018), and coeditor of the incipient book series Rhetoric + Digitality, both from the University of Alabama Press. His essays have been featured in *Quarterly Journal of Speech, Philosophy and Rhetoric, Journal for the History of Rhetoric*, and other venues.

Daniel Rosenberg is professor of history at the University of Oregon. His publications include *Cartographies of Time* with Anthony Grafton (Princeton Architectural Press, 2010) and *Histories of the Future* with Susan Harding (Duke University Press, 2005). Rosenberg has received awards from the National Endowment for the Humanities, American Council of Learned Societies, Max Planck Institute for the History of Science, and Stanford Humanities Center. His current work concerns the history of data.

Haun Saussy is University Professor at the University of Chicago, teaching in the Departments of Comparative Literature, East Asian Languages and Civilizations, and the Committee on Social Thought. His books include *The Problem of a Chinese Aesthetic* (1993), *Great Walls of Discourse and Other Adventures in Cultural China* (2001), *The Ethnography of Rhythm* (2016), *Translation as Citation* (2017), *Are We Comparing Yet?* (2019), and other edited collections and translations.

Chad Wellmon is professor of German studies, with appointments in history and media studies, at the University of Virginia. He is the author or coeditor of several books, including *Organizing Enlightenment: Information Overload and the Invention of the Modern Research University, Becoming Human: Romantic Anthropology and the Embodiment of Freedom*, and *Charisma and Disenchantment: The Vocation Lectures* (NYRB Classics), a new edition of Max Weber's vocation lectures. His latest book, *Permanent Crisis: The Humanities in a Disenchanted Age*, will be published early in 2021.

Geoffrey Winthrop-Young teaches in the German and Scandinavian programs of the Department of Central, Eastern, and Northern European Studies at the University of British Columbia, Vancouver. His main research focus is on media theory and cultural evolution. He is currently working on a study of catastrophes and chronopolitics in the Third Reich.

INDEX

abundance: effects of information, 22–23; and emotional excess, 23–24; fears and fantasies of information, 18; interpretability of, 26–28
Adorno, Theodor, 24
Aquinas, Thomas, 135
algorithm, 11–12, 17, 31–40, 82, 84, 85, 123, 130, 133–36, 142–44, 157, 174, 176–79, 181, 193, 195–96
Amazon, 31, 33, 35
Anthropocene, 81
Anthropology, 138
archive: archive/s, 7–9, 46–49, 141, 195; the archive, 49–51, 94; as verb, 51–53
Aristotle, 2, 20, 135, 183
art, 6, 8, 9, 46, 125, 131, 138, 170, 174, 181, 183, 195–96, 204
artificial intelligence, 17, 37, 116, 199. *See also* machine learning
artificial life, 57, 67, 69, 82
assemblage, 45, 64, 163, 165–71, 189–93, 195–96
authority, 8, 21–22, 44, 47, 79, 93, 95, 124, 139, 143–44, 146

Bacon, Francis, 138
Ballard, J. G., 100–1
Baudrillard, Jean, 25
Beniger, James R., 2
Benjamin, Walter, 5–6
Benkler, Yochai, 26
Bennett, Charles, 79
big data, 3, 6, 17–18, 27, 35, 133
Bijsterveld, Karin, 149–50
Bimber, Bruce, 22
bioinformatics: and code, 61–66, storage and manipulation, 59–60
biosemiotics, 68, 73, 77, 79, 82–83
Blair, Ann, 2, 10, 21, 139
Bogost, Ian, 83
Brecht, Bertolt, 6, 114
Bucher, Taina, 36

Calvin, John, 21
Campt, Tina, 51
Canon, 44, 60
Carey, James, 150
Castells, Manuel, 2, 26–27
Caswell, Michelle, 45
Cavell, Stanley, 170
de Certeau, Michel, 51
Chambers, Ephraim, 138
Cheney-Lippold, John, 38
Christian, Brian, 32

Chun, Wendy, 33, 36, 39
classification, 7, 12, 44, 47, 51, 176–77, 181
cloud, 31, 90, 195, 200, 201
code, 22, 32, 35, 39, 58–66, 77, 84,c127, 135, 154–59, 202–3
cognition: animal, 73–75; cognitive planetary ecologies, 85–86; human, 72–73; machine, 82–85; and meaning, 77–82; plant, 75–77
cognitive psychology, 72
cognitive science, 72
communication, 2–3, 10–11, 19, 22, 25–27, 33, 35, 39, 59–61, 66, 68–69, 77, 81, 89, 91, 96, 98, 110–12, 115–16, 119, 148–57, 162, 192, 194, 199, 208
computer science, 3, 31–32, 57, 84, 187
Craig, Robert, 154
Crawford, Kate, 37
Crick, Francis, 61–63, 65–66
culture, 8–10, 18, 23, 25–26, 124–28, 131, 140, 149, 154, 168–69, 177; algorithmic, 35–36, 39; digital, 17, 25; mass, 24; material, 184; networked, 43n71; oral, 25, 95; political, 89, 95; pop(ular), 9, 190; print, 20, 23; western, 149; visual, 172n15
Cvetkovich, Ann, 50
Cybernetics, 2–4, 34, 98, 156, 208
Czitrom, Daniel, 27

D'Alembert, Jean-Baptiste le Rond, 138
Darton, Robert, 150
Darwin, Charles, 75, 107
Deacon, Terrence, 80
Dean, Gabrielle, 47
Debord, Guy, 6, 25
Deleuze, Gilles, 5, 165, 167
Derrida, Jacques, 47–48, 50–51
Descartes, Rene, 51
Dewey, John, 22, 83
Diderot, Denis, 138
digital humanities, 3, 181
digital media, 25, 34
distance, 12, 76, 151, 162, 171n1, 199–204, 206–8; conceptual, 44, 180, 182
Dourish, Paul, 84
Dunbar, Robin, 92
Durkheim, Emile, 138

Echevarria, Roberto, 47
Eco, Umberto, 153
Eichhorn, Kate, 45, 51
Eisenstein, Sergei, 170
encyclopedia, 10, 21–22, 138, 141, 144, 202
engineering, 2–3, 34, 62–63, 67, 131, 150–57
entropy, 2, 58–61, 151, 153, 156, 159
environmental humanities, 81
Erasmus, 20–21, 183
erasure, 45, 50
Ernst, Wolfgang, 83
Eubanks, Virginia, 2, 37

Facebook, 31, 33–35, 37–38, 155, 162, 177–78
file, 8, 10–11, 50, 183
Fontaine, Henri la, 7
Freud, Sigmund, 73

genomics, 57
Gessner, Conrad, 21, 139
Gibson, William, 117
Gitelman, Lisa, 28
Gleick, James, 33
Google, 33–38, 85, 105, 108, 118, 121–23, 127, 131, 133–34, 142–45, 174–76, 178, 184
gossip: as commodity, 94; and gender, 91; and law, 93; lifespan of, 97–98; as meta-communication, 89; and politics, 95; and rumor, 90; and truth, 91–92
Griffiths, Tomi, 32
Grossman, Sara, 16 no. 14, 52

Habermas, Jurgen, 22–23
Harris, Verne, 52
Hartman, Saidiya, 50
Hayles, N. Katherine, 34
Hayot, Eric, 1
Hegel, G. W. F., 141
Heidegger, Martin, 4–5, 91, 148, 183
Helmholtz, Herman von, 140–42, 145
Helvey, Tibor Charles, 4
Heraclitus, 34–35
Herder, Johann Gottfried, 138
Hill, Robin, 32
Hoffmeyer, Jesper, 77–81
Horkheimer, Max, 24
humanities, 1–5, 7–8, 44, 46, 48, 52, 81, 154–56, 159, 181

information: and emotion, 22; ethics of, 3; fantasy of, 18–19, 150; fear of, 6–7; fear of abundance, 17–19, 26; genetic, 61, 66, 68–69; as a humanistic concept, 1, 112; information age, 1–4, 7, 9, 11, 18, 27, 34–36, 121, 150–51, 159; information society, 1, 4; overload of, 2, 11, 17, 21, 139; regimes of, 35, 37–39; resistance of, 4; studies, 3, 5, 7, 123; theory, 18, 28, 67–68, 115, 123, 151–57, 159
index, history of, 102–7
Ingraham, Christopher, 35
intel: and fiction, 112, 114; history of, 113–14; human, 115; signals, 115–16; and war, 111–12
intellectual property, 49
interpretability, 19, 23, 26–27

Jacob, François, 64–66
Jakobson, Roman, 154–55
Janich, Peter, 59–60
Jenkins, Henry, 25

Kant, Immanuel, 135, 137–38
Kaplan, Alice Yaeger, 47
Kauffman, Stuart, 79
Kearns, Michael, 32
Kennedy, Kathleen E., 2
Ketelaar, Eric, 49
keyword: commodification of, 127; history of 123–26, 128–30
Kittler, Friedrich, 116
knowledge, 133–47
Kracauer, Siegfried, 170

labor, 9, 44, 48, 52, 106, 108, 143, 149
Lacan, Jacques, 5
Lanham, Richard, 18, 35–36
Latour, Bruno, 78, 167
Lawrence, T. E., 114
le Carré, John, 112, 114, 116–17
Leibniz, Gottfried, 21
Lévi-Strauss, Claude, 154
library science, 3
life, 6, 7, 18–20, 34, 36, 39, 44–45, 48, 57–58, 61, 67–69, 77–78, 80, 82, 89, 93, 95, 97, 124–25, 127, 133–34, 177, 187–88, 191, 194
Lippmann, Walter, 23
Locke, John, 135, 137

loss, 23, 50, 57, 67, 94, 182, 195
Luhn, Hans Peter, 123–24, 127–31

machine learning, 134–36, 145. *See also* artificial intelligence
Marder, Daniel, 2
Marx, Karl, 126, 138
Masuda, Yoneji, 4
Mbembe, Achille, 52
McLuhan, Marshall, 25, 27
media archaeology, 171
media ecology, 25
media history, 27
media studies, 3, 98, 189
memory, 9–10, 23, 44–45, 47–48, 50–51, 60, 76, 138, 170–71, 182, 187, 189–90, 193
Merleau-Ponty, Maurice, 149
Michotte, Albert, 170
Mifsud, Mari Lee, 8
molecular biology, 57, 63, 66, 68
Monod, Jacques, 63–66

Nakamura, Lisa, 9
National Aeronautics and Space Administration (NASA), 9
neoliberalism, 37, 38, 81, 194
network, 2, 8, 25–26, 39, 78, 80, 82, 96, 136, 143–44, 155, 162, 166, 169, 175–76
Neumann, John von, 67–68, 152
neuroscience, 72
Noble, Safiya Umoja, 2, 37–38, 176
noise: and industrial modernity, 149–50; and information theory, 151–54; and listening, 155; and silence, 148; and sociality, 148; and social science, 154; types of, 157–58

O'Neil, Cathy, 36
order, 8, 12, 18, 22, 31, 34–37, 39, 45, 47, 49, 51–52, 58, 62, 101–4, 106–8, 122, 137, 141–43, 167, 205; and disorder, 17, 59
Otlet, Paul, 7

Parikka, Jussi, 83
Pariser, Eli, 32, 34, 39, 178
Pasquale, Frank, 35
Paulson, W. R., 154
Peirce, C. S., 77

Perritt, H. Hardy, 2
Peters, John Durham, 2, 32, 34, 150
Pfister, Damien Smith, 33
phenomenology, 155, 194
Phillip, M. NourbeSe, 51
Plato, 18–20, 23, 34–35, 69, 133, 135
Poe, Edgar Allan, 5
politics, 18, 21–22, 27, 31, 33, 45, 95, 176–77, 183, 190–91, 196
Postrel, Virginia, 8
propaganda, 6, 17, 23–24

race, 2, 9–10, 27, 38, 55n28, 114, 184
Rice, Jenny Edbauer, 25
Richards, Thomas, 50
Riggsby, Andrew M., 2
Robertson, Craig, 10
Roth, Aaron, 32
Roth, Joseph, 170
Rousseau, Jean-Jacques, 138
Rouvroy, Antoinette, 33

Schlegel, A. W., 138
Schleiermacher, Friedrich, 138
Schmitt, Carl, 110–11, 120
screen: as assemblage, 165–68; cinema, 169–70; electronic, 162; future of, 171; genealogy of, 164–70, radar, 163–64
Seaver, Nick, 32, 36
Schrödinger, Erwin, 57–59, 61, 67
Shafer, R. Murray, 148
Shannon, Claude, 11, 33, 60, 67, 72, 110, 115, 152–56, 202
social media, 6, 89, 162, 165, 187–88
Socrates, 19, 23, 27, 135–36, 138, 144
Sorge, Richard, 115
Stiegler, Bernard, 19

Stoler, Ann Laura, 46–48, 50
Sun Tzu, 113, 115
surveillance, 47, 111–13, 116–17, 134, 165, 167, 193, 195

Taylor, Diana, 51
technics, 7, 18, 27–28, 31, 40
"The Index" (Ballard), 100–2
Three Days of the Condor, 118
Thorburn, David, 25
transcription, 52, 66, 69
translation, 57, 66, 68–69, 84, 133, 204
Trewavas, Anthony, 75
Trouillot, Michel-Rolph, 47, 49–50
Tufekci, Zeynep, 35, 38–39
Turing, Alan, 60, 67, 116, 152, 206

Uexküll, Jakob von, 75, 77–79, 81
Umesao, Tadao, 4
Umwelt, 75, 77–78, 81–83

Vaidhyanathan, Siva, 37
Vergil (Virgil), 90–91, 96, 98

Waleys, Thomas, 106
Watson, James, 61–62
Weaver, Warren, 60, 72, 152–56
Weber, Max, 138
Weld, Kirsten, 47
Wheeler, Wendy, 80
Wiener, Norbert, 33, 152–53, 156, 208
Williams, Raymond, 123–31
Wolf, Friedrich August, 138
Wollaeger, Mark, 23

Zagzebski, Linda, 145
Zwinger, Theodor, 139

GPSR Authorized Representative: Easy Access System Europe, Mustamäe tee
50, 10621 Tallinn, Estonia, gpsr.requests@easproject.com

www.ingramcontent.com/pod-product-compliance
Lightning Source LLC
Chambersburg PA
CBHW021944290426
44108CB00012B/962